MANY PATHS WITH MARY

MANY PATHS WITH MARY

Popular Piety and the Future Church

Michael J. Rogers

ORBIS BOOKS
Maryknoll, New York 10545

Founded in 1970, Orbis Books endeavors to publish works that enlighten the mind, nourish the spirit, and challenge the conscience. The publishing arm of the Maryknoll Fathers and Brothers, Orbis seeks to explore the global dimensions of the Christian faith and mission, to invite dialogue with diverse cultures and religious traditions, and to serve the cause of reconciliation and peace. The books published reflect the views of their authors and do not represent the official position of the Maryknoll Society. To learn more about Maryknoll and Orbis Books, please visit our website at www.orbisbooks.com.

Copyright © 2025 by Michael J. Rogers

Published by Orbis Books, Box 302, Maryknoll, NY 10545-0302.

All Vatican documents are available online at Vatican.va.

All rights reserved.

No part of this publication may be reproduced or transmitted in any form or by any means, electronic or mechanical, including photocopying, recording, or any information storage or retrieval system, without prior permission in writing from the publisher.

Queries regarding rights and permissions should be addressed to: Orbis Books, P.O. Box 302, Maryknoll, NY 10545-0302.

Manufactured in the United States of America

Library of Congress Cataloging-in-Publication Data

Names: Rogers, Michael, author.
Title: Many paths with Mary : popular piety and the future of the church / Michael J. Rogers.
Description: Maryknoll, NY : Orbis Books, [2025] | Includes bibliographical references and index. | Summary: "Focuses on how Mary, Mother of God, comes to be translated into different times and places"— Provided by publisher.
Identifiers: LCCN 2024044338 (print) | LCCN 2024044339 (ebook) | ISBN 9781626986138 (trade paperback) | ISBN 9798888660683 (epub)
Subjects: LCSH: Mary, Blessed Virgin, Saint—Devotion to. | Catholic Church—Customs and practices. | Sensus fidelium. | Catholic Church—Doctrines.
Classification: LCC BT645 .R64 2025 (print) | LCC BT645 (ebook) | DDC 232.91—dc23/eng/20241113
LC record available at https://lccn.loc.gov/2024044338
LC ebook record available at https://lccn.loc.gov/2024044339

To Hannah

Contents

Acknowledgments ix

Introduction: Here, the Word Became Flesh xiii

1 Copacabana: Conflict and Compromise 1
   When They Came to the Birthplace
      of the Sun 4
   One Culture's Heaven and Another Culture's
      Hell: Conflict and the Need for Exorcism 8
   Casting Out Deception 12
   When Meanings Merge: Our Lady
      of Copacabana 21
   Mary, Genius of Inculturation 24
   A Soil Already Tilled 25
   A Bolivian Mother of God 34

2 Lourdes: At the Horizon of a New Era 41
   1858 42
   A Word on Apparitions 45
   Jean-Baptiste Estrade's Narrative of Change and
      Perdurance 49
   Going in Procession: Corporate Cultural Expression of Psychological Meaning-Making 65
   The Known Unknown at Lourdes 80

Contents

3 Patronage and Lament: The Curious Case
   of Santa Muerte 86
   The Emergence of the Skeleton Saint   87
   Patronage When God Won't Listen   90
   The Problem of Idolatry: Santa Muerte
      as a Mirror   99
   Lament toward Theodicy: Making Sense
      of the Cry of the Poor   103
   Death as an Idol   111
   The Death of God: When the Postmodern
      Problem Emerges in Our Devotion   114

4 Trickle-Up Devotion: From Tepeyac
   to Vatican Hill 119
   The Lady Clothed with the Sun   121
   Sensus Fidelium: The Dynamic Assent of the
      People of God   146
   Bubbling Up from Below: From Tepeyac
      to the Universal Church   162

5 E Pluribus Unum: When Many Faces
   Become One 165
   The Parable of the Elephant: Communication
      from Different Perspectives   168
   Gravity: A Thought Experiment   177
   Walking Together: Popular Piety
      toward a Synodal Church   189
   Many Paths with Mary   194

Bibliography 197

Index 207

Acknowledgments

In 2019, just before the Covid-19 pandemic hit, I completed the pilgrimage to Santiago de Compostela. Along the way, I met so many people who helped and supported me such that I have come to view so many projects with a destination like this one as a journey toward the God who loves us with people who help us learn how to love. This work is the result of a journey, across many continents, across a global pandemic, and across what even feels now like different lifetimes. I am filled with gratitude for so many people who have been a part of this journey along the way, and I am also painfully aware that I could never name them all here. Still, a few deserve special mention.

First and foremost, I thank my supervisor, Sr. Gill Goulding, CJ, for her patience, her wisdom, her guidance, and her prayers as I wrote this work. I have been privileged to work with someone who understands that the best theological work comes from a foundation of prayer. Examining that foundation is very much at the heart of this work. I am also indebted to Dr. Ephraim Radner and Dr. Thomas Reynolds for their guidance, particularly early on in this work, which helped to broaden the scope of the work and gave me the critical tools to think beyond the conventions of my own tradition in forming my ideas.

This work would never have come to be without the trust, guidance, and support of so many members of the Society of

Jesus. I will forever be in the debt of that least Society. I thank Pope Francis, who in a private conversation in February of 2014 encouraged me to rethink the topic of my dissertation to pursue something that "wouldn't be boring." I will leave it to you, dear reader, to determine whether I have met that standard. I would also like to thank Fr. James Corkery, SJ, who, over too many cups of coffee one morning, helped me begin to hash out the idea behind this work. My gratitude also goes to Fr. William Reiser, SJ, and Fr. William Clark, SJ. The opportunity to reflect on many of the themes that appear in this work with them while teaching at the College of the Holy Cross, and the opportunity to join Fr. Reiser on two journeys to Bolivia, were crucial to the development of the insights contained herein. Although there are more members of the Society of Jesus than I could mention here to whom I owe a debt of gratitude, Fr. Thomas Worcester, SJ, president emeritus of Regis College, is owed a particular debt of gratitude. Tom's faith in my ability to do this work and companionship during the doctoral program are foundational to so much of this work, and I will be forever grateful.

This work is also the result of the care of so many benefactors who have supported the research behind it. I thank Meg Lyons, who supported my research in Lourdes. That research enabled me to begin to really understand the power of popular religiosity, and the people that I was blessed to work beside at the sanctuary helped me to better understand what we mean by "the people of God." I also thank Patrick and Melanie Ferguson, who welcomed me into their home and gave me a space to think and pray about this work. One of my most important academic benefactors was my late aunt, Dr. Mary Rogers-Beckert, who funded the purchases of books for this work and also funded a significant part of my tuition costs through an educational trust set up in her memory. As a woman who achieved her doctorate in astrophysics in the mid-twentieth century when women weren't necessarily welcome in the field, Aunt Mair inspired us to be intellectually curious as children. I trust that she is smiling on from the communion of saints as this work reaches its happy end. A little bit of Chapter 5 is a nod to her. I am sure that she'll correct me on my ideas about gravity when we next meet.

Finally, my greatest expression of gratitude goes to my wife, Hannah Ferguson. She has, so often, been the final and most consequential of my theological interlocutors while I have worked on this. From her willingness to act as a research assistant at times, to her warm smile, laughter, and embrace, to the times she has fed both my body and spirit so that this could happen, I am, and will forever be, eternally grateful and overcome with joy at the surprise of her love.

Introduction

Here, the Word Became Flesh

In the dim light of an early morning mass, hemmed into the small chapel by roughhewn stone walls on three sides, I knelt before the altar. As a friend of mine celebrated mass at 5:30 in the morning, I struggled to maintain consciousness. My eyes flew all over the chapel as my stomach growled and my head ached from lack of sleep and lack of coffee. The dark walls that surrounded me weighed as heavily as the baroque thuribles did from the ceiling. The places where thousands, and maybe even millions, of pilgrims had touched the stone walls of the chapel in an act of veneration over the years showed the weathering that can only be left by the patina of prayer. In the darkness and heaviness, I found my eyes pulled upward to the brightness of the lighter marble and the bejeweled and crowned statue above where my friend José was celebrating the Eucharist. The conical statue of Mary, carved from Lebanon cedar, with the head of the infant Jesus poking up from behind the garment in which they were both swaddled was lit from below and was the brightest point in the chapel. As my friend genuflected after the consecration, my eyes looked down and were caught by the inscription below the altar: "*Hic Verbum Caro Factum Est*": Here, the Word became flesh.

The bold claim of the prologue of the Gospel of John, that

the Word became flesh and dwelt among us, has echoed down through the centuries as the central claim of the Christian faith. In places like that chapel in Loreto, Italy, in between the walls that pious tradition holds came from the house at Nazareth, where the Archangel Gabriel visited Mary, the addition of *hic*—here or in this place—reminds us of something that has long been deeply felt by the people of God and expressed in their popular piety and devotion: Jesus did not just become flesh in some foreign place long ago, the Incarnation is not a remote event. Through these devotions, local churches are reminded, while they in turn remind the universal Church, that God enters into our history and our culture to communicate his love to us. As *Dei Verbum* affirms in the time of the second Vatican Council: "Jesus Christ, therefore, the Word made flesh, was sent as 'a man to men.' "[1]

The presence of the Incarnation, expressed in a place, a history, and a culture extends itself to the stories that justify and explain why a place, or a practice, is meaningful to the people who engage it. When we listen to the stories of the Church told within a particular community, as ethnographers of religion do, we see the elements of common meaning that allow the universality of the faith to be communicated in a particular context. The common expression of faith in a community is most evident when shrines are built, when enculturated images are made, and when the dances, songs, and gestures of a people become expressions of faith built out of common meaning. The stories of the faith of a people are often first communicated in the gestures and language of the private, personal, pious exercises that grow into communal devotions, in which pious exercises come to be shared by a larger group. Those devotions then, in turn, become a part of

---

[1] Paul VI, *Dei Verbum,* no. 4, November 18, 1965.

the overall popular piety of a people, which means that they become elements in the overall cultural instantiation of the lived faith. The practices of each people, when brought into dialogue, can speak across difference and speak to us of a shared faith through the phenomenon of popular religiosity.

Thus, even the smallest pious gestures, considered within a localized lived community, might enter into dialogue with the faith of a universal and globally extended ecclesial reality. These levels express an ecclesial understanding as it is often experienced by the people of God and allow for it to be read through the stories that are told by the practices and devotions that make up their own particular popular piety. Here, the work of the ethnographer or historian has its greatest force. As someone who is outside of the community, either by birth or by education, they enter in to record and transmit the stories that the other tells. As a theological source, these testimonies can be employed in an attempt to find common meaning across the broader *Cattolica*.

This book asserts that the phenomenon of popular religiosity, where the practice of the Catholic faith has a cultural instantiation in the particular piety of a given people or culture, can provide us with a valuable model for rethinking a contextualized ecclesial communion. This communion is understood as a unity of the universal Catholic Church across cultural difference within a diverse global context. I focus on Mary, the mother of God, in particular because there are innumerable representations of one historical person who is embodied wearing the clothes, speaking the language, and even sharing the faces of the people who ask her intercession. The universal referent of the mother of Jesus plays in ten thousand places such that, in the cloak bathed in the stars in the image of Guadalupe, in the bleached white of a French sodality gown worn at Lourdes, and in the mountainously shaped dress which adorns her image on the shore of Lake Titicaca high in the Andes, the historical figure of Mary of Nazareth points us to the interplay between the lived faith of a local church and unity of the whole *ecclesia*.

Marian popular piety, which will serve as a heuristic tool for this thesis, is by no means a dynamic unique to Mary, as images of Jesus, God the Father, and the saints often serve as powerful sacramentals. They remind us of the presence of God and of those who dwell forever in God's presence, while reminding us of our friendship with, and relationship to, them. Bernard Lonergan would remind us that, as ecclesial expressions of the Christian message grounded in a local community, these expressions of faith are instantiations of a message that is "incarnate in Christ scourged and crucified, dead and risen."[2] Thus, our human reactions in novenas and rosaries, pilgrimages and processions enter into the divine economy of friendship in which the local incarnation of a universal religious reality takes on the *hic et nunc*—here and now—of popular piety. When those images meet with our concrete acts of devotion, they enter into our own personal and communal history such that, as with the words emblazoned across the altar in both the Cave of the Annunciation at Nazareth and the Holy House of Loreto, Italy, the adherents of the many localized forms of popular piety proclaim not merely *that* the Word became flesh, but rather here the Word became flesh: *hic verbum caro factum est.*[3]

As those expressions eloquently communicate the reality of God-with-us to the cultures into which they enter, popular piety becomes a lived reality in a place that is also an active annunciation of the Kingdom of God among us. For this rea-

---

[2] Bernard Lonergan, *Method in Theology* (Toronto: University of Toronto Press, 1971), 364.

[3] "Here . . ." or "in this place" the Word became flesh.

son, Pope Francis is able to assert: "Expressions of popular piety have much to teach us; for those who are capable of reading them, they are a *locus theologicus* which demands our attention, especially at a time when we are looking to the new evangelization."[4]

Catholic Magisterial Teaching and Studying Popular Piety

Pope Francis's assertion of popular piety as a *locus theologicus* stands in a postconciliar tradition that is concerned with the importance of the embodied nature of religious expression as a means of evangelization across cultures. That is, Roman Catholicism has increasingly recognized how the physical and cultural practices and stories of a people are valuable for spreading the Christian message across difference since Vatican II. The value of such a movement was first highlighted by Pope St. Paul VI in the 1975 apostolic exhortation *Evangellii Nuntiandi*. Reflecting on the role of popular piety in the life of the Catholic Church, Paul writes: "One finds among the people particular expressions of the search for God and for faith, both in the regions where the Church has been established for centuries and where she is in the course of becoming established."[5] During his very brief reign, Pope John Paul I made special reference to his own devotional life when, on the feast of St. Gregory the Great, he noted a saying from the north of Italy that "every good thief has his devotion."[6] Noting how popular piety often arises from interplay between a more established ecclesial reality and an

---

[4] Francis, *Evangelii Gaudium*, no. 126, November 24, 2013.
[5] Paul VI, *Evangelii Nuntiandi*, no. 48, December 8, 1975.
[6] John Paul I, Audience, September 3, 1978.

emerging one, Pope St. John Paul II emphasized the particular importance of such an exchange when, at the Mexican shrine of Our Lady of Zapopán, he asserted: "This popular piety is not necessarily a vague sentiment, lacking a solid doctrinal basis, a kind of inferior form of religious manifestation. How often it is, on the contrary, the true expression of the soul of a people, since it is touched by grace and forged by the happy meeting between the work of evangelization and that of local culture."[7] The moment of meeting that he describes understands the relational reality of evangelization, in which the hearts of those engaged are often opened to the message of the Gospel through signs familiar to them from which they can draw common meaning. Pope Francis adds a particular emphasis when, in the exhortation *Evangelii Gaudium*, he writes that popular piety in this context is not "devoid of content; rather it discovers and expresses that content more by way of symbols than by discursive reasoning, and in the act of faith greater accent is placed on *credere in Deum* than on *credere Deum*."[8] Thus, these searches for faith find their evangelical vigor in the ability to inspire and encourage a particular people in a relationship with God and the saints, rather than simply suggesting assent to propositions of divine truth.

Methodological Considerations

The magisterial development around the role of popular piety points to several important methodological considerations

---

[7] John Paul II, Homily at the Basilica at Zapopán, January 30, 1979.

[8] *Evangelii Gaudium*, no. 124. Pope Francis is here insisting that, more than simply believing that God exists, *credere Deum*, the practices of popular religiosity help us to put our faith in God in such a way that a relationship can develop from that faith, *credere in Deum*.

Introduction: Here, the Word Became Flesh

for such a study: First, if such a work is to be truly "popular," it requires sources that listen to the people who are engaged in the practices of popular piety that it describes as central to understanding the larger phenomenon. Simply, ethnographic research is important. The ethnographic research of Harvey Whitehouse, Ambrose Mong, Robert Orsi, Thomas Landy, Timothy Matovina, Xavier Albò, Alison Spedding, and Victor and Edith Turner, among others, has recently allowed us to better grasp how those engaged in practices of popular piety understand the theological meaning behind the individual practices that grow to popular devotion. By recognizing the voices of those engaged in the practices that surround particular religious images, relics, and shrines, ethnographic approaches can allow such reflection to be more faithfully "popular." They can encourage us to listen to the voices and the reflections of the people who are actively practicing their devotion, faithfully aligning us to the emerging synodal process in the Catholic Church.

Second, in considering ethnographic sources, it becomes clear how overarching phenomena are discussed as specific instantiations play out in particular images and ritual actions. Particularly when considering the manner in which ethnographers consider the reality in front of them, this book uses the term "popular religiosity" to refer to the overarching common phenomenon of such practices within the Church and "popular piety" or "piety" to refer to a specific devotional culture. In this sense, I speak broadly of the popular piety of a place like Mexico, for example, where specific popular devotions like Our Lady of Guadalupe, Our Lady of the Remedies, or even the newly popular heterodox devotion of Santa Muerte, all interact with and shape each other.

Third, when thought of in the broader context of the phenomenon of popular religiosity, the ethnographic evidence from a particular devotion helps us look beyond a local church to the broader ecclesial reality. The new understanding that surfaces from such insights can, in turn, allow us to begin to distill the commonly held theologies that underpin the practices of popular religiosity.

Many particular devotions of popular religiosity also have vast documentary sources that arise around them, ranging from interviews with visionaries to sermons delivered at various shrines and during various feasts. These documents often provide insight into how the people involved in the originary events of a given popular devotion understood what was happening to them as an act of faith. They also illustrate how the competent ecclesial authorities first attempted to interpret the growing cult around various devotions as they began to evolve. Looking to the archival literature from two specific examples of popular piety in particular, I demonstrate the ways in which theological reflection on popular piety has developed over time. The different methodologies that I use both demonstrate a growth in ecclesial reflection and reveal something about the manner in which the external world brings its influence to bear on the faith of any particular people. Furthermore, I show how they come to express that faith as they encounter God through their devotional life. Paying attention to this documentation helps us understand how the universal Church often incorporates the devotions, feasts, and images of one people into the life of all of the faithful. In a globalizing ecclesial reality, we must understand how the religious experience of a few might become the devotion of the many.

A methodological approach that understands the experience of the people of God as a primary theological source has a rich foundation in Catholic theological discourse. In the work *On Consulting the Faithful in Matters of Doctrine*, St. John Henry Newman makes the consistent assertion that, particularly when it concerns the types of theological truths that touch on matters of liturgy and devotion, the hierarchy often ends up affirming that which arises from the lived faith of the people in the *sensus fidelium*. In the same text, though, he refers to a pastoral letter of an English bishop to assert that there is a movement between the faithful and magisterium such that "pious belief, and the devotion which springs from it, are the faithful reflection of the pastoral teaching."[9] In noting the interplay between the belief of the faithful and the role of pastoral teaching, Newman illustrates an important tension in popular piety, namely the need for a Church that listens for the Spirit moving in all of its members while also properly discerning the Spirit's presence and action.

While the Church has often sought the voices of the faithful as a theological source in the context of the *sensus fidelium,* the methodological novelty of this book is the use of ethnographic sources to identify their voices. Ethnographic reports bring a valuable added candor in the faithful's responses to researchers who are not ecclesial authorities. Reflections on specific devotions and practices, offered without concern for the approval of authorities, might offer a fuller picture of how the faith takes hold in a given culture in both its power and its peril. Aware that social scientists might have their own secular biases, however, I look to the ways in which theological convictions are commonly expressed in ethnographic thick descriptions across devotions as a baseline for understanding the broader phenomenon of popular religiosity.

The commonalities that arise might help establish boundaries of popular religiosity and clarify what sort of dialogue might occur between different peoples who are speaking

---

[9] John Henry Newman, *On Consulting the Faithful in Matters of Doctrine* (London: Geoffrey Chapman, 1961), 172.

within the one *sensus fidelium* of the universal Church. Such commonalities across popular pieties that are rooted in different cultures and places could, to paraphrase Tertullian in *De praescriptione haereticorum,* serve as a signpost that takes seriously the guidance of the Spirit within the Church of Christ while also setting boundaries for that common expression.[10]

Outlining the Argument

The interplay between particular devotions that are a part of a given culture's piety as well as universal popular religiosity can be a significant model for the intra-ecclesial communion that characterizes the Catholic Church today. In order to demonstrate this model effectively, this book is divided into five chapters. Each of these chapters exhibits the usefulness of this model from different perspectives.

First, as a question of the origins of such expressions, it should help us better understand how our use of religious images, particularly within Christianity, are often connected to prior, pre-Christian, religious sensibilities in a given culture. Next, a clearer picture of that relationship might then also help us gain a clearer understanding of the role of religious images and practices when they arise as the result of times of crisis, when processes of meaning-making might drive our need to connect to transcendent principles. Conscious of the potential of devotion to play itself out in excess, and even perhaps to turn to idolatry, the third chapter deals with a case where the hierarchical Catholic Church is at odds with a developing

---

[10]See Tertullian, "*De praescriptione haereticorum,*" in *Ante-Nicene Fathers*, vol. 3, ed. Alexander Roberts, James Donaldson, and A. Cleveland Coxe (Buffalo, NY: Christian Literature, 1885), 21.

devotion and outlines ways in which a given local devotion may or may not be a popular expression of universal Catholic piety. Such a reflection then asks us to consider the manner in which devotions might contribute to the overall development of doctrine and how the dominant religious images and practices that emerge from local devotion become formally enmeshed in Catholic teaching. This is an interplay of *Lex orandi, Lex credendi*—the law of prayer is the law of belief—as magisterial authority in the Church listens to, affirms, and incorporates lived expressions of the faith that arise from the *sensus fidelium*. Not all devotions that are properly popular are indeed pious, however. Finally, with a renewed appreciation for the role of popular religiosity in both its promise and peril, I return to examine how the same missionary impulses that fueled so much of the origins of popular devotion might now foster dialogue in a globalized Christianity through a commonality of belief that bears a diversity of expressions.

Copacabana: Conflict and Compromise

What happens when a newly evangelized people seeks to express Christian faith from their own cultural perspective? The first chapter illustrates the value of Pope St. John Paul II's argument, that popular piety is often the expression of the soul of a people precisely because it stands at the intersection of local culture and the initial work of evangelization. I focus on the still emerging church among the Indigenous people of the Andes, using the ethnographic descriptions of an enculturated faith among the Aymara and Quechua-speaking peoples. In addition to this scholarly work, I incorporate testimonies from an Indigenous perspective, namely the Roman Catholic Deacon and Incan *Yatiri* Calixto Quispe. These sources help us address some of the issues around syncretism, the interplay of Catholic belief and animist sensibilities, and the interaction between the cosmic and meta-cosmic levels of religion.[11] The relationship between Our Lady of Copacabana and the traditional Aymara concept of the *Pachamama* is particularly important for illustrating the tensions and synergies that arise when a strongly rooted folk religion interacts with the message of the Gospel. With theological underpinning in both *Redemptoris Missio* and *Querida Amazonia*, this chapter opens us to Timothy Matovina's question: Are these interactions truly evangelization, or do they represent mere "Christianization" of the old folk religion, imposing a certain civilization rather than proposing a lived faith?[12]

Lourdes: At the Horizon of a New Era

While the first chapter demonstrates the dynamic development of many devotions, the second chapter attends to popular devotion that does not arise from the fresh appropriation of the faith by a newly evangelized people. How do we account for popular devotions that surface not as the merger of a new faith in an established context but rather in a place with an already very deeply seated Catholic culture and practice? The second chapter argues that, in these instances, we usually see popular devotions gain strength in relation to an event or an object in a time of crisis. A people's devotions are often primed by experiences of crisis into which divine intervention allows for a re-stabilization of the culture and community. In these moments, popular devotion still stands at the intersection be-

---

[11] Ambrose Mong, *Power of Popular Piety: A Critical Examination* (Eugene, OR: Cascade Books, 2019), 43.

[12] Timothy Matovina, *Theologies of Guadalupe* (Oxford: Oxford University Press, 2019), 7.

tween new and old ways of life, as it did in the first chapter, addressing a crisis through robust acts of meaning-making.

The second chapter will carefully examine the devotion that arose around the visions of Our Lady of Lourdes, as witnessed by St. Bernadette Soubirous, in Lourdes, France, from February until July of 1858. These events did not happen in a vacuum. They were marked by the delayed arrival of both Enlightenment values and the industrial age in a small enclave at the foot of the Pyrenees which until then had its own language, culture, and way of life. The interviews with the visionary after and the hagiographical testimonies of members of the community at Lourdes at the time contextualize the development of the devotion. Ruth Harris, Victor Turner, and Edith Turner point us to a broader sociological and historical context in which we begin to understand how Our Lady of Lourdes became a rallying cry for a people who were engaged in a rich process of meaning-making at the threshold of a new era in their town.

Patronage and Lament: The Curious Case of Santa Muerte

While many practices of local popular devotion become a part of the universal reality of popular piety within the Church, not all do, and perhaps not all should. How do we properly discern what is worthy of approbation as an expression of popular piety for the Universal Church? This chapter particularly considers what can happen when excesses of idolatry begin to emerge within a local devotion. It will examine the growing devotional practices surrounding the narco-religious image of Santa Muerte, which has gained increasing traction in Mexico in the past twenty years, as a counterpoint to Our Lady of Guadalupe in the broader context of Mexican popular piety. Paying attention to the ways in which the Church has theologically understood idolatry, the chapter turns to the icon and its perversion, under the pretense of gaining power over the divine within local contexts.[13] The chapter will consider Jean-Luc Marion's assertion that the distinction between idol and icon is, at base, a distinction between narcissism and self-transcendence. While this distinction identifies the idolatry of Santa Muerte in stark terms, the chapter also identifies how this practice echoes as a lament from within situations of poverty and oppression. The Church must hear the cry of the poor.

Trickle-Up Devotion: From Tepeyac to Vatican Hill

What happens when devotions that are local and particular to a people expand beyond the bounds of a specific church, into the reality of the larger *Cattolica*? The fourth chapter explores how the *sensus fidelium*, expressed in a local church, is given expression through popular devotion, often becoming a part of the universal understanding of the faith as well. The centuries-long development of devotion to Our Lady of Guadalupe is a significant case for understanding this dynamic. An image of Mary that has been venerated on a small hill outside of Mexico City is not just the provenance of the small community around Tepeyac hill. It has become the object of universal veneration, eclipsing even its Old World namesake in renown. Such an image, far from being understood as simply the intercessory patroness of a small

---

[13]See Hans Urs von Balthasar, *The Truth Is Symphonic: Aspects of a Christian Plurality* (San Francisco: Ignatius Press, 1987), 67. "Magic is an enterprise issuing from human power that, at most, would seek to hold the divine fast before us (if such a thing were possible); it could never admit the divine into us."

local community, takes on meaning as the patroness of an entire hemisphere, as a patroness for the poor and marginalized, and, poignantly today, as patroness for the migrants of a continent who seek a new life through their travels. As local legends evolve into universal piety, the law of prayer of a local community, touched by that initial moment of grace described in the first chapter, can often become the law of belief of the whole people of God through a sort of reverse evangelization. Thus, those who may have been evangelized become, themselves, evangelizers, telling the good news of how God has moved in their midst.

E Pluribus Unum: When Many Faces Become One

Having paid attention to popular religiosity's initial development, its outgrowth as a response of faith in times of chaos and crisis, its peril when misappropriated, and the ways that it has contributed to the continued development of doctrine in the Church, the book concludes with a call for intra-ecclesial cross-cultural communion along our many paths with Mary. Popular religiosity is a heuristic for understanding our walk together as the Church. Each devotion reveals something new about Mary and the People of God across different cultures, allowing us to work out a vision of a communion in diversity. Since each culture brings its own metanarratives, foundational cosmological views, and aesthetics to its devotion to the same historical figure, the many paths that we walk together with Mary represent the possibilities for intercultural, intra-ecclesial dialogue that is richly subjective in its cultural foundations and confidently objective in how it unifies the People of God, through the person of Mary of Nazareth, in love with Jesus, her son.

Walking Together: How Popular Piety Binds the Global Church

Although I use a particular type of popular devotion to illustrate most of my thesis, I use and compare other devotions throughout the text to further demonstrate how that particular type of devotion, while having properties unique to it, participates in a broader context of a lived form of religion in which people make meaning of the world around them. The dynamic relationship of emerging popular piety and developing doctrine, in both its promise and peril, provides us with possibilities for thinking about how different cultures across the world already contribute to the Church, as they have down the ages. Popes John Paul II, Benedict XVI, and Francis have emphasized the need for a new evangelization, and this book offers further insights into such a process precisely because it seeks to understand how cultures come to be evangelized at all. This book helps us rethink previously held conceptions about the dominance of a singular cultural perspective in ecclesial life. As we rethink church and cultures, this book provides a constructive heuristic model that can correct that domination where it is needed, grounding our theological attention in the traditions of the People of God.

1

Copacabana

Conflict and Compromise

Some places are just holy.

Communities often acknowledge that certain places bear an inherent sense of transcendence that a religious instinct then seeks to express. We often experience that religious instinct clearly in the resulting myth, image, and practices that surround these places. Pilgrim trails run through vast plains, over mountain ranges, and are trod down through the generations.

In Mecca, the Kaaba was a place of pilgrimage before Muhammad made it the center of Islam, an act that reformed previous pagan practices at the holy site. In Jerusalem, long before Solomon built his temple, the people of Israel held Zion as the sacred spot where Abraham almost sacrificed Isaac, as the previously pagan patriarch emerged into the new life of the covenant. In Santiago de Compostela, the tomb believed by tradition to be that of the apostle James rests at the end of a pilgrim trail long trod by pre-Christian people on their way to what they believed was the end of the world. In Ireland, the pilgrimage to Croagh Patrick in county Mayo, where St. Patrick is said to have spent forty days and nights in prayer, was also clearly, as evidenced by the archaeological markers that surround it, a place of pre-Christian worship.

Some places are just holy. As each generation adds their layers of meaning to the sanctuaries that have warranted such pilgrimages, foundational myths often merge with Christian faith in ways that give rise to popular piety. One of the less well-known places where this has clearly happened is on the shore of Lake Titicaca, on the border between Bolivia and Peru, high in the Andes Mountain range.

Here, the transcendent richness of the place, to the people who live there, assures that the original meanings attributed to the place have never been exhausted. Rather, they seem to have been enriched by the coming of the Augustinian Catholic missionaries such that:

> This popular piety is not necessarily a vague sentiment, lacking a solid doctrinal basis, a kind of inferior form of religious manifestation. How often it is, on the contrary, the true expression of the soul of a people, since it is touched by grace and forged by the happy meeting between the work of evangelization and that of local culture.[1]

When the evangelistic efforts of missionaries can allow for a robust appropriation of the faith into a local culture, the emergence of an Indigenous devotional culture is one of the most obvious expressions of missionary success. Such a devotional culture can blend the faith of the evangelizer and the evangelized, giving new expression to Christian faith. This happened at the shrine at Copacabana and at a hundred *huacas*—Indigenous holy places—that dot the Andean countryside: from the great mountain of Potosi, to the shores of

---

[1] John Paul II, Homily at the Basilica of Zapopán, no. 2, January 30, 1979.

the Island of the Sun, to the temple to the Indigenous deity *Viracocha* that became the shrine of Our Lady of Copacabana.[2]

Through the narrative of the shrine of Our Lady of Copacabana, this chapter examines how place is foundational to religious observance and practice, demonstrating its centrality in popular religiosity. This chapter considers three distinct moments in the evolution of popular piety in a particular place. First, I engage how the myths and legends already present in an Indigenous culture interact with those carried by missionaries to an area, both in matters that are essential to Christian faith and in the structures of the missionaries' own cultures that they bring with them into a new context. This is the question of the difference between a work of evangelization and a Christianizing project. Next, I examine the images and symbols that arise from that interaction, in this case the statue of Mary, which is venerated at Copacabana, and consider how the cultural interactions between Indigenous and imported religions play in the evolution of popular devotion within a people's broader popular piety. Finally, I trace the role of place through sites of pre-Christian worship that are now Christian sanctuaries. That these locations are still places of worship can remind us of the importance of place in the religious development of a people.

When we pay attention to actual place in the stories of religious sites over time, we can better recognize and understand the function of archaic holy places as contemporary shrines.

---

[2] *Huaca* is an Aymara word which can mean either religious object or place. In Andean culture, these objects and places were known to speak through the local *yatiris*. Missionary records argue that one of the great moments of cognitive dissonance for the Inca was that, with the arrival of the gospel, the *huacas* ceased to speak. Contemporary practice seems to demonstrate that that is not entirely true, but that often the shamans who hear the speaking of the *huacas* do so with some Christian culture at least in the background.

Through religious and cultural appropriation of images and practices in a place, a people begin to change. When that which remains distinctly of the culture is allowed to complement Christian doctrine in this change, we gain a rich perspective on how Christianity began to spread in the first place.

When They Came to the Birthplace of the Sun

Once, I was standing on the shore of Lake Titicaca and was handed a small square of sugar. I was visiting Calixto Quispe, an Inca *yatiri*,[3] Roman Catholic deacon, and well-respected Indigenous theologian. We stood by the small *huaca* that was carved out of the cliff on the edge of the lake near his village, an archaic pre-Conquest holy place where Calixto was seeking to build a small retreat and rehabilitation center that could blend the best of Inca and Christian spiritualities. The square of sugar was emblazoned with a small green snake in food coloring that, in order to form a circle, seemed to be chasing its own tail. Calixto told me proudly, "This is your symbol!" I was a bit taken aback.

In no small part due to their role in the third chapter of Genesis, snakes can be unsettling symbols for a person from a dominantly Christian culture. A snake is considered to be cunning, sneaky, slimy, and venomous. To be called "a snake"

---

[3]See Tomás L. Huanca, *El yatiri en la comunidad Aymara* (La Paz: Ediciones CADA, 1990). People often refer to an Aymara *yatiri* as a shaman. Contrary to an understanding of the role of a shaman as a religious leader, the *yatiri* is more the leader of a community that itself has strong religious undertones. As Tomás L. Huanca points out, that the *yatiri* lives within the community, experiences some level of formation for the role, and is only chosen to do so after he has been shown worthy distinguishes him from the shamanic tradition where the shaman lives outside of the community and trains himself before being recognized by other shamans. The *yatiri*, rather than being a specifically religious functionary, is more importantly a community leader.

is broadly considered in my own culture to be insulting, and a man who was well respected among the people I was visiting thought of me as a snake.

"No, Miguel," he chuckled, "don't think of it that way. For us, a snake is a symbol of rebirth, it sheds its skin and emerges into new life."[4]

As it became obvious that our religious imaginations were different, another thing became abundantly clear. The place where I was standing, with the deep blue waters of the lake reflecting the clouds above and the whole delineated by the surrounding tan and snow-capped peaks of the Andes, was truly a holy place. Even if our symbols were different or needed some explanation, surely the beauty of the world's highest navigable lake spoke to all of us of something more than ourselves.

Successive peoples have made their home around this lake, for thousands of years. Before Bolivia and Peru existed, Francisco Pizarro's Spanish Conquest found its way across the sea and up into the mountains in 1532, where he conquered the Inca Empire, which had just consolidated its power one hundred years earlier.[5] Before the Inca came to the lake from Cuzco in the fifteenth century, people had long been living and worshipping at specific holy sites around the lake. On the Island of the Sun, at the present site of the Basilica of Copacabana, particularly in the great earthen pyramid of Tiahuanaco,

---

[4]Personal conversation, March 2018.

[5]See R. Alan Covey, *Inca Apocalypse: The Spanish Conquest and the Transformation of the Andean World* (Oxford: Oxford University Press, 2020). One of the things that Covey notes is that the Inca conquest of the area was itself marked by a certain religious impulse. The Incas made claims to be descended from the gods, and that no mortal would ever be able to match them in warfare. Their making peace with and incorporating the local deities into their pantheon less than a century before the arrival of the Spanish sets the stage for the evangelizing mission of the conquistadors.

they had established their own civilization with its customs, culture, religious practices, and foundational myths.

In the alcoves and beaches, cliffs and islands, people who are indigenous to the area find the place where life began. Here is the spot where the sun rose out of an island with scorched rocks on top that still tell the tale. Here is the proof of the patronage of the mother of Jesus in the image of Our Lady of Copacabana.

Something peculiar happened when the first missionaries reached the Altiplano. They reported back that they had heard stories that had vaguely familiar resonances with the narratives that they had sought to bring to the people above the crest of the La Paz valley. The Indigenous people told them stories of the creation of the world that held eerie resonances with the one that they knew from Genesis: a separation of waters, a time of chaos and darkness, God bringing humanity out of the earth. They heard stories of a great flood to punish wickedness that two righteous people survived by climbing into a great drum and waiting until the flood waters resided, leaving them on the holy island in the middle of the lake. They heard stories of a god who walked among them, working great signs and wonders. They also heard the stories of a saint-like figure who, through what could best be described as intercessory prayer, was a thaumaturge with the specific ability to heal. Those conquistadors took that perhaps to be a sign that either the apostle St. Thomas or St. Bartholomew had somehow been there before them.[6]

---

[6]See Verónica Salles-Reese, *From Viracocha to the Virgin of Copacabana: Representations of the Sacred at Lake Titicaca* (Austin: University of Texas Press, 1997). In her discussion of the succession of Indigenous religious myths at Lake Titicaca Salles-Reese notes the similarities to Christianity, but also makes clear that there are legitimate questions about whether the resonances with Genesis, or the legends which surround the far-flung travels of

As they read Andean Indigenous religion through the lens of their European culture, the first missionaries, according to the records, perhaps unwittingly, created a new religious reality by weaving together the strands of their own belief with those of the people whom they encountered. Sometimes gently, though more often than not forcefully, the missionaries who arrived on the shores of Lake Titicaca brought their cultures, their religious charisms, their national interests, and their theology, supported as it was by Greek and Semitic cosmologies, with them.[7] When they encountered a cosmology that had resonances with their own, they seemed to employ two distinct approaches as they considered how to bring Christianity to the people of the new world. Some approached these commonalities in an extension of the thought of Church fathers like Justin Martyr: perhaps what was afoot was demonic influence, providing a distorted view of religion in juxtaposition to the true faith. Others, however, took the view of those like Gregory the Great: while still cautious of the idea of demonic influence, there are possibilities for building the new on top of the old.

---

the Apostles, are a bit forced because the records that we have of those myths are often first recorded by Christian missionaries.

[7] See Joseph Ratzinger, "Europe: A Heritage with Obligations for Christians," in *Church, Ecumenism, and Politics: New Essays in Ecclesiology* (New York: Crossroad, 1988; original German 1979), 230. It is interesting to note that Ratzinger, later Pope Benedict XVI, emphasizes that Christianity itself is born from a synthesis of two cultures. He writes that "Christianity is the synthesis mediated in Jesus Christ between the faith of Israel and the Greek Spirit." The interchange which occurs in Acts 16:9 in which Paul is summoned to Greece for the first time is also, for Benedict, the birth of Europe as we know it. A cultural interchange, not entirely dissimilar to the one which they themselves were participating in, was something that Benedict would argue was already inherent in the identity of these Christian and European colonizers when they arrived in the Andes in the sixteenth century.

One Culture's Heaven and Another Culture's Hell: Conflict and the Need for Exorcism

While believers in the book of Genesis have long lost a notion of the actual location of the Garden of Eden, many Indigenous cultures still point to a place where creation, or at least a certain creative ordering of the universe, began. Tiahuanaco is one such place for the people of the Altiplano. In a valley between mountain peaks that runs down to Lake Titicaca, one encounters the ruins of a great earthen pyramid, a subterranean temple of the dead, with imposing walls that predate the Inca stone masons who would later come to rule this valley, gateways that align with the solstice solar patterns, and gargantuan sandstone monoliths. As is common in places like Tiahuanaco, places of commerce and social organization emerge where holy sites emerge. Among the ruins, archaeologists have identified homes, places where goods were bought and sold, and implements for the agricultural life that surrounded the city.

The meaning of Tiahuanaco—signified in the way it expands out to the hills and down to the lake, in the evocative way that it stretches up into the heavens on the ledges of its pyramid, while digging down into the earth in its temple of the dead—becomes clear when we take account of Andean myth. As Sabine McCormack notes: "At Tiahuanaco, the Maker Contiti Viracocha made the sun and the day, the moon and the stars, and turned those earlier people into stone for having offended him. Out of stone he made distinct kinds of people, with lords to rule over them, with pregnant women, and babies in cradles."[8] The ancient city was more than just

---

[8]Sabine MacCormack, *Religion in the Andes: Vision and Imagination in Early Colonial Peru* (Princeton, NJ: Princeton University Press, 1991), 109. MacCormack's main source for this is the account of Juan De Betanzos, a

the site of the creation of the human beings that currently roam the earth. It was also the origin of the polis because the creator god of the Inca created people specifically to be lords among the people in that place. The account also makes clear that it was from that spot that humanity spread out into the world and, importantly for the Inca myth, made it to Cuzco.

Tiahuanaco is a holy site for the Inca and the people who preceded them in the region not simply because of the beauty of its location. It is holy because of the idea that something remarkable happened there. Holy places are often marked out by that same belief, yet in the face of the interaction between two diverse groups in the same space, the question of precisely what happened comes into question. What serves as one group's Eden could well be the playground of the devil for another. Historian of religion Mircea Eliade, in considering what makes a place holy, notes that these places are often marked out by a foundational narrative that includes what he calls a hierophany, or a sort of breaking into the world of what Rudolph Otto would call the numinous. "Numinous," for Otto, implies a certain pre-ethical understanding of holiness, a word that itself already evokes an ethical judgment of goodness. In discussions about missionary efforts, when two religions interact, "numinous," which Otto says extends across cultures, allows us to faithfully attend to that which is common to both.[9] In concert with Otto's insight into the use of the word "holy," Eliade introduces us to the importance of the holiness of place through the familiar words of God to Moses in Exodus 3:5: "Put off thy shoes from thy feet, for

---

sixteenth-century Spaniard who had moved to Peru, married into a noble Inca family, and sought to act as their translator.

[9] Rudolph Otto, *The Idea of the Holy: An Inquiry into the Non-Rational Factor in the Idea of the Divine and Its Relation to the Rational,* trans. John W. Harvey (Oxford: Oxford University Press, 1936), 7.

the place whereupon thou standest is holy ground."[10] In reference to the divine rejoinder to be conscious of the holiness of place, Eliade marks the common importance of such belief for many cultures, noting that such a sense is not exclusive to the Abrahamic religions. From his perspective as a historian of religion, marking out the holiness of a place is a fairly universal phenomenon.

Eliade holds that holy spaces break up the homogeneity of the world and serve as points of orientation. This is often nowhere stronger in his account than about places that function as the center of the world or the locus of creation for people of belief. These places, more than just orienting us within the plane of our own mundane existence, often mark connection to transcendence as well. The orientation provided by these spaces provides a compass and serves as a sort of altitude indicator of the type one might find on an airplane, orienting us both across the horizon and to the horizon itself. For Eliade, these centers also push outward toward the horizon. Such an orienting reality finds a home in specifically Christian thought because, as Hans Urs von Balthasar reminds us:

> THE VERY FORM OF THE CROSS, extending out into the four winds, always told the ancient Church that the Cross means solidarity: its outstretched arms would gladly embrace the universe. According to the Didache, the Cross is *sēmeion epektaseōs*, a "sign of expansion," and only God himself can have such a wide reach: "On the Cross God stretched out his hands to encompass the bounds of the universe" (Cyril of Jerusalem).[11]

---

[10]Mircea Eliade, *The Sacred and the Profane: The Nature of Religion,* trans. Willard R. Trask (New York: Harcourt, 1987), 20.

[11]Hans Urs von Balthasar, *Heart of the World,* trans. Erasmo S. Leiva (San

The cross is far from an abstraction. The cross existed within history, at a specific place and in a specific time, and Christians still orient themselves from Calvary today. That place still serves as a point of orientation for Christians, as it likely did for the missionaries who sought to bring the faith to the Andes. The cross stands as a place of origin from which the divine mission extends into the world through the sacrifice of Christ.

In breaking up the homogeneity of the cosmos, sacred spaces allow us to orient ourselves to the world around us, and to the world that lies beyond us. These sites not only mark off the geography of a religious culture on Eliade's account, they often implicitly make the case for the *raison d'être* of a community in the context of their religion. Namely: "All these beliefs express the same feeling, which is profoundly religious: 'our world' is holy ground *because it is the place nearest to heaven,* because from here, from our abode, it is possible to reach heaven; hence our world is a high place."[12] The spaces where one can feel, touch, and be present to foundational religious understanding serve an important role in religious practice and belief and in making an "ours" at all. These places are important for creating the concept of belonging to a group or people.

Victor Turner has a similar sense about the role of such spaces as binding a group. He notes that our pilgrimages to the sites create a certain "normative communitas" that delineates groups through "a nonutilitarian experience of brotherhood and fellowship."[13] While Eliade's understanding allows for the sorts of conflicts that may, and indeed did, occur on the

---

Francisco: Ignatius Press, 1979), 13. *Emphasis his.*

[12]Eliade, *The Sacred and the Profane*, 38–39.

[13]Victor Turner and Edith Turner, *Image and Pilgrimage in Christian Culture* (New York: Columbia University Press, 2011), 135.

Altiplano through successive conquests, both Turner and Eliade point to the important idea that spaces matter in the creation of a people and the subsequent creation of cultural, religious, and social norms.

If sacred spaces play such a role in delineating a people, the question arises: What happens when actors foreign to the established Indigenous group, often with their own unique connection to another place that is marked off as holy, enter the sacred space of another thinking it to be profane? For the Spanish missionaries who climbed into the Andes and conquered the Inca empire, perhaps Santiago de Compostela, the Shrine of Our Lady of the Candelaria in Tenerife, or Jerusalem were such locations. They were places marked off by a hierophany that provided an origin of their identities as Spanish or Christian. As identity can be multivalent, it is important not to overlook the role place might play for the members of religious orders who came as missionaries. The connections of those missionaries to European cultures and their particular charisms might also have influenced how they preached the gospel and spoke to the Indigenous people of the area. When such groups interact in a sacred space, conflict seems inevitable. When those cultures intermingled in Bolivia, however, something new came out of the initial conflict.

Casting Out Deception

In the ruins of Tiahuanaco one finds evidence of what happened when cultures clashed. On the great sandstone monoliths that stand on the site, and in the few removed to a small museum nearby to protect them from the ravages of the environment, one can trace a physical impact on the site itself. As one approaches the Ponce Monolith, which, in Andean myth, represents the race of stone giants who populated the world before humans came to exist, one notices something on the left shoulder of the large statue: a cross carved into the stone in an almost graffiti-like form.

The cross on the arm of the monolith was intended as an exorcism. Unconscious of the Andean creation myth and the great stone giants purported to have roamed the land, the marking of the monolith with the cross was, to the Spanish, the destruction of an idol. There is a sense in which the exorcism by the Spanish missionaries was, however, both repudiation and consecration. Participating in the same dynamic that the Inca did when they arrived at Tiahuanaco, the Spanish were seeking to claim this space for themselves and for their God.

As the Inca had first colonized and converted Tiahuanaco to their own purposes after conquering the area shortly before the arrival of the Spanish, even incorporating the creator myth of Viracocha into their own religion and instituting a pilgrimage to the already ruined site, so the Spanish would place their own symbols there.[14] Layers of meaning have been added on by each successive group that arrived in these ruins.

Far from being a mere act of colonization, often enough these were rich acts of religious meaning-making. Eliade sees events like this as a natural extension of how religions work and an expression of the sort of dominion with which Adam is charged in Genesis 1:28: "It must be understood that the cosmicization of unknown territories is always a consecration; to organize a space is to repeat the paradigmatic work of the gods."[15] Guardini perhaps best explores this insight from the specifically Christian perspective when he notes that: "When we examine the motives of human endeavor and the play of

---

[14] See Covey, *Inca Apocalypse*, 202–203.
[15] Eliade, *The Sacred and the Profane*, 32.

forces set in motion by historical decisions we discover everywhere a basic will at work, the will to dominion."[16] Romano Guardini understands that such dominion, as expressed in the sorts of cosmicization that Eliade takes it to be, is characterized as a permission to rule by divine consent. When placed in the context of an obligation to do so, it is best understood as divine mission. Guardini continues: "Behind the attempts at world-renewal beckons an image by which man attempts to express the essence of things, of his own being, and of the meaning of life. The struggle for dominion is the struggle to realize that image."[17] Such a struggle, in the case of the Spanish arriving at Tiahuanaco, became evident in the image of the cross as an expression of the meaning of life in the midst of a religious reality completely other than their own.

Expressing what is other as "demonic," and therefore feeling the need for a cleansing or an exorcism, was by no means new in Christian history nor to the Spanish missionaries who arrived in Bolivia. Even a passing glance at the works of Justin Martyr or Irenaeus shows that the fathers of the Church perhaps grappled with the same sorts of realities that the Spanish missionaries did. Some rites, stories, or symbols that they observed in pagan practices may have seemed vaguely similar to the Christian practice. Still, many of those same things that were cherished in the classical pantheon caused a moment of *aporia* for the fathers. These sorts of moments, when we feel confused, blocked, or simply wonder why the world is the way it is, force us to ask questions to make meaning of the worlds we inhabit. The question of the similarities was not merely a theological one. Remember that these questions

---

[16]Romano Guardini, *The End of the Modern World*, trans. Elinor C. Briefs (Wilmington, DE: ISI Books, 1998), 172.

[17]Guardini, *The End of the Modern World*, 173.

arose from deeply felt experiences of a persecuted Church, and they motivated the Fathers' inquiry existentially. As Michelina Tenace notes, this was also a religious experience of what the community was suffering in that moment: "The incomprehensible violence that the pagans unleashed against the Christians was provoked by demons, and it was against the demons that they needed to struggle."[18]

That persecution makes it easy to see why, in the first *Apologia*, Justin Martyr condemns the religious practice of the Romans as idolatry and blames the origins of the beliefs and practices connected to Roman idolatry on the appearance of demons who were meant to deceive the Christian people into worshipping dead statues.[19] Irenaeus echoes Justin, quoting the psalms in *Adversus Haereses* to make the point further:

> As with David: The gods of the heathen are idols of demons; and, You shall not follow other gods. For in that he says the gods of the heathen—but the heathen are ignorant of the true God—and calls them other gods, he bars their claim [to be looked upon] as gods at all. But as to what they are in their own person, he speaks concerning them; for they are, he says, the idols of demons.[20]

Holding fast to the proscription of idolatry in the first commandment of the decalogue, the Fathers understood that the

---

[18] Michelina Tenace, *Cristiani si Diventa: Dogma e vita nei primi tre concili* (Rome: Lipa, 2013), 77. Translation mine from: "l'incomprensibile violenze che I pagani scatenavano contro i cristiani era provocata dai demoni, ed era contro di lor oche bisognava lottare."

[19] Justin Martyr, *The First Apology of Justin Martyr: Addressed to the Emperor Antoninus Pius,* trans. John Kaye (Edinburgh: J. Grant, 1912), 11.

[20] Irenaeus of Lyon, *Against Heresies,* trans. John Keble (London: James Parker, 1872), 214.

only way to make sense of the claims that the statues of the classical pantheon had some meaning, or at least some efficacy in the lives of those who worshipped them, was to impute that meaning and efficacy to demons. Since there is no other god than the triune God for the Christian, if people imputed personality to these statues and told stories of how the worship of idols somehow helped them, such action by the idol could only be the act of a demon deceiving them.[21] While the persecution of the early Church might have provided the impetus for such a line of thinking to develop, the same logic perdured in theological discourse, particularly in the realm of missiology, well beyond its original motivating historical circumstances. This logic found its way into the heart of the Andes when the Spanish missionaries carved the cross into the side of the monoliths, sure that the monoliths were objects of worship at an Inca pilgrimage site and that they must be manifestations of the devil.

The Spanish often extended beyond simply carving a cross into the arms of statues that they perceived to be idols. In practices that became common among the Spanish missionaries throughout the so-called New World, Native religious practices would be banned and the conversion of Indigenous peoples would often be used to justify slavery under the *encomienda* system.[22] Broadly, as Verónica Salles-Reese notes, in

---

[21]Obviously, the logic entails that this could not be an angelic act since, as messengers of God, they could only direct humanity to the one true God.

[22]The *encomienda* system was established by the Spanish crown in 1501. In essence, Indigenous people were "entrusted" to the conquistadors for the purposes of their religious and cultural conversion. The system itself was tied to the doctrine of discovery, initially established by Pope Nicholas V in 1455 with the bull *Romanus Pontifex*, which gave the Portuguese crown power specifically for the enslavement of the Muslim peoples of Africa under the understanding that, as such, they could be converted to Christianity for their own good. For the purposes of the Americas the principle was extended in

many circumstances, the *encomienda* system as it was practiced and supported by the priests of Catholic religious orders intended to set up a new version of feudalism for the purposes of Christianizing the Indigenous population. The subjugation of Indigenous peoples in the Americas, for mining gold and silver in particular in the Andes, was often justified through the lens of evangelization. The pitfalls of such a project were evident beyond the obvious and abject abuses of human rights almost from the very beginning. Bartolomé de Las Casas, famously himself an *encomiendero*, saw that the system was incompatible with the faith and had a conversion experience on the vigil of Pentecost in 1514, while praying with the text of Ecclesiastes 34:18, seeing the need for "worship acceptable to God." He spent the rest of his life, first as a priest and then as a bishop, heroically advocating for the Indigenous peoples of the Americas.[23]

Even for the more cynically minded among the missionaries, the *encomienda* was clearly not an effective method of evangelization. In Bolivia and Peru, the missionaries of the sixteenth and seventeenth centuries had their doubts about the genuineness of converts in the context of the system. Salles-

---

1493 by Alexander VI in the papal bull *Inter Caetera*. In that bull, Alexander more explicitly states the purposes and ends of the *encomienda* system. Both bulls, and the doctrine that was subsequently derived from them was used consistently to justify the actions of colonial powers even to the end of what we might now recognize as cultural genocide. In March of 2022, representatives of the Indigenous nations of Canada, who had been subjected to residential schools based in the doctrine of discovery by both the Catholic Church and the Government of Canada as late as 1990, went to Rome to meet with Pope Francis. One of their requests in those meetings was that Francis officially revoke *Inter Caetera* as official Church law.

[23]See Maria Izabel Barboza de Morais Oliveira, "Entre la Espada e a Cruz: Bartolomeu de Las Casas em Defesa do modo Pacífico de Evangelização dos Indígenas na América Espanhola," *Revista Brasileira do Caribe* (São Luís, MA, Brazil) 19, no. 37 (July 10, 2018).

Reese notes one text in particular in which José de Arriaga, a Jesuit missionary in the seventeenth century, held this system under contempt, since the converts apparently held to their old customs:

> On the feast of Corpus Christi, they very covertly put a small *Huaca* at the feet of the monstrance of the most Holy Sacrament. And a curate told me that he found *Huacas* in the holes by the feet of the statues of saints in their altars and yet others under the altar, put there by the Sacristan, and I have seen them myself behind the same Church.[24]

Fr. Arriaga goes on to talk about how the Indigenous people had also constructed an image of Our Lady of the Assumption in order to continue to worship the idol "HuayHuay." There are comparable stories across Latin America, many of which only became apparent as Catholic churches and cathedrals were renovated after the Second Vatican Council. When sixteenth-century altars were removed, small Indigenous symbols were often found neatly tucked away. Even the Spanish knew that the project of evangelization was not working, as Arriaga's text indicates. When the idols were exorcised, they seemed to simply find places to hide behind icons. Where the Spanish missionaries placed crosses on monoliths, Inca people pushed back in expressions of their culture that forced a similar juxtaposition.

---

[24]Salles-Reese, *From Viracocha to the Virgin of Copacabana*, Kindle location 407. Translation mine from: "*Indios, que a acontecido en la fiesta del Corpus, poner una Huaca pequeña en las mismas andas al pie de la Custodia del Santísimo Sacramento, muy disimuladamente. Y un Cura me dixo que avía hallado las Huacas en el hueco de las Peanas de los Santos del Altar, y otras debaxo del Altar, que las avia puesto el Sacristán, y yó e visto detrás de la misma Iglesia.*"

One of the great limits of the *encomienda* system, especially as it was practiced in what is now Peru and Bolivia, was that it fostered cycles of dependence at its best and promoted something akin to slavery at its worst. By making the act of faith part of a socioeconomic arrangement, it likely deprived the Christian message of one of the key points of its anthropology: the very mission of dominion that is shared not just by all believers, but by all human beings by virtue of their creation.

The Indigenous peoples of the Andes often expressed their own mission to dominion by maintaining the rites, cultures, and customs of their prior belief in the guise of their newfound Christianity when they placed idols in altars and at the feet of statues of saints. They were still engaging in the sorts of natural world making that Eliade would point to or exercising the theological mission of dominion that Guardini would describe. In that case, it makes sense that the Indigenous who were caught up in the *encomienda* would see a similar dynamic at play between Catholic symbols and their Indigenous *huacas*. If Guardini is right, the "Modernity" of the moment in this sense meant that the colonizers simply "could bask in the dreams of undiscovered lands, untapped reserves,"[25] while seeking to set up a system of tutelage for the purpose of exploiting those lands, their resources, and their peoples. The subjugation that occurred might have simply driven Indigenous religious practice underground, or perhaps more precisely up into the mountains. Since it lacked the sense of self-appropriation of the faith that is necessary for a person who is exercising their dominion, however, it also meant that the old religious practices endured and continued to evolve alongside the new. Rather than the full-throated renunciations of the Indigenous religion that the Spanish sought under the

---

[25]Guardini, *The End of the Modern World,* 184.

encomienda system, the dominion of the people continued to express itself against their colonial oppressors in the inculturation of the Catholic faith.

When we consider carving crosses on the arms of the Ponce Monolith at Tiahuanaco or the Indigenous talismans placed side by side with the Monstrance holding the Blessed Sacrament in a Corpus Christi procession, it is clear that we are talking about not *merely* a religious conflict. These conflicts fall into the many ways in which a people makes sense of their world and exercises their collective dominion over it. As Harvey Whitehouse puts it: "Religion, like any cultural domain, is a distributed phenomenon. That is to say, it inheres not merely in the thoughts and feelings of an individual devotee but also in the recognizably similar or complementary thoughts and feelings of a population of religious adherents."[26] In this sense, while the dominion that humanity exercises as a process of world making and sanctifying begins on the individual level for Guardini, it expresses itself as religious reality in the collective experience of a people. As a social scientist, Whitehouse is also correct to point out in a note that has resonances with the epistemology of St. Thomas Aquinas: "Our cosmologies, eschatologies, ethics, ritual exegeses, and so on, are all firmly constrained by what we can encode, process, and recall. Only once we begin to understand these restraints can we begin to disassemble and explain the constituents of religion."[27] Our cognition of the divine begins in the sensory experiences of the world around us and in our religious practices, which are generally experienced corporately. When one people comes into contact with another, as we have seen, the

---

[26] Harvey Whitehouse, *Modes of Religiosity: A Cognitive Theory of Religious Transmission* (Walnut Creek, CA: AltaMira Press, 2004),16.

[27] Whitehouse, *Modes of Religiosity*, 16.

resulting interaction can lead to conflict. It might also lead to a moment in which, in the translation of terms and cultures, a new understanding might emerge.

It may be that, in such a moment, a respectful dialogue about the nature and meaning of symbols in diverse cultures can yield meaning common to both, as it did for Calixto and I that day on the shores of the lake with the symbol of a snake. However, as Eliade demonstrates, and Guardini seems to understand well, the constraints of the worlds that we inhabit and the meanings that we are able to derive from them are often constitutive parts of who we are. These also push us forward and out from the centers of the religious meaning we create.

The problems that arise when adherents of one center of religious meaning encroach upon the boundaries of another might not be a matter of conflict. In the end, they may be a matter of translation. One of the places where this becomes most obvious is on the ruins of the Inca temple that purified those who were preparing to journey in pilgrimage to the temple of the Sun. Today, a basilica to Mary, the mother of Jesus, stands there. Her feast is celebrated on the memorial of the purification in the temple recorded in the Gospel of Luke. She is known more popularly as "Our Lady of Copacabana."

When Meanings Merge: Our Lady of Copacabana

When most people hear the word "Copacabana," it evokes images of a sun-soaked beach in Rio de Janeiro, Brazil. Few consider that the neighborhood that boasts that beach is named for a nearby church. That church is devoted to Our Lady of Copacabana, one of the earliest Marian devotions in Latin America.

Often enough, in a postcolonial world, the meaning that

can be derived from place arises from a common understanding of value that is translated between different peoples. These places become places of reconciliation rather than conflict, as a certain liminality is present in these sorts of spaces that speaks to a common humanity. The pale white Spanish church on the shores of Lake Titicaca, which holds the roughly sculpted statue of the Lady of the Candelaria, is itself a mix of Christian and Islamic architectural elements and is one such place because of the way in which the stories surrounding her can capture different religious imaginations. The pre-Christian religion of the area speaks to the ways in which the already fertile ground of devotion at the site of the shrine was cultivated before Christianity arrived such that a new devotion could take root. That certain elements of the original indigenous religion remain at the site is apparent to this day. How these elements now coexist offers insights into the continued dialogue between the two cultures that has been forged at a place that both consider holy, and these insights might offer us a path forward in a global Church.

Nearly four thousand kilometers away from that Brazilian beach, nestled in the mountains on the border of Peru and Bolivia, the shrine of Our Lady of Copacabana is one of the earliest, and most difficult pilgrimages, in the Americas. The pilgrim path starts at the Basilica of St. Francis in downtown La Paz, itself one of the oldest churches in the Americas. Winding up out of the canyon, the pilgrim encounters miles of the windswept and often desolate Altiplano as they approach the shores of Lake Titicaca. From there, over and around the hills that hem in the lake, the trail leads to the small village of San Pablo de Tiquina, where it is necessary to board a small ferry boat to cross to the other side and onto the peninsula, where the basilica sits along with so many Indigenous holy sites. The road trails up into hills until, coming down the other side, one sees the Basilica of Our Lady of Copacabana looming prominently over the small town.

In front of the basilica, Indigenous women dressed in *cholita* fashion, often in brightly spun wool garments and bowler hats, sell small devotional items.[28] They sell bright synthetic flowers that are to be used in the blessing of cars, a noted intercessory concern of Mary in her guise as Our Lady of Copacabana. They have small statues and large rosaries mixed in among Indigenous talismans and brightly colored cloths that have often been woven by hand from llama and alpaca wool. When compared with other major Marian shrines, the scant number of these booths just outside the gates speaks to the remoteness of the shrine. Just past the gates and beyond the booths, the pilgrim crosses into the plaza of the basilica and then enters a side door into a darkened church.

Above the main altar, the statue is noticeable in the brightness of the gold that adorns it and stands out amid the drabness of the wood that surrounds it. Standing a meter and a half tall, the statue has a remarkably Indigenous face and holds lightly to an infant who appears to be wiggling loose of her embrace. Crowned and venerated, the statue was once thought too ugly to be an object of devotion. Now, hundreds of years later, people still make pilgrimage seeking healing and peace through the intercession of an image of Mary, the mother of Jesus, which is pregnant with the possibility that she could be one of them.

---

[28]*Cholita* is the typical style of traditional Bolivian dress for women. It generally involves a felt bowler hat and a large hoop like skirt. In recent years, among Indigenous communities, the intentional choice of this style of dress has also been a symbol of resistance.

Mary, Genius of Inculturation

Consider the panoply of Marian devotions in the Catholic Church and even some Protestant churches. A common thread almost immediately emerges: Mary seems to always match the place in which she finds herself. Just north on the same continent, at the same time as the devotion to our Lady of Copacabana was evolving, Our Lady of Guadalupe appeared speaking Nahuatl and dressed as an Indigenous princess. At Lourdes, Mary wore the attire of the local Marian confraternity and spoke the local patois, and even in Walsingham, an object of devotion for some Anglicans, the holy house that was built used English styles and materials at the order of an apparition of Mary to bring the reality of the Holy Family to the English countryside. Wherever Marian devotion arises, it seems to fit the culture that surrounds it. This pattern, especially where such a devotion arises out of an originary event of a local church, has profound theological implications.

In order to better understand the inculturation that seems consistently at play, it might be helpful to look back even further than the conquest of the Andes, into Christian antiquity. Looking back, we can consider how the role of Mary took hold in the Church of classical antiquity and why, perhaps, given an ancient Mediterranean worldview, Mary played a significant role in the growth of the faith in a previously pagan country. Recognizing parallels in the development of the devotion from the ground of similar pre-Christian realities helps clarify the common features of such a movement and allows us to consider whether a similar dynamic was, and even still is, at play in Bolivia as it was in the ancient Mediterranean. Finally, having considered the role that Marian devotion might play in missionary work, we might consider the possibility that

Marian devotion bears a certain liminality that both invites us forward and shapes our understanding of Christological truths from an enculturated perspective.

A Soil Already Tilled

As we are reminded in the parable of the sower in the synoptic Gospels, seeds must be sown into well-prepared ground in order to flourish. The ground of the Mediterranean world in which the Church first took root is an obvious example of how the metaphor offered by Christ in the parable practically plays out. The Mediterranean soil was tilled by the classical religions that inhabited the area. The search for meaning, the openness to transcendence, and the quest to clarify what order there might have been in the cosmos, as Eusebius reminds us, all constituted a certain *praeparatio evangelica*. As Eusebius himself noted, however, the religions that prepared the ground extended far beyond just the Greek and Roman pantheon. Wherever the Gospel spread in those early days, rather than simply encountering a rival school of thought or belief, it also encountered what Thomas Aquinas calls the *desiderium naturale vivendi Deum*, that desire for God present in humanity as the desire for the universal good.[29] The early Church did not *only* see rivalry and errors in these religions. It also understood that the same desire for God that underpinned Christianity could be present within their adherents. When, as Eusebius points out, the Egyptians and the Phoenicians looked at the sun and the moon and worshipped them as gods, even in their error, they "looked up to the clear sky and to heaven itself,

---

[29]Thomas Aquinas, *Summa Theologica* I-II, q. 2, a 8.

and in their souls reached up unto the things there seen."[30]

If Eusebius is right, then, when the people of the Mediterranean encountered transcendence in nature, it began a preparation that led them to being able to accept the Gospel. As Hugo Rahner notes: "Observation of nature, combined with a kind of awe for the myths to which the processes of nature give rise, was a universal ingredient of the religious feelings of antiquity."[31] The theological imaginations of the people of Mediterranean antiquity were, in a sense, primed by their pre-Christian religion. The seeds of the Gospel were planted in soil that was rich because of their desire for the universal good that allowed them to see the hand of some sort of providence in the natural world around them.

There is a noticeably clear line from the ways in which the early Church began to speak about Mary of Nazareth that stretches on to just the same interpretation of her role in Bolivia under the title of Our Lady of Copacabana. Whether the missionaries most responsible for the growth of the devotion to our Lady of Copacabana understood this link, whether it is something which evolved organically from the faith of the people, or whether such a connection is a construct which seems to have been imposed upon the narrative at a later date is initially unclear. The lack of clarity comes, in no small part, because most of what we know of the faith of the people of the Altiplano in the wake of the Spanish Conquest comes from chronicles and letters of Spanish priests, outsiders interpreting the experience of Indigenous religious practice through European archetypes and biases. More contemporary sources

---

[30]Eusebius Pamphili, *Evangelicae Praeparationis,* trans. E. H. Gifford (Oxford: Oxford University Press, 1903), 17.

[31]Hugo Rahner, *Greek Myths and Christian Mystery*, trans. Brian Battershaw (London: Burns and Oates, 1963), 114.

that are more attentive to Indigenous experience might offer clearer insight into just how the devotion to Mary, the mother of Jesus, arose as an important part of Bolivian Catholicism.

The well-known Bolivian anthropologist, Xavier Albó, notes that there is a distinct understanding of what constitutes the good life for the Indigenous communities that surround the shrine of Our Lady of Copacabana. The Indigenous culture of the region emphasizes the importance of an agent's connectedness to all of creation and the importance of living well together; this is expressed in the Aymara phrase *suma qamaña*, or *vivir bien*, as it is often translated into Spanish. This concept of connectedness extends beyond interpersonal human relationships and to the world that surrounds us. While far from being considered gods, all created things have a certain agency in the Indigenous Aymara culture. Humans have ethical commitments that extend beyond humanity. In this sense, rather than simply being an object that benefits or is exploited by man, nature becomes a personal reality with which humanity is in constant contact. *Suma qamaña* is thus best expressed as a commitment to live for the common good, in community with human subjects as well as "coexistence with nature, with Mother Earth or the *Pachamama*."[32] The gratitude or requests expressed in the words of the Indigenous *yatiri* toward the *Pachamama* are, thus, less supplications to a god than they are expressions of gratitude toward any other patron with whom we are in relationship. Even food sources, like potatoes, are understood as having some agency in Andean Indigenous culture. As Calixto Quispe, with whom I once had the conversation about the symbol of a snake on the

---

[32]Xavier Albó, "Suma qamaña = convivir bien. ¿Cómo medirlo?" *Revista de Estudios Bolivianos* 25 (2019): 101. Translation mine from: "la convivencia con la naturaleza, con la Madre Tierra o *Pacha Mama.*"

shores of Lake Titicaca, offered in an interview with Abraham Colque, "The potato speaks to us and in many ways. . . . It is a relation of a you to a you, of subject to subject. You talk to it, you ask its pardon, you celebrate it. . . . You speak to it as another living being."[33]

The interconnectedness of the created world in Andean culture is considerably less anthropocentric than a traditional Western perspective, but it still understands the importance of an intersubjectively ethical reality. The key difference between the Euro-American approach and the Andean experience is an intentionality within the Andean culture that recognizes that the earth, animals, and even the potatoes have a certain active relationship to me, and I to them. The other things that exist are not gods. More properly, they collectively fall under the category of "thou," by recognition of their subjectivity and the role that they play in *suma qamaña*. The *Pachamama*, or "mother earth" as Albò translates the term, is the personification or subjectification of the sustaining realities of nature for the Andean peoples. In the same way in which St. Francis of Assisi, in the Canticle of the Sun, praised the created realities of nature as brother, sister, and mother who relate to and benefit humanity, so the Aymara peoples of the Andes have developed a rich ritual language to praise those same realities. In this way, such an understanding is not far afield from the way that Pope Francis understands the connection when he says, in the opening lines of his encyclical *Laudato Si'*: "Our common home is like a sister with whom we share our life

---

[33] Abraham Colque, "Sobre papas que lloran y otras cosas: Diálogo sobre la espiritualidad ecológica andina," *Fe y Pueblo* (Instituto Superior Ecuménico Andino de Teología) 19 (October 2011): 6. Translation mine from: "las papas nos hablan y de muchas formas. . . . Es una relación de tú a tú, de sujeto a sujeto: Le hablas, le pides perdón, le festejas. . . . Le hablas como a otro ser viviente."

and a beautiful mother who opens her arms to embrace us."[34] While the Indigenous of the Altiplano might remove the word "like" and simply claim our common home as a sister, it is easy to see why the expansion of subjectivity beyond humanity that Indigenous Andean cosmology maintains seems to find a home within Christianity for so many on the Altiplano. It also suggests the possibility of an understanding of the role of Mary and the saints that fits uniquely within the culture.

A gathering of Aymara catechists in 1987 expressed the connection between their Christian and Indigenous beliefs in ways that many cultures have before them. Their statement of faith echoes the Church of antiquity as it sought to make sense of its own connections to the pantheons of Mediterranean antiquity. The gathering of Catholic catechists, as well as Methodist and Lutheran pastors, expressed the synthesis of their belief and culture in ways that have powerful resonance with some of the Fathers of the Church. Rereading Deuteronomy 6:20–25 and 26:6–10, they speak of the moon as a mother and the sun as a father but still recognize the transcendent God who has always walked with them. In an inculturated reformulation of the Creed, the catechists make a comparison between Mary and the *Pachamama* that is not entirely dissimilar to the ways in which Hugo Rahner would argue that the early Church began to elucidate the role of Mary in salvation history: "I believe in Mary who is the mother of us

---

[34]Pope Francis, *Laudato Sí*, no. 9, May 24, 2015. Pope Francis would also affirm the importance of Indigenous traditions in the Americas in making this important connection in an address to a convocation of FIDA, the International Agricultural Development Fund, which took the role of Indigenous peoples as its main theme. He affirmed the importance of this connection in his address when he said: *"Y ustedes, en sus tradiciones, en su cultura—porque lo que ustedes llevan en la historia es cultura— viven el progreso con un cuidado especial a la madre tierra."*

all, as is the Pachamama [Mother Earth]."[35] The equivalency of Mary and the *Pachamama* may be potentially problematic for Euro-American theologies, but it highlights two important features of the enculturation process with the *Pachamama* and its similarity to and difference from Mary. First, the distinction between worship and veneration is important in understanding rituals that focus on the *Pachamama*. Second, the comparison of Mary and the *Pachamama* implies a difference between the two. With these features, we can also recognize the processes connecting Mary and realities for the Fathers of the Church. Together, this helps us understand how the Lady of Copacabana might have been initially accommodated in the place it came to be venerated and why it still plays a vital role today.

First, the comparison between Mary and the *Pachamama* draws out the important theological principle that rituals that focus on the *Pachamama* are not understood by most Christian Indigenous communities to be an act of worship. The self-understanding of the community seems to place the rituals more in the context of the veneration of saints. As John of Damascus points out, helpfully, veneration is not offered only to the saints, however, but also to things sacred to God.[36] Beyond the personification of mother earth as the *Pachamama*, the rituals surrounding the *Pachamama* are events of veneration because

---

[35]Sinclair Thomson, Rossana Barragán, Xavier Albó, Seemin Qayum, and Mark Goodale, eds., *The Bolivia Reader: History, Culture, Politics* (Durham, NC: Duke University Press, 2018), 553.

[36]See Saint John of Damascus, *On the Divine Images: Three Apologies against Those Who Attack the Divine Images*, trans. David Anderson (Crestwood, NY: Saint Vladimir's Seminary Press, 1980), treatise 1, para. 14. John, precisely because of the Incarnation, is clear that matter can be venerated because salvation was worked through matter in the person of Jesus of Nazareth. John goes on to discuss the Ark of the Covenant as an object of devotion and veneration among the people of Israel and is careful to point out that, through it, it is clearly the case that we properly venerate objects which are sacred to God.

the earth itself is held as a manifestation of divine care and concern by the people of the Andes. As Hugo Rahner points out, this sort of an understanding of the divine manifest in nature is neither new nor unique in the life of the Church. Just as in the pre-Christian Mediterranean world the moon was seen as the "primal cause of all birth" because of the life-giving power of the morning dew that was thought to be left by the moon each morning, so Mary took on a similar role for the early Church as being the primal cause of all birth in the act of giving life to Christ.[37] Rahner notes that the moon was used as an important symbol for understanding the connection between Mary and the Church: "Mary is the spiritual Luna of this Christmas union between God and humanity and the Church is the true full moon of Easter, and in the Christian sense the 'primal cause of all birth.'"[38] Understanding and benefiting from those connections between the Incarnate Word and the pre-Christian tradition of a people has always been a part of the Church's self-understanding. Just as holy day processions in Europe often mark the veneration of a specific saint and often follow the seasons of the year and have resonances with pagan feasts, so the Catholic and Christian communities of the Andes, precisely because they view subjectivity and agency as extending beyond human beings, angels, and God, invoke and venerate the beneficence of the earth itself in the name *Pachamama*.

Second, it seems important to note that the comparison implies a difference. Mary and the *Pachamama,* while accorded a similar function, are mentioned as distinct entities. That which is true of Mary is *not necessarily* always the same of *Pachamama*. The important distinction might be how Hans Urs Von Balthasar understands it:

---

[37]Hugo Rahner, *Greek Myths and Christian Mystery*, 160.
[38]Hugo Rahner, *Greek Myths and Christian Mystery*, 161.

In one relationship, (woman) is the answer that is necessary if the word that calls to her is to attain its full meaning; in the other relationship, she herself is the source ("Mother of all the living": Gen 3:20), and hence she is the primary call addressed to the child. If absolute significance is attributed to this second aspect, it leads to the cults of the Magna Mater, the principle of reproductive fruitfulness—often depicted with an array of breasts—understood as the ultimate source.[39]

The distinction between pre- and post-Christian understandings of the role of *Pachamama* offer an important insight. Where the words used in veneration of the *Pachamama* may still allow outsiders to infer a role as an ultimate source, the juxtaposition of *Pachamama* and Mary by the catechists in the Indigenous appropriation of the Creed implies that something more akin to Balthasar's first understanding of fruitfulness is at play. The catechists, in drawing the comparison between Mary and the *Pachamama*, illustrate in a straightforward way that neither is the ultimate source. Rather, their fecundity is bound in relationship to the living God, who is source of all and the foundational belief in their creed: "I believe that God has created the earth, the mountains, the lake, and so it is that they produce our fields."[40] Drawing the distinction between them also implies different, but interconnected, orders of existence. On one hand, the distinction implies parallels in the Andean and European Christian metanarratives. On the other hand, it seems to understand that the same God who brought

---

[39]Hans Ur von Balthasar, *Theo-Drama: Theological Dramatic Theory*, vol. 3: *The Dramatis Personae: Persons in Christ* (San Francisco: Ignatius Press, 1992), 292–293.

[40]Thomson et al., *The Bolivia Reader*, 553.

the order of Christian salvation into the world also created the *Pachamama*, mother earth. *Pachamama* sustains and blesses the people's mundane existence through gifts of subsistence over thousands of years in the harsh terrain and climate of the Altiplano and Andes Mountains.

The soil was and still is tilled for the message of the Gospel through the culture of the people of the Andes. The Andean concept that they were and still are subject to a sort of special maternal care and understanding is also clearly nothing new for cultures who encounter Christianity for the first time. The Fathers using the image of the moon, from Ambrose and Augustine down and beyond the Patristic era, echo the cries of pre-Christian antiquity. Hugo Rahner, borrowing a line from Giselbert of Westminster, notes that "even in the early Middle Ages, the miniatures of the crucifixion preserve this echo of antiquity in the lamenting moon, for the moon appears above the Cross 'like a sorrowing virgin veiling the shining horns of her light.'"[41] These images and ways of thinking endure, especially when Christian missionary interaction with non-Christian religions finds a place of connection to a local non-Christian culture in shared concepts such as maternal care and beneficence. Attentiveness to the commonalities across cultures in what comes to the Church as a "spoil of Egypt," to borrow a line from Origen, echoes the universality of the Gospel message in the ears of the believer.[42] If we can be as comfortable with the spoils of Tiahuanaco, which have made their way into the enculturated faith of the Andes, as we are with the spoils of Egypt, Rome, Greece, and the Frankish

---

[41] Hugo Rahner, *Greek Myth and Christian Mystery,* 170.

[42] See Origen, *Letter to Gregory*, paragraph 2 in volume 4 of *Ante-Nicene Fathers*, edited by Alexander Roberts, James Donaldson, and A. Cleveland Coxe (Buffalo, NY: Christian Literature, 1885).

courts that have made their way in to an enculturated Euro-American faith, then we might find something wonderfully consoling in the resonances between the two. The story of Our Lady of Copacabana is a powerful example of cultural negotiation for a common understanding of the faith in Spanish Colonial Bolivia. Here, the symbolic language of one culture met the other's narrative about the importance of a place, yielding a new, shared commitment.

A Bolivian Mother of God

How do we translate the holiness of a place across cultures? Even if there are latent similarities between those cultures, it may well be that the reality at which they are grasping resists translation. Otto's description of the numinous, rather than the holy, and Eliade's use of it are helpful in the invitation to look beyond our value judgments to the matter at hand. The question becomes how the interaction of the two cultures and two different metanarratives can come to commonly express the importance of a place as connected to God. Often enough, the importance of a place is adequately expressed in a symbol or a common narrative that can maintain the prominent features of what each culture brought to the conversation. By the shores of Lake Titicaca, Our Lady of Copacabana is clearly one such symbol. Beyond the exorcisms of monoliths and the struggles to understand the perdurance of the *Pachamama* long after Christianity had taken hold, that shrine is an image that appears fleetingly European but has a clear Andean origin. It speaks for both cultures and to the truth of the maternal care of the Mother of God.

In many cases across Latin America, an image of Mary was adopted by the people of a place that had a connection to one that was popular in Europe. As we shall see in a later chapter, such a practice is why the image of Mary found on the outskirts of Mexico City is known as Our Lady of Guadalupe rather than Our Lady of Tepeyac. The story is no different at Copacabana. Nestled high in the mountains, the missionaries brought devotion to Our Lady of the Candelaria—made famous in the Spanish empire because of the devotion of the people of Tenerife in the Canary Islands—to Bolivia as a "Peruvian Guadalupe."[43] According to the contemporary chronicler Alonso Ramos Gavilán, the devotion was chosen to match the season and the place. February was a time when the people of the area had feasted in honor of the pre-Christian gods in hope of protection. When considering the place, Ramos Gavilán extensively describes the pre-Christian uses of the temples of the area, noting that the place was full of "pagan" worship, specifically parallel to Rome before its conversion. Those two key elements come to be connected in Christian worship in the devotion to Our Lady of Copacabana.

Ramos Gavilán, in considering the observance of holidays on the Altiplano, notes that all of January was given over to festivals celebrating a coming harvest, offered with sacrifice to the supreme god of the Andean pantheon, Viracocha. The sacrifice of the animals would be allowed to flow into the rivers, where "Viracocha would receive them."[44] A contemporary of Ramos Gavilán, Bernabé Cobo, noted the interesting point that even the llamas that were sacrificed to the sun during this time were intended still, even in that instance, to be "offered on the Sun's behalf" to Viracocha. This offering

---

[43] Alonso Ramos Gavilán, *Historia de Copacabana y de la Milagrosa Imagen de su Virgen* (Lima: J. Enrique del Campo, 1867), 60.

[44] Ramos Gavilán, *Historia de Copacabana y de la Milagrosa Imagen de su Virgen*, 36.

seems to dimly indicate that offerings to sun, moon, or earth were understood, even in pre-Christian understanding, to show that there was one supreme deity.[45] Ramos Gavilán notes that, in the Andean calendar, the festivals of January gave way to feasts that included purification and marriage in February.

The choice of the time for a feast for Copacabana was not accidental in this sense. Celebrating on February 2 each year matched the feasts of the people in the transition from a time set aside for feasting that roughly corresponded to the European season of Christmas, to a time in which purification, specifically of young women, and offering in marriage was the rule of the day. Ramos Gavilán notes that the sacrifices to the sun that had existed before might, however, have had another purpose: January and February were the most feared months of the year because the frost would ruin the flowering fields. The Indians would be extremely afflicted by hunger and famine as a result.[46] They asked for the beneficence of the sun so that their crops might survive the frost. Supplications and prayers during this time of year were normal among the Andean people who inhabited the peninsula of Copacabana. Seeking such a feast, Ramos Gavilán notes that this is why they themselves chose to found a confraternity dedicated to "Our Lady of the Candelaria or the Purification," whose feast

---

[45] Sabine MacCormack, *Religion in the Andes: Vision and Imagination in Early Colonial Peru* (Princeton, NJ: Princeton University Press, 1991), 167. It seems helpful to note that this is not a remote practice of the past. Llamas are still first plied with alcohol and then sacrificed in a similar manner in many Aymara communities in the Andes seeking a good harvest. One can find, especially in La Paz, fetal llamas for sale hanging from the rafters of specific stores intended for this purpose.

[46] Ramos Gavilán, *Historia de Copacabana y de la Milagrosa Imagen de su Virgen*, 60.

the Augustinian missionaries had brought with them.[47]

The waters of the lake and the peninsula itself had special purpose and meaning to the entirety of the Inca Empire at the time of the Conquest. These were places that served as sources of life, affirmation of mission, and purification. As we have already seen, the lake is one of the places that the people as a whole counted as their place of origin. The rulers of the Inca Empire, and Inca Roca in particular, were anointed with water from the lake called "water forming drops of crystal to make kings."[48] The Copacabana peninsula was set aside as a place of final purification for those arriving on their pilgrimages to the Island of the Sun, to see where the Sun had emerged from the rocks. R. Alan Covey notes that, on entering the peninsula, pilgrims "changed into their finest clothing and jewelry" before embarking on the final phase of their pilgrimage.[49] This translated into a new way of thinking at the site after the arrival of the missionaries, as Salles-Reese notes, because "the new Christian belief in the need to purify the soul prior to its entrance into Paradise left the natives little choice but to invoke the intercession of the Virgin, since the ancient gods possessed no jurisdiction over an afterlife."[50]

In considering the place that Mary holds at Copacabana, Ramos Gavilán also noted the presence of a pre-Christian temple in the area at the time with an idol that served as a referent to the temple on the lake. Contemporary images that surround the shrine point to this blue stone as having been an

---

[47]Ramos Gavilán, *Historia de Copacabana y de la Milagrosa Imagen de su Virgen*, 60.
[48]MacCormack, *Religion in the Andes,* 298.
[49]Covey, *Inca Apocalypse*, 42.
[50]Salles-Reese, *From Viracocha to the Virgin of Copacabana: Representations of the Sacred at Lake Titicaca,* Kindle location 795.

object of worship in the place at the time. Understanding the place, its relationship to the Island of the Sun, and the role that the pre-Christian idol that was once there held for the people, Gavilán concludes: "Because, in fact, what long ago saw idolatry from those rocks, was the other Titicaca rock: and today the blessed image of Mary is placed here, what is seen and venerated on those stones is the door of heaven, as from the stones of Bethel the Lord let Jacob see."[51]

The Christian devotion, especially given the time of year and place, clearly paralleled the Indigenous memory of the place and the significance of the time of the year. Copacabana was and still is a place where people feasted in celebration of divine protection, celebrated the idea of ritual purification, and understood the role of that which is venerated there in reference to something far greater. Both in Catholic Marian devotion and the prior pre-Christian practice, the internal religious logic of the place remains intact to this day. Its sense of the numinous at the site as a locus of the origins of the world remains intact both as an Indigenous place and as an origin of the Bolivian Catholic community. In that sense, the translation of old values at the site was worked through a symbol common to both the European conquerors and the Indigenous community and forged the shrine as a new center. The shrine was born out of the conflict of the two peoples, with two distinct cosmologies, merging into one in the image of a woman who looks Bolivian while wearing the vestiture of a European queen in the niche above the altar of the basilica.

---

[51] Ramos Gavilán, *Historia de Copacabana y de la Milagrosa Imagen de su Virgen*, 45. Translation mine from: "Porque, en efecto lo que tiempo atrás veía desde esas penas la idolatría, era la otra pena Titicaca: y hoy colocada acá la imágen bendita de Maria, lo que se vé y se venera sobre esas piedras es la puerta del cielo, como desde las piedras de Bethel viera Jacob al Señor."

The statue itself was cast as a symbol of the confraternity of Our Lady of the Candelaria, and it was not without controversy when it was sculpted. Its sculptor, Francisco Tito Yupanqui, who was himself a recent convert when he cast it, was discouraged when the priests of the area told him it was too ugly to be an object of devotion. In retrospect, what they likely meant was both that it was too rudimentary in its technique and too Bolivian in its appearance to represent the Mother of God. Still, the proof for the people present came in the miracles in which the Lady seemed to take on the role of protector of the people. Ramos Gavilán notes tales of her intercession: providing rain in times of drought, protecting a local magistrate when a large cross fell on him while the image was carried in procession from La Paz to Copacabana, and even raising a woman murdered by her husband from the dead. Especially as she plays a part in local agriculture, Our Lady of Copacabana came to be associated with maternal care in parallel to that of the *Pachamama*. In this sense it is perhaps because of, rather than in spite of, their previous devotion and their understanding of place that so many converts came to understand the role of Mary and find a way to begin to embrace the Christian message.

Some places are just holy, or we can at least agree that there are many places that are numinous. They can speak to us and to those who might be essentially other to us of the presence of God. Countless pilgrimage sites that have been holy to generations and across religions attest to that fact. For the Christian, when a place that is at the heart of a people can be touched by the grace of the Gospel, we are privileged to witness something akin to the first generations of the Christian faith. We witness a seed planted in good soil and can watch it grow. Just as it was for the early Church, so it was in Bolivia—the advent of a Christianity that could allow people to understand God though the lens of their home and their culture, providing a firm foundation in which the lived faith of a people could take root. As we will see, the fruit of that faith can often bring life to the whole Church.

2

Lourdes

At the Horizon of a New Era

"When I saw [the vision] I rubbed my eyes, I thought I was deceived."[1] Saint Bernadette of Lourdes introduces to us the grounding question for this chapter: Is seeing believing, or is believing seeing? In the small town of Lourdes, the tension between Enlightenment values and the local culture was growing. At the core of that tension was, in part, an account of what counted as meaningful or worthy of belief in the first place. The battle between old and new ways of thinking at Lourdes had cultural, psychological, and spiritual implications for the dynamics of religious patronage and its ability to accommodate the trauma of the shifting paradigm.

What happened both to Bernadette and to the people of Lourdes in those days in 1858 captured the imagination of the world. To this day, movies, books, and even a recent musical have told this story. Bernadette's story isn't particularly novel, however. Pious legend holds that people have reported seeing

---

[1] René Laurentin, *Lourdes: Histoire Authentiques* (Paris: P. Lethielleux, 2002), 46. Translation mine from: "quand j'eus vu cela, je frottai mes yeux, je croyais me tromper."

Marian apparitions since the end of the Apostolic Era. Spanish legend holds that Mary, during her earthly life, appeared to St. James while he was preaching the Gospel in Zaragoza, Spain, and encouraged him to return to Jerusalem to aid a persecuted Church. In the nineteenth century, there were at least two other well-known apparitions of Mary in France alone, and another in the town of Knock in County Mayo, Ireland. Lourdes still seems to have stood out in capturing the world's imagination. Hundreds of thousands still travel on pilgrimage to the foothills of the Pyrenees each year. Many arrive at the shrine seeking healing; some go to accompany the sick; others go out of simple devotion; and more than a few go out of sheer curiosity. In recent years, in addition to the myriad Catholic pilgrims who cross the gates into the sanctuary, many Hindu immigrants to Europe have taken to making pilgrimage to the shrine, to bathe in the waters, and even to leave offerings of flower garlands in front of the image of Mary nearby.

1858

On February 11, 1858, St. Bernadette Soubirous, a teenage girl from an impoverished family in the town, left the small, converted jail cell in which she lived with her family to go in search of kindling to keep the family's fire lit. While walking along a stream that ran by a mill on the outskirts of Lourdes, she had a vision of a young woman that seemed to emerge from one of the many caves that dotted the landscape just outside the town's gates in the foothills of the Pyrenees. Bernadette was initially suspicious of the apparition. Such a suspicion likely arose, in no small part, because of what historian Ruth Harris notes was a local belief that fairies lived in this particular cave: "The site of the apparition was inhabited by the fairies, the dragas, damizélos, hadas, fadas, encantadas—the term varied as the patois changed across the Pyrenean chain—who inhabited the forests, bushes, fountains and, above all, grottoes of the region."[2] When Bernadette returned to the grotto, she brought holy water to hurl at the apparition. When the apparition smiled at Bernadette's attempted exorcism, Bernadette was satisfied that whatever she was seeing was not of demonic nature and agreed to return to the grotto to speak and pray with the apparition over the course of the next two weeks and beyond.

Over the course of eighteen apparitions, the woman spoke to and prayed with Bernadette, entrusted Bernadette with a message of prayer and penance, and revealed a spring from which Bernadette was to wash and drink. This spring was quickly found, almost by accident, to be a site of miraculous healing. The healings that would occur, and that are said to continue to this day, would eventually be used by the local bishop as the most objective demonstration of the veracity of Bernadette's claims. Pilgrims today travel from around the world to bathe in those same springs, many hoping for a miraculous cure.

The local parish priests, not sure of what to make of the apparitions, kept pressing Bernadette to ask the lady for her name. Bernadette simply called the lady "Aquerò," the formal version of "her" in the local patois, but she asked the lady of the apparitions for her name at the request of the town clergy. On the morning of March 25, 1858, the young woman of the apparitions revealed herself, after much prodding from Bernadette, to be "the Immaculate Conception." This was not a name, but rather a title for Mary with roots in the Council

---

[2]Ruth Harris, *Lourdes: Body and Spirit in the Secular Age* (London: Penguin, 1999), 77.

of Ephesus. It had been promoted by John Duns Scotus, but it had only been solemnly defined by Pope Pius IX in the encyclical *Ineffabilis Deus* just four years before the apparitions to Bernadette.[3] The giving of this title finally affirmed for those who believed that Bernadette had been talking with Mary, the Mother of God.

When the apparitions ceased, Bernadette became something of a recluse, living in the local hospice and eschewing the attention that the story of her experience had garnered. She would eventually join the one nearby convent—in Nevers—that did not seem overly impressed by her status as the visionary of Lourdes.[4] There, she would live out the rest of her life, eventually serving as something of a pharmacist in the convent's infirmary before dying at the age of thirty-five. She would later be canonized by Pope Pius XI in 1933, and the apparitions would reach universal recognition in the Catholic Church through a liturgical celebration established each year on February 11, the anniversary of the first apparition.

When the story is told of what happened around St. Bernadette in those days, the narrative tends to focus on Bernadette herself, and reasonably so. However, attention beyond Bernadette, especially given what happened with the parish sodality

---

[3] It seems helpful to note here that the dogma of the Immaculate Conception, that Mary was conceived without original sin by virtue of the merits of the salvific work of her Son, was not settled teaching up to this point. Even august theologians like St. Thomas Aquinas held, for various reasons, that it could not be the case. (For Thomas the issue was one of when ensoulment occurred, a good Aristotelian, he held that it was at quickening as a principle of motion.) The affirmation of the promulgation of the Dogma of the Immaculate Conception that came as a part of the apparitions at Lourdes likely was a part of the reason why the devotion spread so quickly.

[4] At least one account has the mother superior making Bernadette, in her first days in the convent, dress in the traditional clothes of Lourdes to tell the story of those days. Unfortunately, despite her best efforts, Bernadette was unable to escape notoriety.

known as the Children of Mary and the hagiographical narrative of John-Baptiste Estrade, illustrates how apparitions break through expectations and, because they imply relationship, can often more directly connect us to the underlying movement of God through the dynamics of patronage.

A Word on Apparitions

Apparitions and allocutions can all too often sound like "a knowledge given by revelation, which has been made available only to the elect who are capable of receiving it, and therefore has an esoteric character," to borrow a part of the definition of Gnosticism from Kurt Rudolph's seminal study.[5] While apparitions seem to be experienced by only a select few, the obvious distinction is that the character of the knowledge imparted to the visionary, rather than being saved for a select few, is shared publicly, almost immediately and often to the chagrin of ecclesial authorities. Far from being marginal realities, the scriptural precedents for apparitions, the sharing of the contents of the apparitions, and the careful discernment that occurs around them within the Church point to something different from mere esotericism or Gnosticism. The Church ultimately never rules that the contents of contemporary apparitions are postulates of faith that must be believed by all the faithful as necessary to their salvation. They are, rather, understood as perhaps being helpful to the faith of at least some of the faithful. In the life of the Church, apparitions are understood as a potential means to bolster the life of faith of a believer and not to serve as a soteriological sine qua non.[6]

---

[5] Kurt Rudolph, *Gnosis: The Nature and History of Gnosticism*, ed. Robert McLachlan Wilson (Edinburgh: T&T Clark, 1987), 55.

[6] Unfortunately, in some instances this is not as clearly understood as it

Remember that the life of Christ begins and ends with apparitions. The first passages of the Gospel of Luke recount the apparition of the Archangel Gabriel to Mary, announcing the good news of the birth of Jesus. Mary's response to this apparition brings about the Incarnation and the mission of Christ in the world. These sorts of apparitions are by no means novel to Christian Scripture. Angels appear to humans throughout the Hebrew Scripture and, in the case of the book of Exodus, God appears to Moses. Far from being an esoteric new development, these sorts of apparitions of angels and even of God are a long-entrenched part of Jewish and Christian scriptural traditions. Of course, for Christians, the apparitions of Christ, physically present in his glorified body after the resurrection, are the apparitions par excellence. Thus, at a second glance, apparitions are far more ubiquitous in the Christian tradition than one might have initially thought and play a significant role in salvation history.

Although apparitions might be more commonplace than would allow them to be an esoteric matter in Christianity, it seems important to note that, in scripture, these apparitions and allocutions were generally directed to the end of the mission of an individual in the context of the whole community. The missions of Abraham as the father of faith, Moses as the leader of the people of Israel, Samuel as the prophet of Israel, Mary as the mother of God, and even the disciples as witnesses of the Resurrection—all came as apparitions or allocutions that were specific to an individual or a group of individuals and not intended as dispersed realities. As John Henry Newman

---

perhaps could or should be by some of the faithful. As we will see in Chapter 3, one of the excesses of practices of popular piety is unfortunately the manner in which some devotees understand their devotion to a saint or an event to be more crucial to their salvation than the paschal mystery.

notes when considering the witness of the resurrection: "It is, indeed, a *general* characteristic of the course of His providence to make the few the channels of His blessings to the many."[7] The primary purpose of the resurrection appearances, according to Newman, was to instruct the early Christian community and prepare it for its mission moving forward. On Newman's account, the divine pedagogy inherent in apparitions like those of Jesus at the time of the resurrection limits itself to the few human instruments that can best carry the message to all. In that sense, a visionary is also always meant to be a missionary. Although, as was the case during the Apostolic Era and at Lourdes alike, miracles and signs seem to stand as evidence attesting to the veracity of a visionary's claim, the message is the source of the divine motivation and the purpose of an apparition.

Given that many of the apparitions that have garnered the devotion of the Catholic faithful, particularly from the early nineteenth century on, are of a specifically Marian nature, it seems important to make one key theological point about how those apparitions connect to what has been previously stated about the resurrection appearances of Jesus and the scriptural tradition of apparitions as a whole. The dogma of the Assumption, as solemnly defined by Pope Pius XII in the apostolic constitution *Munificentissimus Deus* of 1950, clarifies what had long been a point of theological debate both within the Catholic Church and in conversation with the Orthodox east. The Catholic Church views Mary's present existence as that of the resurrected in anticipation of the final resurrection of the dead. As Pius XII puts it: "Like her own Son, having overcome

---

[7] John Henry Newman, "Sermon 22: Witnesses of the Resurrection," in *Parochial and Plain Sermons* (London: Longmans, Green, 1907), 286. (Emphasis his.)

death, she might be taken up body and soul to the glory of heaven where, as Queen, she sits in splendor at the right hand of her Son, the immortal King of the Ages."[8] It is precisely because of this claim that, as the noted theological expert on apparitions René Laurentin puts it, "her glory, glorified by the Assumption, is visible and can therefore manifest itself."[9]

It would be tempting in that line to think of apparitions as some odd sort of superpower afforded to Mary because of her role, but it is important to remember that, as Joseph Ratzinger reminds us, "what the dogma of the assumption tells us about Mary is true of every human being."[10] What we understand to be true of Mary as a result of the assumption, according to Ratzinger, we hold to be true of all of us. "Owing to the timelessness which reigns beyond death, every death is an entering into the new heaven and the new earth, the Parousia and the resurrection," he writes.[11] Entering into the new life of the resurrection, which scriptural accounts of the resurrection attest to including the ability to appear in an apparition after death, means that Mary could certainly appear. That line of reasoning also means, as the Church affirms in the *nihil obstat* that is given to Marian apparitions that seem to be credible, that there is no theological reason in Catholic theology that stops us from believing that Mary could appear, or indeed did appear, at Lourdes in 1858.

---

[8] Pius XII, *Munificentissimus Deus,* no. 40, November 1, 1950.

[9] René Laurentin, *Pilgrimages, Sanctuaries, and Icons*, ed. William Fackovec (Milford, OH: Riehle Foundation, 1994), 98.

[10] Joseph Ratzinger, *Eschatology: Death and Eternal Life* (Washington, DC: Catholic University Press, 1988), 108.

[11] Ratzinger, *Eschatology: Death and Eternal Life*, 108.

Jean-Baptiste Estrade's Narrative of Change and Perdurance

While the idea of apparitions is made reasonable by an eschatological understanding of Mary that regards her as participating in the timelessness of the resurrection, they still happen at a given time and in a specific place. They happen within our history, as they did in 1858 at Lourdes. The foreword to one of the more popular accounts of the miraculous events of those days notes that "extraordinary changes seem to be passing over the world in which we live."[12] As was the case at Lourdes, moments of extraordinary change often also yield extraordinary stories of the intervention of the supernatural into daily life. It may well be that God breaks into those moments in a particular way, though perhaps it could also be that we are just more attentive or attune to the possibility of narrative-changing supernatural or divine events when the world seems in flux. Cognitive psychology offers the perspective that we naturally engage in the process of meaning-making in such moments. Our need to understand, when met with the limits of our ability to know, produces a moment of aporia in us. Perhaps that is why moments of this sort may well be where the constancy of God's communication of divine love meets human receptivity.

Jean-Baptiste Estrade offers a particularly rich testimony to the events surrounding the visions of 1858 at Lourdes. In his lucid telling, the apparitions came in the context of the robust arrival of a nationalizing French culture and language

---

[12]Jean-Baptiste Estrade, *The Apparitions of Lourdes* (Lourdes: Imprimerie De La Grotte, 1958), vii.

into a strong local culture and dialect. Contemporary cognitive psychology and sociology offer us perspectives on what happens when one person needs to make sense of what seems contrary to their normal understanding of the world and, perhaps, what also happens when a larger group attempts to put such a moment into perspective. The psychological reality, however, seems to point to that moment of aporia, which, because it is grounded in a desire to understand, can only be answered by a faith that implies relationship.

The Town of Lourdes and the Peculiar Case of Jean-Baptiste Estrade

When people think of Lourdes, their attention often focuses on the visionary, St. Bernadette, and Mary, whom she claimed to have seen. In the narrative surrounding the 1858 apparitions, the network of people that surrounded Bernadette is often overlooked. These people include those who were inclined to believe the visions, people like some members of Bernadette's family, the members of a pious confraternity called the "Children of Mary," and the hundreds who would make the trek out of town to the site of the apparitions over uneven ground. There were also those who were skeptical, like the police commissioner, the imperial commissioner, and the self-styled freethinkers of Lourdes who would gather at the Café Français.

Somewhere in the middle of those two groups was Jean-Baptiste Estrade, the local French imperial tax collector. Estrade is an interesting figure in the narrative for two reasons. First, Estrade tells us that he felt pulled between two worlds, the old and the new. By his account, the local customs and traditions of Lourdes, and his own connection to them, weighed as heavily on him as his role as an imperial official.

Second, the strength and zeal of his account on behalf of the validity of the apparitions constitute more of an apologia than a historical account. Estrade clearly wants his reader to know the facts of those days, but he is also committed to making sure that one believes that the apparitions occurred. Estrade's work reads like a conversion narrative in which a once proud and arrogant man, who scoffed at the idea that St. Bernadette was receiving visions, had a religious experience of his own and became a witness to it to the ends of the earth through his book. Ultimately, Estrade clearly takes Our Lady of Lourdes as his patroness and asks for her to intercede for him at the moment of his judgment.

While Estrade claims to have felt initially caught between the two worlds, his account is clearly not a disinterested one. From the very beginning of his work, the abundance of religious and specifically theological language belies his assertion that he is merely reporting what he witnessed in those days, and not interpreting it. Later in the work, Estrade takes a strong position as a believer in the vision, up to and against those whom he once called his closest friends among the bourgeois elite of the town of Lourdes. Estrade even recounts one moment in which he felt compelled to give encouragement to the local priests, who themselves had decided to stay neutral as the events of those days played out. For someone who went to great lengths to claim objectivity in his account, Estrade takes a strong position on what happened at Lourdes. In those claims, he is clear that some people have a right understanding of what happened and that others are simply wrong. Even if Estrade is overstating his claim of having mocked the apparitions until he experienced them, it is evident in the text that Estrade is, at the very least, hoping to explain why he believes so strongly and also why he is seeking to justify that belief. The question then becomes one of motivation. What motivates a man who claims to have been skeptical about the apparitions to take such a strong stance in favor of them? Is this a mere rhetorical device, or is there something more behind the passion with which he makes these claims in his text?

Estrade's motivation for writing might be best understood through a cognitive process that points us toward an important dynamic in popular religiosity. Estrade's own account of his religious experience at the grotto outside of Lourdes points to his having experienced something that the cognitive psychologists Travis Proulx and Michael Inzlicht might call a particular type of "meaning violation."[13] Conversion, in this sense, came as a meaning violation when Estrade was faced with a cathartic moment that forced him to see the world differently. This moment also brought him to a deep sense of the patronage of Mary. Estrade's work, qua apologia, may be a way of drawing attention to an experience in order to set it apart, or it might also be a means to make sense out of that which went against his understanding of the world as it was. Estrade's account of the day that he first went to the grotto seems to offer a clearer understanding of the text built around it. It also might offer insight into the ways in which adherents of devotional movements view themselves in the context of their world.

Estrade tells a story that places the people of Lourdes in a vital role. Internal drama can seem to magnify the place or the importance of any community, but Lourdes, at this time, was little more than a backwater town. Estrade's text provides us with some details that are affirmed by historians. Because of its unique geographical position at the junction of seven valleys, Lourdes effectively served as the capital of a small

---

[13]Travis Proulx and Michael Inzlicht, "The Five 'A's of Meaning Maintenance: Finding Meaning in the Theories of Sense-Making," *Psychological Inquiry* 23, no. 4 (2012): 317–335.

nation and was the traditional seat of the counts of Bigore. The large medieval castle that looms over the town, now as then, demonstrates its past strategic significance in this remote part of France.

At the same time, Lourdes was removed from the rest of the world around it in many ways. The historian Ruth Harris notes that, absent the railway, it took thirty-two hours to arrive in Lourdes by coach from Bordeaux, a distance that can now be traversed in four hours by bus over the highways. "One traveler," she wrote, "claimed after the experience that Dante should have used the vehicle in his *Inferno* to punish sinners."[14] Importantly, though, the trains had recently arrived in the nearby towns of Pau and Tarbes at the time of the apparitions. Estrade's account notes that, slowly but surely, this once remote outpost found itself frequented by visitors from as far off as Paris, seeking the idyllic setting of the Pyrenees in the prevailing romanticism of the era. The ways in which the people corporately made meaning of the events of the world as it evolved around them demonstrates a second movement that seems consistent to the development of devotion and for which Harvey Whitehouse might later offer us some insights into the development of communities centered around devotion.

February 23, 1858, Lourdes, Hautes-Pyrénées, France

It was not the first time that the fourteen-year-old girl had reported seeing the Lady coming out of a golden cloud on the rock of the cave. For about a week, the town was abuzz with the news that the eldest daughter of a destitute, unemployed miller and his wife was seeing something in the rocky outcropping by the river where many of them had sheltered

---

[14]Ruth Harris, *Lourdes: Body and Spirit in the Secular Age* (London: Penguin,1999), 24.

their pigs during storms. The girl's family "were by no means what is commonly called *devots,* but they always performed the essential duties of their religion."[15] If there was something going on in the cave, how could the people of the town make sense of it? The interpretations of the events of those days show the ways in which the people of Lourdes were not just trying to make sense of the events of the grotto, but of the world around them.

One group of particularly pious women, known as the "Children of the Virgin," held to the belief that souls could return from purgatory to warn the living about their lives or ask for prayers for their release from temporal punishment. They thought that the girl might be seeing a revenant, a ghost, of one of their dear friends who had just passed away.[16] They noted a similarity to their own uniforms in Bernadette's description of how the lady had dressed and hoped that this vision could be their friend reaching out from beyond the grave.

Others in town held to the belief that the land was enchanted and full of all sorts of spirits. To this day, talismans of various types meant to ward off evil spirits and witches mark houses on either side of the mountain range. Given Bernadette's description of the youthful appearance of the Lady, perhaps a fairy was making herself known. Clearly, Lourdes was a place where the supernatural wove its way into the narrative of the culture.

Still others in town thought the girl to be delusional at best or a fraud at worst. Georges Bertrin's account of the matter

---

[15] Estrade, *The Apparitions at Lourdes,* 16.

[16] See Harris, *Lourdes: Body and Spirit in the Secular Age,* 57. This belief was by no means specific to the culture of the Pyrenees. The ghost of Hamlet's father in the eponymous play is perhaps the most well-known example in literature, but there are clear examples of this belief dating back to the Patristic era, as Tertullian and St. Gregory the Great both recount similar visitations by ghosts from purgatory.

notes that many in town thought Bernadette to be a particularly melancholy person and that her melancholia may have been a source of her vision. Delusion, not a miracle, was at play.[17] The official account of the French prefect, Baron Massy, concluded that "a gleam of light coming from the side of the grotto doubtless arrested her attention; her imagination naturally predisposed in that direction, gave to that gleam of light a form which had already struck her, that of the statues of the Virgin, as seen over the churches' altars."[18] Even the parish priest doubted that something was really going on, when, on February 22, he said to Estrade, who was planning on accompanying his eager sister to the grotto the next day:

> I don't see any harm in you doing what your sister asks and if I were in your place I should have gone before now. I, like you, think that there is nothing but a child's delusion in it all, but I really don't see how you compromise your dignity by going to witness a thing which takes place in broad daylight and of which everyone is talking.[19]

In the tension between those who believed a vision was occurring and those who did not, Jean-Baptiste Estrade set out on

---

[17] Georges Bertrin, *Histoire critique des événements de Lourdes apparitions et guérisons* (Lourdes: Bureaux et Magasin de la Grotte, 1922), 106. It is interesting to note here that Bertrin's manner of describing Bernadette's mental state is an almost direct quotation from the third volume of Pope Benedict XIV's treatise *"On Heroic Virtue,"* in which he uses St. Thomas Aquinas's rudimentary understanding of psychology to discuss the various and sundry ways in which we might know a seer in the cases of a Marian apparition to be less than reliable. This same treatise is cited extensively in the ecclesial approbation of the Bishop of Tarbes of the cult that would later evolve around the apparitions at Lourdes.

[18] Estrade, *The Apparitions at Lourdes*, 184.

[19] Estrade, *The Apparitions at Lourdes*, 83.

the morning of February 23, 1858, to the grotto of Massabielle with his sister.

From the limits of the old town of Lourdes, one descended into the Gave de Pau river valley, crossed the old bridge, and then had to climb over a hill to get to the grotto. The route in the 1850s would seem today to be a fairly roundabout path. The geography of the river largely dictated this path in the 1850s, and the space that is largely occupied by the Shrine at Lourdes today would have been a fairly inhospitable flood plain at the time of the apparitions. Estrade took this path, along with his sister, slightly before 6 a.m. on that February morning. Estrade claims that, along the way, he joked with his sister and her friend about how silly such a hike was. When they arrived at the grotto at just around 6 a.m., Estrade recounts that there was already a group of about two hundred people, mostly women, and a handful of men who were asked by the women to station themselves at the edge of the cave for the safety of the crowd. There, they waited as Bernadette approached.

Estrade writes that everyone's eyes were riveted on Bernadette when she arrived. She knelt down, took out her rosary and begin to pray. In Estrade's recollection, she next looked up toward the rock as if she were waiting for something. Then:

> Suddenly as in a flash of lightning an expression of wonder illuminated her face and she seemed to be borne into another life. A light shone in her eyes; wonderful smiles played upon her lips; and an unutterable grace transfigured her whole being. The seer's soul within the narrow prison of the flesh seemed to be trying to reveal itself to the outward sight and to proclaim its joy and happiness. Bernadette was no longer Bernadette; she was one of those privileged beings, the face all glorious with the

glory of Heaven, whom the apostle of the great visions has shown us in ecstasy before the throne of the lamb.[20]

At this point, Estrade says that he noticed a change in himself; he removed his hat and knelt. He called it a "heavenly scene" and noted that, while he didn't see or hear anything, those present knew that a conversation was going on between Bernadette and the unseen Lady, whom Bernadette would only refer to during that time as *Aqueró*. The ecstasy lasted for about an hour that morning. At the end, Estrade recounts:

> I felt like one in a dream, and I left the grotto without remembering the ladies for whom I was responsible. I could not shake off my emotion and a crowd of thoughts invaded my soul. The Lady of the rock might hide herself from my bodily eyes, but I had felt her presence and I was convinced that she had looked on me with maternal love. It was indeed a solemn hour of my life and deeply was I moved to think that I, the omniscient and superior person who had mocked and scoffed at such things, had been allowed to come so near to the Queen of Heaven.[21]

Estrade thought that he had a religious experience that day. Despite recounting an experience of the lady through the experience of Bernadette, Estrade's account seems to match William James's classical description of a religious experience. Though he wrote of the experience, ultimately, Estrade recognized that the experience that he had was ineffable. His lengthy description demonstrates that this moment in his life defied explanation. His appeal to it having been an "experience of heaven" further evidences its ineffability. In the insights

---
[20] Estrade, *The Apparitions at Lourdes*, 84–85.
[21] Estrade, *The Apparitions at Lourdes,* 86–87.

that caused his change from skeptic to true believer, the noetic quality of the experience is clear. That same insight not only changed his mind, it pragmatically changed who he was and how he would later respond both to Bernadette and to others in the town. Intriguingly, Estrade realizes that this is not merely his own experience. Somehow, he and all present shared in it together with Bernadette.[22]

In the end of his account of that morning, Estrade addresses the Lady of Lourdes, writing,

> When at the last great hour I have to appear before thy Divine Son, vouchsafe to be my protectress and to remember that thou hast seen me on my knees and believing, beneath the sacred vault of thy Grotto at Lourdes, in those wholly happy days when *thou didst reveal thyself to Bernadette, and through Bernadette to me.*[23]

Elsewhere, he recounts that Bernadette had told him that, during one of the visions, the Lady looked around at those present as if she were looking at friends. Recounting the famous March 25 apparition, when the Lady revealed herself as the "Immaculate Conception," Estrade writes that those present "were conscious of intense happiness within their souls."[24] Recounting his own experience is significant unto itself, but, if his text is to be believed, that he offers a vision of a communal experience that was felt in the presence of St. Bernadette during the apparitions is monumental.

Something happened at Lourdes in 1858. By at least one

---

[22]See William James, *The Varieties of Religious Experience: A Study in Human Nature: Being the Gifford Lectures on Natural Religion Delivered at Edinburgh in 1901–1902*. Lecture XVI (New York: Modern Library, 1902).

[23]Estrade, *The Apparitions at Lourdes*, 87. Emphasis mine.

[24]Estrade, *The Apparitions at Lourdes*, 143.

account, what happened was not *just* Bernadette's experience. It was at least one other person's experience, and it was likely the experience of a whole community. How do we make sense of the religious experience if it is more than simply a moment of meaning violation for an individual? How do we make sense of the religious experience of an entire community when the experience itself might actually be a motivating factor toward the resolution of the tensions inherent in the community? How do we make sense of the religious experience of an entire community when that experience helps the community to express something deeper about itself?

Meaning and the Girl Who Saw Mary

Change is difficult. Few would deny that moments of cognitive dissonance take their toll on us both individually and corporately. Estrade's narrative is a glimpse into a moment of cognitive dissonance during a time of profound change for both himself and for the people in Lourdes. The difficulties embodied in such a moment are not merely notional. At least one study in cognitive psychology suggests that there are even physiological implications involved in the threat posed by change. Beyond the implications for any given subject of such a moment, some anthropologists also argue that the religious responses that emerge in the corporate meaning-making caused by cognitive dissonance may be grounded in the behaviors that helped our ancestors survive. The events of Lourdes and the popular devotions that arise from them offer insights into the ways in which a particular popular devotion can grow because of who and how we are as human beings and how we are predisposed to understand and appropriate such an experience. Growth might not be simply because of a moment of divine or heavenly inbreaking. We might just have a built-in need for the sort of saintly patronage that is expressed by the popular devotion to Our Lady of Lourdes. Such a predisposition, in addition to telling us something about our own makeup as human beings, might also point us to the nature of how we express relationship to God and to the Church. It might also help us reckon with why experiences like the one at Lourdes are so important to us.

Estrade's Dis- and Re-orientation

Given the choice between experiencing physical pain or not feeling physical pain, common sense dictates that human beings will generally choose the latter rather than the former. The same can also normally be said to be true of psychological pain. What is not always immediately apparent to us is how the two are connected. The connection is even less obvious for experiences that do not prima facie seem to be particularly psychologically traumatic. Psychologists Travis Proulx and Michael Inzlicht have demonstrated that, when faced with moments of disorientation, particularly when our way of life or the narratives that help us make sense of the world break down, we do our best to find a certain homeostasis. Interestingly, though, psychological processes through these moments primarily serve a palliative function. Our minds ease, dull, or eliminate that which is, in fact, both psychologically and even physiologically painful in order to set us aright. The community at Lourdes, faced with a crisis of meaning in 1858 as the narratives of the quiet provincial town broke down around them with Enlightenment values finally at their doorstep, engaged in acts of meaning-making through their religious experience.

For Proulx and Inzlicht, meaning offers explanations for the *what* and the *why* of the world around us. The *what* of meaning is "an epistemological understanding of the world, a sense of what things are made of, how they are similar or different from other things, and how they interact in space and time."[25] This would cover complex things like the laws of science and physics, but it also covers the basic sorts of things that we learn as we develop as human beings, like object permanence. *What* senses of meaning provide the basic rules of nature, and miracles violate those rules by their very nature. For Estrade, violations of meaning of this sort, especially as one who associated himself with the "freethinkers" of the town, would have included the miraculous healings that occurred at the spring that arose at the site of the apparitions in those days.

The other, and perhaps more important for our purposes, meaning violation that Proulx and Inzlicht mention, are the violations that get at the "*why*" of reality. The *why* of meaning can "provide a teleological account of our experiences, most often understanding reality as a means to some end, as shaped by a purpose determined by some or other intentional reality."[26] For Estrade and for many others at Lourdes, the Church and their own cultural understandings of the supernatural provided some teleological foundation for their everyday belief and practice. Whether in superstition or religion, the small world around them seemed to be passing away as the greater world began to arrive at their doorstep via the cultural and technological revolutions that were taking place in nineteenth-century France.

When those conflicts with our basic sense of meaning come about, Proulx and Inzlicht's study argues that we have "meaning violation": a moment when our basic sense of understanding has been undermined, arousing genuine psychological

---

[25]Proulx and Inzlicht, "The Five 'A's of Meaning Maintenance," 319.
[26]Proulx and Inzlicht, "The Five 'A's of Meaning Maintenance," 319.

discomfort. When the "why" of a situation is upended, when the underlying meaning we presume to be at play no longer makes sense, or when the reasonable expectation that our understanding was universally applicable no longer applies, we face a moment of meaning violation. Such a violation can be exacerbated in a moment where there might be different interpretations of a situation in a given community. As Proulx and Inzlicht note: "This may be especially true in the moral domain, where similar others value dissimilar things, often not playing by the interpersonal rules that we assumed were universal."[27]

We know that the experience of the grotto was contextual for Estrade, and we know that that context shaped his reactions to what he encountered. He went thinking extraordinarily little of Bernadette and the possibility of the truth of the apparition. He was encouraged by his friends and even his pastor to approach the situation with just this sort of skepticism. He also went alongside his sister and her friend, both eager to experience what they thought might be real.

While the experience of the grotto and the miraculous events that occurred there over the course of the visions likely constituted a meaning violation of the *what* type, it is clear that there was a meaning violation of the *why* type already within the community.[28] The events of those days violated the sorts of meanings that we construct around the natural order. They also brought into stark relief the sorts of explanatory meaning violations that were already under the surface in the community.

---

[27] Proulx and Inzlicht, "The Five 'A's of Meaning Maintenance," 320.

[28] The Catholic Church has recognized sixty-seven healings at Lourdes since 1858 to be of a "miraculous nature"; the medical bureau at Lourdes also contains records of thousands of other unexplainable healings. These would still constitute "what" type violations.

It seems too easy to put the individuals involved in the apparitions into two camps, those who were ready and excited for such an event as the apparitions and those who might have been more skeptical. Estrade's account, however, when combined with Proulx and Inzlicht's insight about the nature of these moments reveals that people fell more along a spectrum than fit into some sort of forced dichotomy. The people of Lourdes were proud of their home, culture, and history and, at the same time, did not want to appear backward. They both held fast to their faith and culture and were proud of their place in an emerging French nation in a new modern era. Holding those things, no doubt, meant a certain tension for the people of the town, and the apparitions seem to have brought that tension to the fore. At the time of the apparitions, which unto themselves constitute meaning violations, the town of Lourdes was already struggling with other meaning violations as it sought to define itself anew as the world crept in on it.

Meaning violations are not neutral events. They cause a certain amount of psychological and even physical pain. Proulx and Inzlicht coined the word "*disanxiousuncertlibrium*"[29] to describe what we feel in these moments. It is a sense of meaninglessness, a state of disequilibrium, and their study shows that it has psychological and physiological consequences. Our physiological response to meaning violations are close to our feelings of being threatened. Surprisingly, we have this reaction regardless of whether that meaning violation could be deemed a positive or a negative overall experience. We experience physical symptoms like elevated heart rates and constricted blood vessels in those moments. "More broadly," Proulx and Inzlicht conclude, "these expected relationships may organize either the *what* or the *why* of our experiences,

---

[29]Proulx and Inzlicht, "The Five 'A's of Meaning Maintenance," 322.

and regardless of what they organize, violations of these meaning frameworks evoke a common physiological state that we refer to as aversive arousal."[30]

A state of aversive arousal, because it is unpleasant, demands a reckoning. As such, we engage in certain behaviors that seek to ease the pain and begin to cognitively process the world around us with primarily palliative intent, seeking a sense of equilibrium. Proulx and Inzlicht categorize our approaches to resolving such disequilibrium into five distinct categories. Jean-Baptiste Estrade's experience can be read as an example of accommodation.

Estrade's account of those days at Lourdes is a particular expression of how he accommodated this violation. Faced with the need to account for those days, expressing that the Lady of the Grotto is his patroness makes sense of all of it for him. Whether he is coping with the *what* violation of the miraculous events surrounding the apparitions or the *why* violations of the various and sundry incursions of the outside world into the citadel of Lourdes, Estrade's narrative acknowledges that his own view of the world at that point was insufficient. He uses the construct of patronage to try to account for this insufficiency. The patronage model allows him to accommodate the new schemata of the relationships that make up meaning in the world.

Proulx and Inzlicht, when thinking of this approach to meaning violations, write, "Experiences that are inconsistent with our schemata will arouse a sense of *disequilibrium*, which in turn motivates an *assimilation* of the experience so that it matches our schemata, or an *accommodation* of our schemata so that they account for the experience."[31] Estrade's account

---

[30]Proulx and Inzlicht, "The Five 'A's of Meaning Maintenance," 324. Emphasis theirs.

[31]Proulx and Inzlicht, "The Five 'A's of Meaning Maintenance," 325.

of his experience on February 23, 1858, serves as the violation of meaning. The expository nature of his book, perhaps especially as he recounts the earlier apparitions for which he was not present, is "a revision of [his] familiar understanding" such that it is consistent with the event.[32] The account of his own experience of his first time at the grotto, which we read above, both gives us an understanding of the meaning violation and serves the palliative function of reorienting Estrade, who had been disoriented by feeling the presence of Mary, the mother of Jesus, when he had previously been sure that such an apparition was not occurring and perhaps not even possible. That Estrade tells the tale as a testament to the Lady's continued presence in his life after that day reveals something important about how Catholics often appropriate such experiences in the context of relationship to the saints and to God.

Going in Procession: Corporate Cultural Expression of Psychological Meaning-Making

Estrade expresses a type of individual experience that almost always happens in the context of a broader community. The corporate expression of those individual psychological processes often has recognizable expressions. When something like the events at Lourdes occurs in the Roman Catholic tradition, after ecclesial approbation, it is common that a shrine would be built, processions will be made, and masses will be said. When we look at the example of Lourdes, we see that essentially palliative acts of meaning-making were manifest in ritual that became regularized in those first years and are still practiced 160 years later. That ritual is all focused around

---

[32] Proulx and Inzlicht, "The Five 'A's of Meaning Maintenance," 325.

the patronage of Mary, whom those devoted to Lourdes still believe heals people there.

To make meaning in the midst of the apparitions, the people naturally developed ritual, and, from that ritual, an organized cult developed. Responses to the threat of disequilibrium may trigger a meaning-making response in someone like Estrade, but what he describes also points to a people's corporate response, which may well come from the deep-seated evolutionary advantage that religion offers. Considering what Proulx and Inzlicht have described about meaning-making and its function as a response to a threat, the work of Harvey Whitehouse and Victor and Edith Turner describe the ways in which response to a threat may well be the thing that brought the people of Lourdes together to offer expressions of ultimate meaning as a twofold evolutionary and psychological response in and through their processions and practices.

In their study of Christian pilgrimage, anthropologists Victor and Edith Turner note that there is a particular type of pilgrimage, which they call the modern pilgrimage, that stands as the assertion that miracles still do happen. The Turners note that this sort of expression of pilgrimage is usually a reaction to the threat posed by a modern or postmodern narrative that eschews the possibility of divine intervention and purports to explain all through science. The way that the popular devotion of Lourdes came to express itself is a clear example of this kind of devotion. There are certainly tropes in the Lourdes narrative that are consistent with other and older types of pilgrimage. A particular characteristic of popular devotion of Lourdes stands out for the Turners. "In tone, these pilgrimages are actually antimodern, since they usually begin with an apparition, or vision, and they assert that miracles do happen," they write.[33]

---

[33] Victor Turner and Edith Turner, *Image and Pilgrimage in Christian*

In the midst of a moment of threat from the encroachment of the world into their sleepy Pyrenean enclave that could upend their religious expectations, the practices of the people built a certain sense of social cohesion that still holds today. "In Lourdes," the Turners note, "there is a sense of living *communitas*, whether in the great singing processions by torchlight or in the agreeable little cafés of the back streets, where tourists and pilgrims gaily sip their wine and coffee. Something of Bernadette has tinctured the entire social milieu—a cheerful simplicity, a great depth of communion."[34]

While the Turners understand *communitas* as a particular kind of ritual reality, communion as social cohesion is an important communal meaning-making response to a threat. Harvey Whitehouse notes that developing such a sense of communion is an evolutionarily grounded process. Whitehouse notes that there is evidence that scarcity of food during the last Ice Age forced our ancestors into "new and often more dangerous strategies of cooperative hunting." Such a competition among groups made group cohesion an evolutionarily advantageous trait. "Cohesive units formed through the communal performance of low-frequency, high-arousal rituals would have been capable of wiping out, displacing, or absorbing less cohesive bands of hunter-gatherers competing for the same resources (under conditions, of course, of growing scarcity)."[35] In other words, the development of ritual as communal meaning-making is built into our evolutionary makeup. Developing ritual for meaning-making helps us build cohesive groups for mutual aid in survival.

Estrade writes of some angry stonecutters who took up

Culture (New York: Columbia University Press, 2011), 19.

[34]Turner and Turner, *Image and Pilgrimage in Christian Culture*, 230.

[35]Harvey Whitehouse, *Modes of Religiosity: A Cognitive Theory of Religious Transmission* (Walnut Creek, CA: AltaMira Press, 2004), 78.

torches in the early days at Lourdes. When the imperial officials built barriers around the site of the apparitions to keep people away, a band of stonecutters went at night, by torchlight procession, to tear down the barriers. Interestingly, Estrade does not label the torchbearers as just functioning as a mob. He describes the group as united by prayer in their torchlit procession toward the grotto.

This story is an example of the particular kind of ritual development that Whitehouse talks about as an evolutionary response to a threat. Where imperial power was threatening their access to a place of prayer, the stonecutters responded, rather spontaneously, by constructing a "high-arousal" ritual of processing by torch light through the woods and up a steep hill each night. The efficacy of the ritual is made even more evident by the fact that others began to join them in this procession until eventually even the ecclesial authorities joined in.

Originally, such a procession would have been remarkable in its rarity. Today, that first moment is formalized in the candlelight processions, known as the *flambeau*, that one would experience on any given night at Lourdes during the pilgrimage season at the shrine. As the people repeatedly evoke the name of their patroness in the candlelight of the now daily procession, they also connect to each other and to the communion of saints in a manner that hearkens back to our human origins and that, as a theological narrative grounded in apparitions, pulls us forward to the eschatological horizon.

In light of both psychology and anthropology, the *flambeau* procession makes sense. Such a response, evolutionarily grounded, is a meaning-making response for Proulx and Inzlicht, where the new rituals are created as new frameworks for meaning. While religious processions were already a deeply entrenched part of the makeup of Christian Europe at the time, putting those processions together with the belief in the patronage of Mary made this new experience at Lourdes feel familiar when it had been unsettling at first. As Proulx and Inzlicht put it, such a response "may render our experiences familiar feeling, there may be some assembled meaning that we *create to feel familiar*—in the wake of uncertainty, we *make* something that makes sense to us."[36]

This ritual at Lourdes, which already feels familiar because it is, in some way, a part of our evolutionary makeup, offers a response that is both palliative in its ability to ascribe meaning where it had been violated and constructive for group cohesion or communion as an essential response to a perceived threat. The dynamic of ritual-making very well might be inherent in the development of practices of popular piety because ritual-making is a part of who we are and how we respond to the world around us as humans.

"O Mary conceived without sin, pray for us who have come to you for help"

Every day at Lourdes, in the baths where the sick seek their own miraculous healing, in the masses and rosaries by the grotto, and in the torchlit *flambeau* every evening, you hear words that are hardly original to Estrade but joyfully proclaimed in his account: "O Mary conceived without sin, pray for us who have come to you for help."[37] The stories of witnesses of Lourdes in those first days, the rituals and practices performed in the town to the present day, and even the battles that occurred between the warring sides, speak to a people who were disoriented by the newness of a world that was not quite their own yet. They ultimately found meaning and even identity in the events of those days of 1858. They

---

[36]Proulx and Inzlicht, "The Five 'A's of Meaning Maintenance," 329.
[37]Estrade, *The Apparitions at Lourdes,* 144.

built a narrative that reflects the visitation of none other than Mary, the mother of Jesus. They dwell in the dynamics of patronage. Attentive to that particular care, they developed rituals that bound them together and carried forth what they witnessed and experienced in those days. Together, these rituals and stories proclaim the care of the mother of God from whom the faithful asked intercession and protection.

What happened at Lourdes and to Jean-Baptiste Estrade, including the ways in which religious practices and beliefs grew up around it, is by no means unique in the history of Roman Catholicism. Reading Lourdes through lenses of evolutionary and psychological sciences provides us a fruitful approach for considering the growth of popular religiosity broadly. Likewise, approaching the evolutionary and psychological material through the historical events and developments at Lourdes can help us understand the contributions and limitations of these scientific disciplines in considering the development of such shrines and practices of popular religiosity. It might help us to better understand how it is that we find ourselves as capable receivers of divine revelation and religious experience by describing the human processes by which we are capable of doing so in the first place.

The Children of Mary

Although I have focused on Estrade's account, it would be wrong to paint all of the people of Lourdes in 1858 with the same brush. Although the rituals that evolved might point to a corporate resolution of meaning violations, there were likely some for whom no real meaning violation was present. The concept of patronage seems able to accommodate the possibility that something other than a palliative narrative emerged from the life of those who surrounded Bernadette at Lourdes.

For at least one group, the Children of Mary, we see something more akin to an act of faith, which recognized the presence of a familiar relationship. For these women, the arrival of the Virgin almost seems to have been a natural and understandable occurrence. They understood her appearance as an ordinary extension of the patronage that they felt she exercised over them. Their interpretation of the apparitions makes sense of why Mary is said to have appeared to Bernadette in a way that was clearly recognizable to their specific sodality. It also helps us understand why the devotion continued to grow as the recluse visionary took refuge after the events of 1858, first in the town hospice, and then in the convent at Nevers.

The Children of Mary was founded by the Jesuit Jean-Léon Flammingue, the rector of the Roman College, as a sodality in 1565. The sodality grew quickly, and the Jesuit superior general, Claudio Acquaviva, sought official approbation for the sodality and the associated indulgences for the group shortly thereafter from Pope Gregory XIII, who was famously a patron of the works of the Society of Jesus in the days following the Council of Trent.

The sodality's association with the Society of Jesus sparked its own heroines and put forth volumes with narratives of women from among its ranks who had experienced mystical experiences, conversions from Protestantism, and had engaged in works of charity in their respective communities.[38] One of their 1838 manuals, *Les Délices des Enfants de Marie,* reads as a sort of catechism for its members. In one dialogue in that book, Mary speaks to her devotees about what it is like to have been conceived without sin, saying that "God chose

---

[38] One particularly notable account of a Protestant convert who became a member of their sodality is called the "Daughter of Damnation."

and predestined her."[39] That same manual has an office of the Immaculate Conception for the members of the group to pray together. The manuals make clear that the French members of the sodality, even in the decades before the formal definition of the Immaculate Conception by Pope Pius IX in *Ineffabilis Deus* in 1854, had a devotion to Mary under the understanding that she was conceived without the stain of original sin. Their devotion only magnified as the sodality and its leadership followed the lead of Pius IX, recognizing Mary under the title of the Immaculate Conception.

The 1856 *Manuel des Enfants de Marie* tells us something remarkable about the direction the organization had taken as a whole after Pope Pius IX's definition. They had changed their official name. They, of course, maintained their common name, the Children of Mary, but officially they became the Association of the Immaculate Conception of the Blessed Virgin Mary.[40] The organization actively promoted the devotion by upholding the annual December 8 solemnity, by including explicit references to the Immaculate Conception in the rite of reception into the group, by wearing medals with the words "Immaculate Conception" written on them, and by praying an impromptu prayer aloud throughout the day: "Blessed be forever the holy and Immaculate Conception of the Virgin Mary."[41]

Within the list of the indulgences granted to members of the group, their role in assisting in pious meetings and helping the

---

[39] Mélanie Van Biervliet, *Les Délices des Enfants de Marie* (Tournai: H. & L. Casterman, 1837).

[40] Marius Aubert, *Manuel des Enfants de Marie—ou moyens de conduite de royaume des cieux: A l'usage des pensionnants* (Paris: Perisse Frères, 1856), 22.

[41] Aubert, *Manuel des Enfants de Marie*, 66. Translation mine from: "Bénie soit à jamais la sainte et immaculèe Conception de la bienheurse Vierge Marie."

sick took precedence.[42] These indulgences, which read more like directives for the group rather than incentives, would have put the group in touch with those who, like Bernadette, were known to be suffering from illnesses in Lourdes. The indulgences also would have made gathering at the grotto to pray second nature, as they did from the fourth until the sixteenth apparitions.[43]

One of the leaders of the group was a maid-turned-socialite named Jeanne-Marie Milhet. When she first heard news of the apparitions, Milhet's first thought was that the apparition in the grotto could be the ghost of a friend and former member of the group, Elisa Latapie. Latapie had recently passed away and, so Milhet thought, was returning, while in purgation, to offer guidance to the group.[44] When we look at the first engraving of the 1857 *Manual for the Daughters of the Virgin*, Milhet's assumption makes sense. The engraving shows, on the right, a woman dressed in a white dress, tied with a sash, and a white veil, a strikingly similar outfit to Bernadette's description of how the apparition was dressed: "A white dress closed with a blue ribbon, a white veil on the head, and a yellow rose on each foot . . . a rosary in her hands."[45]

---

[42]This list of indulgences is signed off on by the secretary of the Society of Jesus, thus demonstrating the strong connection between the Jesuits and the group, even after the suppression and re-constitution of the Society of Jesus at the turn of the nineteenth century.

[43]Bernadette was an asthmatic and was known as a sickly girl around the town of Lourdes at the time of the apparitions.

[44] Harris, *Lourdes: Body and Spirit in the Secular Age*, 58 This has been a commonly held belief throughout Christian history, even if it has fallen out of our normal patterns of belief today. As an example, Pope Gregory the Great, in book IV of the *Dialogues*, recounts the story of a schismatic deacon who had supported an anti-pope who returned to serve as a ghost in the Roman baths favored by the party of the actual pope until the people of God would pray for him to go to heaven. Milhet's belief was, therefore, actually in line with what some Catholics thought of ghosts.

[45]René Laurentin, *Lourdes: Récit Authentique des Apparitions* (Lethielleux:

The manual that Milhet and her fellow sodalists used, published just one year before the apparition, entreated members of the sodality to promote devotion to the feast of the Immaculate Conception on December 8. Just two months before the apparitions, on a solemnity that required attendance at mass, it is reasonable to think that these women would have been in the parish church at Lourdes, wearing this specific dress and veil for all to see. While Bernadette would have been working as a shepherdess in the nearby village of Bartrès during the celebration of the Immaculate Conception in 1858, the image would have been fresh in the religious imagination of the sodality and faithful of the parish, such that Bernadette's description of the Lady that she saw would have matched their expectations from the local devotion.

Paying attention to a particular form of popular devotion that we know was active in Lourdes in the days leading up to the apparitions reveals a more robust picture of the devotion to Mary that surrounded the apparitions and perhaps even helps us make sense of why the people of Lourdes were so committed to the devotion from the very beginning. We know that a woman connected to the Children of Mary, Jeanne-Marie Milhet, was also connected with St. Bernadette and her family. We know that the Children of Mary, who were committed to promoting devotion to the Immaculate Conception, were present at the grotto during the apparitions and that it is likely that they were praying the litanies prescribed for them by their own prayer manuals in praise of Mary as the Immaculate Conception. At least one source also records that the candle

---

Œuvre de la Grotte, 2009), 82. Translation mine from: "Une robe blanche serré par un ruban bleu, une voile blanche, sur la tête et une rose jaune sur chaque pied . . . un chapelet à la main." Laurentin drew this directly from the transcript of the interrogation of St. Bernadette by the local police commissioner Dominique Jacomet on February 21, 1858.

that St. Bernadette was holding at the time of the apparition of March 25, when the vision declared herself to be the "Immaculate Conception," was a candle of this sodality. Rather than a meaning violation, these events could very well have stood as an affirmation of the patronage they had long felt from the Mother of God. Indeed, the theological foundation of patronage grounds meaning-making for the devout and the converted alike.

Patronage and Mystery

Twenty-one years after Lourdes, another apparition was reported in the impoverished countryside of Knock, Ireland, in 1879. There, Mary appeared on the outside wall of the local church building along with St. Joseph, St. John the Evangelist, and St. John the Baptist. They were together, with Jesus represented as the Lamb of God on a plain altar beneath them. Although not nearly as well known or as popular as Lourdes, Knock draws thousands of pilgrims each year to what would otherwise be considered a remote corner of County Mayo. On a visit there for his own research, Robert Orsi stopped to fill up his car's gas tank. He was somewhat surprised when the gas station attendant, neither a priest nor a scholar, told him that, at Knock, "the transcendent broke into time." Reflecting on this, Orsi notes that:

> What happens when "the transcendent breaks into time," in the phrase of the gas station attendant at Knock, is more confounding and unsettling—socially, culturally, psychologically—than "meaning-making." It may be that some religious stories are too hard to tell or that at the heart of the telling of them there remains a core of uncertainty and even distress that narrative can only circle

but never resolve. And this in turn raises the question of whether or not "meaning-making" is the best way of thinking about religions.[46]

Perhaps Orsi is right. Maybe meaning-making is not the best way to describe what went on at Knock or Lourdes in the nineteenth century. The circling points us to the type of mystery that might only be resolved in the context of patronage. At Knock, as at Lourdes, the story that is told is not just of an event that occurred. It is a story that weaves the people of particular places into the very narrative itself. In Christian patronage, the relationship between a devotee and a patron summons both the Estrades and the Milhets of the world into compelling and inexhaustible mystery as they try to reconcile the reality of the transcendent breaking into time. The devout and the convert encounter a Christological dynamic in patronage that shapes their experience.

Emphasizing the connection between heaven and earth constructed in the dynamic of patronage, Orsi's research has led him to the insight that it is not *merely* the attainment of favors or miracles that drives the connection. The relationship between the devotee and patron is enlivened by a desire to be caught up in the stories of the lives of the saints, and, in a real sense, to imagine ourselves in friendship with them and connected to their story. Texts like Estrade's, for example, are "best understood as a creative process that goes on and on in the circumstances of everyday life, as people add their own experiences of a saint to his or her vita and contemporaries get woven into the lives of the saints."[47] In Estrade's case, while he wants to be a part of Bernadette's story and weaves

---

[46]Robert Orsi, *Between Heaven and Earth* (Princeton, NJ: Princeton University Press, 2005), 111–112.

[47]Orsi, *Between Heaven and Earth*, 113.

himself into it at opportune moments, his address to Mary throughout the text makes clear that he wants to be woven into the story of the mother of Jesus as well. His ultimate hope is in Mary's intercession for his own salvation. For Hans Urs von Balthasar, such a hope is intimately Christocentric in the context of the communion of saints.

> In the "communion of the saints" these bounds are overstepped, and people's intimate personal areas are affected: this is only possible in and through Christ. The "merit," therefore, is exclusively at Christ's service, although, in handing it over, the Christian may link it with some quite specific request or intention.[48]

Rather than meaning-making, relationship resolves the "*disanxiousuncertlibrium*" in these moments for the believer.

The relationality implied by patronage does not exclude the possibility of meaning-making. Rather, it allows for the possibility of meaning that is inexhaustible. Joseph Ratzinger, later Pope Benedict XVI, perhaps offers the clearest understanding of how that search for meaning functions in the context of relationship when considering one of the central tenets of the Nicene Creed:

> The meaning that sustains all being has become flesh; that is, it has entered history and become one individual in it; it is no longer simply what encompasses and sustains history but a point in it. Accordingly, the meaning of all being is first of all no longer to be found in the sweep of mind that rises above the individual, the limited, into the universal; it is no longer simply given in the world of

---

[48]Hans Urs von Balthasar, *In the Fullness of Faith* (San Francisco: Ignatius Press, 1988), 38.

ideas, which transcends the individual and is reflected in it only in a fragmentary fashion; it is to be found in the midst of time, in the countenance of one man.[49]

Jesus, as the inescapable source of meaning for the believer, points us to the nature of meaning itself. We are reminded that meaning is inexhaustible as a knowable thing and that, in the context of interpersonal relationship, meaning grows and changes. It would be a violence to the nature of meaning itself if we concluded that we somehow could have it all figured out, thematize it, or provide some apodictic reduction to its most basic terms. Relationship directs meaning toward a horizon that seems to always escape our final arrival until the ultimate, eschatological fulfillment. Within the dynamic of patronage, we experience this arrival when, to borrow a line from Ratzinger's eschatology, "the believer holds the mirror of the Savior up to the face of the Judge"; when our pilgrimage on Earth is ended.[50]

Lourdes, Knock, and many other shrines and sanctuaries engage the faithful in the dynamic of patronage, directing us to the person of Christ. Often through the communion of saints, we are oriented toward meaning and reminded that meaning is always bound up in holy mystery. Relational framing in patronage echoes the words of Pope Francis. Popular religiosity implies an incarnate connection between Heaven and Earth:

> Genuine forms of popular religiosity are incarnate, since they are born of the incarnation of Christian faith in popular culture. For this reason, they entail a personal relationship, not with vague spiritual energies or powers,

---

[49] Joseph Ratzinger, *Introduction to Christianity* (San Francisco: Ignatius Press, 2004), 193.
[50] Ratzinger, *Introduction to Christianity*, 11.

but with God, with Christ, with Mary, with the saints. These devotions are fleshy, they have a face.[51]

Relationship, including patronage, animates the core of popular religiosity and devotion.

One might demur that patronage is a merely transactional reality. Pilgrimages, processions, and candle lightings are done merely to curry favor with a particular saint or with God for a particular intention. Yet intercession is something more.

Hans Urs von Balthasar, while quoting Luther, draws our attention to our place within the dynamic relationality of the communion of saints. "With this love I appropriate not only their goods, but themselves; and so, in virtue of their honor, my disreputable self attains repute; my lack is supplied from their superfluity; in virtue of their merits [*eorum merita*] my sins are healed."[52] Patronage reminds us of our connection to the whole Church throughout salvation history, bringing us into a communion that, as Pope Francis notes, is "capable of fostering relationships and not just enabling escapism."[53]

How do we make sense of meaning-in-relationship at Lourdes? Meaning-in-relationship is inexhaustible. Within the context of inexhaustible mystery, meaning-in-relationship resolved the perceived conflict between faith and reason in Lourdes. Specifically in the person of Mary, patronage featured prominently in accounts of the time as the relationship that resolved the presenting conflict.

For the remainder of this chapter, attending to the treatments of mystery that Bernard Lonergan and Jean-Luc Marion offer in their work will help clarify our definition of mystery in the context of the patronage relationship. Lonergan can help us

---

[51] Pope Francis, *Evangelii Gaudium,* no. 90, November 24, 2013.
[52] Balthasar, *In the Fullness of Faith,* 70.
[53] Pope Francis, *Evangelii Gaudium,* 90.

understand the cognitive nature of mystery, and Marion can help us understand the dialectical nature of mystery as a part of the dynamics of revelation. Each, in his own way, helps us understand potential theological underpinnings to the psychological and sociological realities that Proulx and Inzlicht, Whitehead, and the Turners have highlighted.

The Known Unknown at Lourdes

There was a great deal of curiosity about what was occurring at Lourdes during those days. From the interrogations of Police Commissioner Jacomet to the ecclesiastical investigations, the questions posed to Bernadette and the records of onlookers reveal heartfelt belief. They also reveal no small amount of skepticism. There was, and still seems to be, an open question of what happened—and is perhaps still happening—in the healings that occur at Lourdes. From the chemical analysis of the waters in which pilgrims bathe at Lourdes, to the thousands of carefully kept records of unexplained healings held in the medical bureau, there is a sense in which Lourdes compels its devotees toward a horizon of always wanting to know more. "Man's unanswered questions," Bernard Lonergan notes, "confront him with a 'known unknown,' and that confrontation may not be dodged."[54] We are compelled always toward the next question. Even as one question seems to be answered with an adequate description for what is occurring, it is clear that the "known unknown" cannot ever fully be eliminated. Each answer at Lourdes seems to lead to more questions such that, left to its own devices, it appears that we could encounter a never-ending spiral.

---

[54]Bernard Lonergan, *Insight: A Study of Human Understanding* (Toronto: University of Toronto Press, 1992), 569.

Lonergan reminds us, however, that the sorts of meaning-making that can take place in relationship have a certain built-in foundation that is porous enough to allow for the continued search for meaning without the fatalism that might seem inherent in a never-ending quest. Relationship may render the interminable Aristotelian moment of aporia actually terminable. The search itself, and perhaps the ultimate palliative result about which Proulx and Inzlicht talk, is not meaningful just because it can occasion an accommodation of new truths into old narratives. For the believer, the search is meaningful because it is a *conversion grounded in love*.

Although Proulx and Inzlicht themselves admit that "meaning is relationships,"[55] they perhaps mean it more in the sense that Lonergan means when thinking about knowledge itself. They could mean relationship in this sense as they consider relationality in a superstructure of ideas such as schema, narratives, and so on. Relationship to God, however, is a relationship to transcendent mystery. For Lonergan, such a relationship, in line with the teachings of Lateran IV, is something that is spoken of in analogy to our own human relationships, yet the Incarnation provides for the possibility that transcendent mystery can speak to human subjects. Borrowing a line from John Henry Newman, Lonergan notes:

> *Cor ad cor loquitur*. Incarnate meaning combines all or at least many of the other carriers of meaning. It can be at once inter-subjective, artistic, symbolic, linguistic. It is the meaning of a person, of his way of life, of his words, or of his deeds.[56]

---

[55]Proulx and Inzlicht, "The Five 'A's of Meaning Maintenance," 319.
[56]Bernard Lonergan, *Method in Theology* (Toronto: University of Toronto Press, 1971), 73.

Although Lonergan is careful to note that this kind of meaning applies beyond the person of Jesus, even saying that it might be the case that this is why we find meaning in literary characters such as Hamlet and Don Juan, the search for incarnate meaning speaks to our hearts in an expansive way that admits of mystery particularly in the context of those like Jesus and the saints. Heart speaks unto heart such that patronage can make meaning without exhausting mystery.

Patronage and Revelation

In two testimonies that she wrote in her own hand, one in 1864 and one in 1866, St. Bernadette makes an interesting choice in describing the moment of the first apparition at Lourdes. Rather than using the verb *"voir"* to describe that first time that she saw Mary, which she used elsewhere, in these two accounts Bernadette uses the word *"apercevoir"* to describe the moment.[57] The difference might seem subtle, but it is meaningful.

Rather than just saying that she saw Mary, Bernadette is conveying that she perceived her and that, perhaps, there was something that remained veiled about the apparition. Throughout her letters and testimonies, it becomes clear that the inexhaustible surplus of meaning found in the patronage of Mary at Lourdes is one that is revealed to Bernadette over the course of the apparitions, becoming apparent to people like Estrade only over the course of time. Bernadette's use of *"j'aperçue"* and Estrade's account of his first time at the grotto remind us that there is a sense in which Mary reveals herself to them, and that, in that revelation, they are able to make meaning of the event.[58]

---

[57]René Laurentin, *Lourdes: Histoire Authentiques 1* (Paris: P. Letheilleaux, 2002), 46.
[58]Laurentin, *Lourdes: Histoire Authentiques 1*, 46.

For Jean-Luc Marion, there is a certain sense in which revealed truth (*apokalypsis*) is different from what we might normally otherwise think of as truth (*aletheia*).[59] *Apokalypsis* has an inverse intentionality about it. For revealed truth, it is the truth *itself* that acts on our wills in love. Normally, we might make meaning through our wills acting on knowledge in the context of a judgment of truth or meaning. Here, the meaning itself acts with love on the will. Thus, meaning in the context of a revelation is not just a judgment of truth. It is, rather, an act of loving. In this sense, the revealed truth itself makes meaning, rather than the other way around.

Revealed truth, because it acts on us, requires an intentionality that can only be born in agency. Marion points to the reality of Christian revelation through the person of Jesus Christ, in which seeing is not believing but believing is, rather, seeing. Karl Rahner once succinctly noted that knowing in this sense is such that "it is the question which is its own answer when it is accepted in love."[60] Perhaps, more easily, to put it in Augustine's classic formulation, such knowing is a matter of "*credo ut intelligam*." Marion makes the critical point that the Spirit must first act on our wills in grace, which is to say in love, for us to be able to believe the reality of Christ. Such an inversion reminds us of something particular to incarnate meaning: the meaning that we make is not about the accommodation of new knowledge into our worldview but is about the summons of love.

Unlike other knowledge, a summons of love cannot be subsumed into a theme because it is the revelation of God in Christ for which the Spirit prepares us. As such, this is a summons that compels us forward so that the aporia of knowledge

---

[59] See Jean-Luc Marion, *Givenness and Revelation*, trans. Stephen E. Lewis (Oxford: Oxford University Press, 2016).

[60] Karl Rahner, *Foundations of Christian Faith*, trans. William V. Dych (New York: Crossroad, 2019), 192.

is not a frustration looking to be sated but a fulfillment calling us into deeper relationship, implying "nothing less than the *conversion* of the *I* that bears this gaze."[61] This conversion, bound to the meaning that arrives in love, is an experience of *apokalypsis* as a moment that grounds the phenomenon Lonergan describes as incarnate meaning. Furthermore, incarnate meaning extends beyond Christ through the saints. As John of Damascus reminds us, the veneration of the saints is nothing less than a veneration of Christ himself though the saints as *alter-Christus*. Such a veneration, as Balthasar reminds us, participates in the kind of revelation that Marion points to in order that, "in the holiness of the communion of saints, the world should come to learn what the holiness [that is, the divineness] of the incarnate Word on earth was."[62]

Patronage, for the person of faith, becomes a hermeneutic through which meaning-making is first a matter of loving so that it can become a matter of knowing. We love so that we might know, and we do not love into an abyss. Meaning violations, for those who live through the dynamic of patronage, are reconcilable because they bring about conversion. This is perhaps why it is that, in an experience of conversion, Estrade can re-find the sort of psychological equilibrium described by Proulx and Inzlicht. It is also perhaps why it seems that the Children of Mary, who already had a sense of Mary's patronage at the time of the apparition, seemed to experience the apparition as an affirmation instead of a meaning violation. In the patronage of a saint, especially in the case of one filled "with an abundance of all the heavenly gifts taken from the treasury of (God's) divinity," popular devotion finds one of its richest theological expressions because it is ultimately con-

---

[61] Marion, *Givenness and Revelation*, 65. Emphasis his.
[62] Hans Urs von Balthasar, *Explorations in Theology I: The Word Made Flesh* (San Francisco: Ignatius Press, 1989), 151.

nected to the revelation of God in the person of Jesus Christ.[63]

Sometimes the worlds in which we live seem turned upside down. Those moments can leave us personally and communally disoriented. They can send us looking for a place of connection to re-ground our sense of self and community. The story of Lourdes teaches us that, for the believer, epochal shifts are ultimately survivable as we realize our continued relationship with the God in whom we live, move, and have our being and our participative life within the communion of saints.

Popular devotions, like the one to Our Lady of Lourdes, remind us of the moments when the transcendent breaks through and divine love becomes all the more evident in our world. Patronage relationships—with God and the saints—remind us that our stories continue on and that meaning itself is inexhaustibly revealed to us in relationship. The dynamics of patronage, foundationally grounded as they are in relationship to Christ, thus allow us to make meaning of a world that might seem to be coming apart at the seams, weaving the threads of salvation history through the remnant.

---

[63]Pius IX, *Ineffabilis Deus*, December 8, 1854.

3

Patronage and Lament

The Curious Case of Santa Muerte

Christ's words from the cross sting our ears whenever we hear the passion proclaimed. His cries echo the psalm,

> My God, my God, why have you forsaken me?
> Why are you so far from helping me, from the words of my groaning?
> O my God, I cry by day, but you do not answer; and by night, but find no rest.[1]

Demanding answers to the Godlessness of the crucifixion is striking but not counterintuitive. Having entered into our humanity, Jesus cried out in the moment of his passion and death with a feeling of God's absence that reaches into the depths of human experience.

People of the barrios of Cancún and Mexico City and others who are materially poor throughout the world powerfully feel this absence in the face of everyday life's adversities. Accord-

---
[1] Psalm 22:1–2.

ing to ethnographic research, their feeling of God's absence often presents as divine deafness or, worse, indifference. When popular religiosity that is expressed in the context of religious patronage becomes confounded by a perceived rupture in the relationship between the faithful and God, the popular devotion can become expressed as lament. In such moments, the prayers and practices of devotional lament can become a sort of performative theodicy that protests a perceived lack of divine action in response to the faithful by substituting other patrons who may be more responsive. When those substituted patrons become idols, rather than icons, the interior dynamics of popular religiosity break. The practices that emerge in this rift can serve as a sort of warning sign of deep-seated problems to the broader ecclesia. Perhaps nowhere is this more clearly the case since the 1990s than in the devotion to Santa Muerte, which has emerged into the light from the back alleys of Mexico City's Tepito neighborhood to challenge devotion even to the Virgin of Guadalupe in Mexican society.

The Emergence of the Skeleton Saint

Daniel Arizmendi López, an infamous Mexican kidnapper known as *el Mochaorejas* for his habit of cutting off his victim's ears and sending them to their families, was arrested at his home in August 1998. As authorities searched his home, they found a small altar erected to Santa Muerte, a Grim-Reapress figure that he venerated like one might venerate an image of the Virgin of Guadalupe or St. Jude.[2] The difference between St. Jude and Santa Muerte, however, is that the latter is not a canonized saint in the Catholic Church. The fantastic

---

[2] See R. Andrew Chesnut, *Devoted to Death: Santa Muerte the Skeleton Saint* (Cambridge: Cambridge University Press, 2018), 14, 98.

story was spread by the press when authorities allowed him to take his shrine with him to jail where he could continue his devotion in his cell.[3] The fantastic stories of this image have grown since then, as has devotion to it.

Unlike most other devotions, this particular devotion cannot be traced to one specific origin story, apparition, miracle, or even proto-icon. Most studies point to the erection of an altar to Santa Muerte by Enriqueta Romero in 2001 in the Tepito neighborhood of Mexico City as the moment when the devotion, as we have come to know it, went public. In the front of what used to be her small food shop, Romero, now affectionately known by devotees as Doña Queta, began the public exposition of her private devotion to Santa Muerte.[4] Since then, the devout have gathered near her house weekly to recite a version of the rosary that is focused on the virtue of a good and holy death and to seek the patronage of death itself. While el Mochaorejas and Doña Queta have brought this devotion to the public, the devotion's roots might be deeper than are immediately obvious.

At first glance, many images of Santa Muerte seem to evoke something of a cross between the grim reaper and Our Lady of Guadalupe. The image is a skeleton wrapped in gowns of an assortment of colors, often correlating to the petitions of her supplicants. Common to images of the grim reaper, she often holds a scythe. Among many other titles, the image is commonly called "*la flaca*," the skinny lady, "*la niña blanca*," the white girl, and even "*Señora de las sombras*," lady of the

---

[3]While *el Mochaorejas* was the most well-known incarcerated devotee of Santa Muerte at the time, most anthropologists who study the devotion, including R. Andrew Chesnut, note that she has many devotees in the Mexican prison system, both among inmates and guards.

[4]Oriana Velázquez, *El libro de la* Santa Muerte (México City: Editores Mexicanos Unidos, S.A., 2007), 7–9.

shadows, by her devotees. There is clear evidence of devotion to Santa Muerte in working-class Mexican villages as far back as the 1940s, though some cite the possibility that an Inquisition document from 1797 also recounts such a devotion.[5] The day of greatest veneration is November 1. One might make connections to the Catholic Feasts of All Saints and All Souls as well as the Mexican celebrations of the dead and *La Catrina*. Scholars who have studied the cult of Santa Muerte, however, seem to be split on the nature of her connection to this well-known Mexican celebration. While some see Santa Muerte as a logical extension of the Indigenous Aztec and Mayan devotion to the gods of death when combined with the plague images that the Spanish brought with them in the sixteenth and seventeenth centuries, others rely on ethnographic evidence to tell them that devotees experience their own connection to Santa Muerte as an explicit expression of their Catholic faith and not necessarily as something connected to Indigenous roots.

As the first chapter clarified when considering Our Lady of Copacabana, the sorts of distinctions that scholars make in anthropological studies of the devotion likely do not pertain to the regular devotee of Santa Muerte. This is to say that, as their own words recorded in the ethnography suggest, many of those devoted to Santa Muerte think of themselves as faithful members of the Catholic Church. These devotees are not concerned with the connection to pre-Conquest belief in

---

[5]See Wil G. Pansters, "La Santa Muerte: History, Devotion, and Societal Context," in *La Santa Muerte in Mexico: History, Devotion, and Society*, ed. Wil G. Pansters (Albuquerque: University of New Mexico Press, 2019), 1. Pansters cites an Inquisition document from 1797 in which Christian authorities note an incident in which Indigenous people in San Luis de Paz "under the influence of peyote, engaged a figurine they called Santa Muerte in a forceful way, 'tying her up with a new, wet rope [and] threatening to whip her and burn her if she fail[ed] to perform a miracle.'"

Mexico, nor do they view their devotion as heterodox in the context of their Catholicism. As we will see, even the explicit condemnation of the devotion by a prominent cardinal and the implicit rejection of the devotion by Pope Francis have not seemed to slow the growth of the devotion to Santa Muerte. The pivotal driving force behind the devotion appears to be one of the perceived efficacy of the devotion. In moments when it seems that the institutional Church would not speak for them, and perhaps more importantly when they felt that they could not turn directly to God for their needs, or that God was silent in response to their supplication, devotees of Santa Muerte turn to a folk saint that they think of as being one of their own to hear their prayers.[6]

Patronage When God Won't Listen

St. Ignatius of Loyola, in his *Spiritual Exercises*, when considering why someone might address their prayers to the Virgin Mary rather than directly to the divine persons of the Trinity, famously had the insight that we should turn to the queen for her patronage when we feel unable to turn to the king.[7] Sovereigns are intimidating. Sovereigns have the powers of life and death. They stand as the representation of the entirety of the state, and, in more liberal societies, they also represent the will of the people. Prudence might dictate that,

---

[6] See Pansters, "La Santa Muerte," 33.

[7] This insight comes in the second week of the *Spiritual Exercises* when Ignatius is introducing a "triple colloquy." While the retreatant goes on to speak with God the Father and Jesus, Ignatius seems to understand that it is easier for us to begin the conversation with Mary. Ignatius's insight is a key point for how most people seem to experience their devotions in the ethnographic evidence and is true in the case of Santa Muerte as well.

given access to a royal court, one might not immediately offer a personal request to the sovereign. Rather, we might ask other, more accessible people in the court to assist us with our petition. Ignatius offered this explanation as a clarification of religious patronage in the midst of Reformation critiques of Catholic devotion, and his words help us understand why we might turn to Mary in prayer. There are some prayers of petition that, for whatever reason, we just do not feel comfortable taking directly to the King.

Ignatius's key insight here is that, for many of us, the thought of making a request of God in prayer can seem intimidating. When our supplications go seemingly without answer, approaching the triune God can become even more daunting. In the context of a place like Tepito, we can understand why a devotion like the one to Santa Muerte might so easily take hold. Considering both social and personal contexts in which the devotion to Santa Muerte emerged, we can recognize some patterns that allow us to begin to make sense of the devotion. Framed by Ignatius of Loyola's insight, such a brief examination also allows us to notice why the dynamics at play are not unique to the case of Santa Muerte but have a more universal application that could indicate deeper ecclesial problems.

In a recent ethnographic study of Santa Muerte devotees in Cancun, Kate Kingsbury draws a distinction between the tourists who visit the sunny beaches and the people who live in the town, surviving by waiting on the wealthy in the tourist industry. Unsurprisingly in the context of the COVID-19 pandemic, Kingsbury notes that the latter population has found their already difficult existence almost untenable.

> While tourism has brought many benefits, such as modern infrastructure, in a region that has long seen hardships, this dependence on gringo dollars has dangers that have

been made more apparent during times of coronavirus. Over eighty thousand people lost their jobs in the formal economy in Cancun in May 2020 and innumerable more in the informal tourist economies.[8]

Life was already precarious for the people who relied on the tourist-based economy before COVID-19. Kingsbury argues that disparities between men and women in the tourist industry, even in the positions that were available before the pandemic, clearly demonstrate her point. While wages are unjustly low for most employees of the tourist industry in Cancun, Kingsbury reminds us that men are much more likely to be employed in positions, like waiting tables, that yield tips. Most women employed in the tourist industry, she explains, work in the more menial and less public-facing tasks of cleaning rooms and doing laundry. Those positions mean long hours without the possibility of gratuities to bolster meager wages. This puts women at a distinct economic disadvantage and gives them disproportionately less voice in their society. In this struggle, many of the women of Cancun have turned to Santa Muerte.

The wealth of tourists stacked against the poverty of the local population in a place like Cancun is immediately jarring. The juxtaposition of luxury and struggle in a place like Cancun perhaps makes it less surprising that the devotion to Santa Muerte has spread remarkably quickly there. In Tepito, where Doña Queta first exposed the image of Santa Muerte that so many mark as the true beginning of the spread of the cult, the situation also demonstrates a context in which the devotion can thrive though it lacks the stark disparities in Cancun. Before the rise of Santa Muerte, Tepito was perhaps most popularly

---

[8] Kate Kingsbury, "At Death's Door in Cancun: Sun, Sea, and Santa Muerte," *Anthropology and Humanism* 46, no. 2 (2021): 246–247.

known throughout Mexico for the number of *luchadores* and professional boxers that came from the neighborhood.[9] In the stalls of its "thieves' market," known for the sale of goods that might have a suspicious provenance, the locals speak their own dialect. The local economy is otherwise dominated by sweatshops and informal work. As a neighborhood, it can be so dangerous that even Doña Queta famously tells people to leave her house promptly after one of her rosary services to avoid being accosted once the sun goes down.

In both Cancun and Tepito, ethnographers have noted that devotees of Santa Muerte turn to the devotion because of a sense of powerlessness. Kingsbury's study demonstrates that, especially for the women of Cancun who are the priestesses of the Santa Muerte cult, this devotion empowers them such that, beyond the traditional gender roles and economic arrangements in place in Cancun, they are able to realize some financial independence and social status that they might not have otherwise. She chronicles the practice of Yuri Mendez, a local healer connected to Santa Muerte in Cancun, who has "acquired significant prestige in her community":[10]

> Yuri is revered as a person of power. Acquired through her role as death's doctor, her prestige and financial autonomy, together with that of her all-women team, speak of an implicit feminism and female empowerment that is quietly at work in a corner of Cancun, where women do not have to work for male bosses in the tourist industry and can achieve financial independence as well as social status.[11]

---

[9] *Luchadores* are traditional masked professional wrestlers.
[10] Kingsbury, "At Death's Door in Cancun," 244.
[11] Kingsbury, "At Death's Door in Cancun," 262.

For women like Yuri and Doña Queta, consigned to economic dependence by virtue of their gender in an already infamously macho culture, being a practitioner of the Santa Muerte cult has afforded them a certain degree of economic independence and status within their own communities. It is important to note, however, that Santa Muerte devotional practice already has something of an internal feminist logic that also appeals to women like Yuri and Doña Queta.

Considering the reasons why people turn to Santa Muerte with their needs, Robert Chesnut notes that associating Santa Muerte merely with narco-culture is a vast oversimplification. Chesnut documents devotees turning to Santa Muerte for help with health problems, with money problems, while seeking protection, and, most traditionally, for help with romance. A red votive candle being lit for romantic purposes in supplication to Santa Muerte, Chesnut notes, is one of the earliest and most diffuse sorts of intentions brought to the folk saint's attention. Chesnut argues that such a devotion is found in anthropological manuals dating back to at least the 1940s. There is something peculiar about this particular manifestation of the devotion, however. Typically, the devotee in this particular kind of prayer is a woman asking not only for a wayward love interest to return to her, but that he wholly submits to her for the rest of their lives.[12] When the economic exigencies of a

---

[12]See Frances Toor, *A Treasury of Mexican Folkways* (New York: Crown, 1947), 141–142. Toor describes just such a ritual. Locating the practice in the Mexican state of Morelos, Toor describes devotees lighting funerary candles and lying on the ground as if they were dead. The devotee had to stay in the position reciting "the prayers of the Christian Creed," until the candles burned out. The supplicant was then to "pronounce the name of the unfaithful one," while invoking the "Soul of Tulimecca, thou who art in Rome." The supplicant finally asks not only that the lost lover return, but that he do so: "Repenting of all of the grief he has caused me by going away." This ceremony was intended to be repeated thrice.

society necessitate connection to a male partner for survival, these are more than just love spells. They can often be a matter of life and death. Chesnut argues that, when these types of love spells occur, the women who engage in them are motivated by the fear of the destitution that might come without a male partner to provide for their needs. This is particularly true in societies where it is difficult for women to provide for themselves without those connections. In other words, the empowerment of a woman over an unfaithful partner and the assurance of a woman's own well-being when they feel most vulnerable is inherent in one of the more popular interpretations of the devotion to Santa Muerte. As Chesnut concludes, "From the love-related spells and curses centuries ago in the Mediterranean to the present-day Americas, patriarchal societies have generated strong demand for such love magic on the part of socioeconomically vulnerable women."[13]

The love prayers associated with the devotion to Santa Muerte, however outlandish they might seem, point us to the devotion's connection to women who find themselves in situations of poverty and misogyny. In such a context, the devotion also reveals something to us about the health of the society in which it is found. The women engaged in these prayers and rituals often do so because, as the prayer itself implies, reuniting with a partner and maintaining that relationship is a matter of survival. The prevalence of the practice of love spells generally points to the status of women within a society, revealing a dreadful cost of misogyny.

The devotion's ritualized connection to women who suffer serves as an indicator of the sorts of gender inequality that both breeds dependence and assaults the agency of women. Both cases are true: the devotion lifts practitioners like Doña

---

[13]Chesnut, *Devoted to Death*, 135.

Queta or Yuri to a place of economic stability and security within their community, and the devotion points us to a deeper problem in which marital infidelity, combined with strong cultural misogyny, leaves women mortally vulnerable. Santa Muerte love spells and the economic security in serving as an acolyte for Santa Muerte both point us to the precarious situations that women must navigate in these cultures.

Devotees to Santa Muerte also call on her for healing, for wealth and prosperity, and for justice. In stark contrast to the prayers for healing offered in devotion to Our Lady of Lourdes or Our Lady of Guadalupe, ethnographic evidence seems to indicate that many devotees to Santa Muerte see the harm of their enemies as an important element of the protection that their saint offers. Santa Muerte is called on both to protect life and to take it.

In this way, this devotion is sadly symptomatic of violence within its host society. The ethnographic work around those two issues reveals a tension that goes beyond the religious practice of Santa Muerte devotion, telling the stories of a people who no longer feel safe in the hands of a loving God or who feel that the canonized saints have not listened to their prayers. When life itself seems interminably precarious, Santa Muerte devotees feel they have a patroness who powerfully holds both life and death in her hands and who can protect them, for at least a little longer.

The prayers for healing to Santa Muerte, like so many of the other rosary and novena-like devotions offered to the Grim Reapress, act like a sort of contract. Other Catholic devotions carry within them a sort of promise to the saint to spread the devotion if the prayer is answered. In devotion to Santa Muerte, people often offer objects to Santa Muerte and are clear in the phrasing of the prayer and in the practices themselves: this is an ongoing contractual relationship. In the case of prayers for healing and health, the consistency of offerings at altars erected to Santa Muerte—fruit, cigarettes, and even intoxicants like alcohol and cannabis—tell us something about how devotees view this saint. They treat her more like one of their own than they would some of the more formally canonized saints, reflecting their own proclivities in her desires.

R. Andrew Chesnut wrote of one prayer left at Tepito for healing. Whoever offered this prayer understands that Santa Muerte might react as we would in a given situation:

> Glorious little saint, today I come to you in a bad state. At 5:00 they're going to take NRL to the hospital for his operation tomorrow. Please make everything turn out fine. And if this is the result of harm sent his way, allow me to see it, and use your scythe to get those responsible out of our way, so they disappear from our lives and from the world—all of them, but especially MBL. Amen.[14]

This particular prayer, left at the feet of Doña Queta's image of Santa Muerte, speaks both to the nature of the many prayers to Santa Muerte around healing and to the way that the particular devotee views the folk saint. In speaking to her colloquially and offering her anger at those who might have caused "NRL" to need an operation, she views Santa Muerte not just as a patroness but as a compatriot. This is a saint who will take her side and who will also visit evil upon her enemies.

Prayers like the one offered above may seem antithetical to the Gospel message. Yet prayers specifically seeking the death or harm of an enemy are a part of the psalms that we pray and the scriptures that we read as Christians. To deny that, or merely gloss over the fact in the wake of devotions

---

[14] Chesnut, *Devoted to Death,* 180.

like Santa Muerte, seems a bit disingenuous. Scripture is full of the sorts of prayers like the one offered to Santa Muerte, including the extreme violence directed at Israel's captors in Psalm 137:9— "Happy is the one who seizes your infants and dashes them against the rocks"—and the consistent claim that God marched in conquest with the people of Israel against their enemies. Prayers for protection from an enemy or for harm to be carried out against an enemy for the purposes of liberation from that enemy are not foreign to the Christian tradition. In that sense, the devotee's prayer above is not *necessarily* beyond the pale of normative devotional practice. Instead, the motives for why devotees turn to Santa Muerte in this context raise the most difficult questions about the devotion.

There is an inner dialectic of power and powerlessness at play in the devotion to Santa Muerte. This dialectic is particularly clear when we consider the way that devotees tie her to questions of life and death. Harm to one's enemies in the prayers to the skeleton saint end up being as much about protection of myself and my loved ones as anything else. In at least one part of Doña Queta's Santa Muerte rosary, those present hold hands to form "a chain through which energy can flow" through someone who is directly touching the altar on which the effigy of the skeleton saint stands.[15] The prayers that channel this energy through the crowd ask for physical protection, but they also ask for protection from harm to one's reputation, from stalkers, and so on. At Doña Queta's shrine, devotees' prayers for protection do not shy away from the possibility that harm might be visited upon an enemy. They view Santa Muerte as acting with just concern for the powerless, who might need her help in visiting such harm.

---

[15]Laura Roush, "Santa Muerte, Protection, and *Desamparo*: A View from a Mexico City Altar," *Latin American Research Review* 49 (2014): 136.

In prayers where Santa Muerte is recognized as the angel of death, with power to grant or take life that is second only to God, the shift seems fairly clear. These are the prayers of a people who pray for life and death, to that reality which they view as having the power of life and death, because they live in the valley of the shadow of death itself. The problems inherent in the devotion seem to be bound up in the fear that comes along with dwelling in that valley when it seems that we might not have a God who would lay a table before us in the presence of our enemies. Fear, in that sense, might ultimately be that which drives a people to the hope that they can force God's hand by venerating a figure of death, a reality that seems all too familiar to their own lives. The devotion becomes a sort of magic, the prayers become spells, and all of it tends toward idolatry because, as Hans Urs von Balthasar reminds us, "magic is an enterprise issuing from human power that, at most, would seek to hold the divine fast before us (if such a thing were possible); it could never admit the divine into us."[16] When we seek to compel God in these devotions, we are really talking about an idolatry that expresses a sort of naïve theological narcissism. Still, devotees to Santa Muerte might be calling out to a God who seems to have abandoned them, and, in the midst of the exigencies of their lives, they demand an answer.

The Problem of Idolatry: *Santa Muerte* as a Mirror

One of the prayers offered in a novena to Santa Muerte begins with the words: "Allow the power that exists within

---

[16]Hans Urs von Balthasar, *Truth Is Symphonic: Aspects of Christian Pluralism* (San Francisco, CA: Ignatius Press, 1987), 67.

me to be unleashed in order to do away with the illness, be it natural or supernatural, which affects men and women. Because I believe in my own energy, which resides in me."[17] This prayer eloquently demonstrates what the devotee praying it believes about their devotion. The appeal of Santa Muerte to so many of her devotees is that she resembles them in their own ways of life, in both virtue and vice. When vicious, unlike other saints, she drinks and smokes and can be both jealous and vengeful.[18] In those moments, she is appealing because the devotees have a saint who can empathize with them by reflecting their own behavior.

The prayers that revolve around Santa Muerte, however, reveal that the devotion can also function as something of a mirror for the devotee rather than as a window that opens on to a genuine relationship of patronage like that which is present in the devotion at Lourdes. In the prayer above, for example, because the devotee asks for the power within them to be unleashed, it lacks the relationality that is so essential to the concept of patronage. The devotion derives a certain power from Santa Muerte's function primarily as an idol, rather than an icon, as it offers comfort in its similitude to the devotee. Even without being devoted to the skeleton saint, considering the dynamics of idolatry, particularly as Jean-Luc Marion outlines them, might remind us of other places in our own life of faith where we are muttering into an idolatrous mirror rather than glancing through the window of the eternal in a relationship of genuine patronage.

The institutional Church sees the devotion to Santa Muerte as a problem. Theologically, the primary problem is best expressed by the simple formulation that Christ, in his death

---

[17] Chesnut, *Devoted to Death*, 85.
[18] Chesnut, *Devoted to Death*, 85.

and resurrection, has conquered both sin and death. As such, neither sin nor death has sway in the world. Thus, devotion to death is a devotion to a reality which is essentially impotent.

In 2013, Cardinal Gianfranco Ravasi, the president of the Pontifical Council for Culture, summed up this argument when he condemned devotion to Santa Muerte while hosting an event in Mexico City that explicitly intended to reach beyond the bounds of the Church, the Cortile dei Gentili.[19] Ravasi called Santa Muerte a "denigration of religion" and noted that "religion celebrates life, but here you have death, it's not religion just because it's dressed up like religion; it's a blasphemy against religion."[20] Pope Francis, in an address to the Mexican Church on the first day of his visit in 2016, reinforced what Ravasi had said three years previously, but a bit more subtly while condemning both the devotion and those who, like Doña Queta, benefit from it: "I am concerned about those many persons who, seduced by the empty power of the world, praise illusions and embrace their macabre symbols to commercialize death in exchange for money which, in the end, 'moth and rust consume' and 'thieves break in and steal,'" he said.[21]

In an interesting turn, Pope Francis hints at the root of the theological problem. He continues his address by proposing a shift in devotion away from Santa Muerte and back to the more traditional devotion to the Virgin of Guadalupe.

---

[19] The Cortile dei Gentili is an ongoing series of events hosted by the Pontifical Council for Culture in various places around the world. The intent of the events is to open a space for dialogue between the Church and the world, as the courtyard of the Gentiles in the Temple of Jerusalem, from which the event takes its name, intended to do for the people of ancient Israel.

[20] "Vatican Declares Mexican Death Saint Blasphemous," BBC News (BBC, May 9, 2013), https://www.bbc.com/news/world-latin-america-22462181.

[21] Pope Francis, Apostolic Journey to Mexico: To the Bishops of Mexico at the Cathedral Church of Mexicopolis, February 12–18, 2016.

By proposing the shift, Pope Francis recognizes the context behind the growth in the devotion to Santa Muerte while he identifies both the potential idolatry in the hetero-devotion to Santa Muerte and its implications:

> In the mantle of the Mexican spirit, with the thread of mestizo characteristics, God has woven and revealed in la Morenita the face of the Mexican people. God does not need subdued colours to design this face, for his designs are not conditioned by colours or threads but rather by the permanence of his love which constantly desires to imprint itself upon us.[22]

Here, Francis extrapolates the problem that created Santa Muerte in the first place. He understands that he is addressing a devotion that arose from a population that was left feeling distant from God by inequities in economic standing, gender, and class. When Francis proposes the Virgin of Guadalupe anew as a counterpoint to Santa Muerte, however, he offers a pastoral solution that reveals his theological principle. Francis offers a reminder that God has been present to the Mexican people through the patronage of Our Lady of Guadalupe. In Our Lady of Guadalupe, Mary is said to have appeared as an Indigenous woman to Juan Diego in Mexico City speaking Nahuatl, wearing Aztec clothing, and imagined with Indigenous symbols.[23] By turning to her, Francis presents a counter-image of God's care and protection that is not linked to the idolatry that is inherent in the cult of Santa Muerte.

The solution that Francis offers points to the two-pronged problem inherent in the cult of Santa Muerte. First, Francis hints that this sort of practice is more often a symptom of

---

[22] Pope Francis, Apostolic Journey to Mexico.
[23] I will deal extensively with this narrative in the following chapter.

the broader sorts of problems that we have already discussed rather than the disease itself. Second, in noting God's closeness through the maternal care of the Virgin Mary as she has been venerated in Mexico since the time of the apparitions on the hill at Tepayac, Francis provides a counterpoint to the lament of God's absence that often drives the devotion to Santa Muerte. When we, with Francis, understand how lament emerges as a human response to the perception of divine absence, we can recognize how devotions like Santa Muerte might be both a form of idolatry and a form of protest in prayer.

Lament toward Theodicy: Making Sense of the Cry of the Poor

In the book of Job, crying out in his final defense, Job addresses God.

> I cry out to you, God, but you do not answer; I stand up, but you merely look at me. You turn on me ruthlessly; with the might of your hand, you attack me. You snatch me up and drive me before the wind; you toss me about in the storm. I know you will bring me down to death, to the place appointed for all the living.[24]

The harshness of the lament is striking. Job does more than just remember days past or note God's absence. He accuses God of indifference. In this moment, the lament takes on a new tone. It becomes theodicy. God is asked to justify his actions, or lack thereof.

For those who turn to Santa Muerte, lack of divine action is one of their primary motivators. Turning away from God and

---
[24] Job 30:20–23.

toward Santa Muerte in prayer, turning to another advocate to plead their case, is a way for the people to accuse God of being indifferent or inactive. The refrains of songs praising Santa Muerte make the belief behind this accusatorial shift even more explicit. A song by the Mexican band Los Cadetes de Linares even explicitly makes the claim, according to R. Andrew Chesnut, that "her power . . . appears even greater than that of God himself."[25] The supplication becomes different in the case of Santa Muerte because the question of choosing a new advocate is not just a matter of divine friendship and the connection to a saint as an *alter Christus*. It is an intentional choice for an advocate who wins devotion because of her power perceived as efficacy.[26] She acts when God, or the saints, cannot or will not. In this sense, as an advocate, Santa Muerte becomes a prosecutor for the supplicant rather than a mediator in conversation with the divine.

Despite being a biblical genre that is present in the psalms, Job, the gospels, and even an eponymous book—Lamentations—lament is difficult to consider theologically. In the end, our laments are often a matter of how we construe justice in the context of divine action. Although our human understanding might think, or perhaps more precisely *feel,* that God has betrayed a relationship of love by not acting quickly on behalf of our personal petitions, it can still be hard to express that. The heterodox devotion to Santa Muerte expresses lament in a manner that, for many who also claim to be faithful members of the Church, allows devotees the symbolic language to express their frustration and desperation in practices that look and feel close to their familiar devotional practices.

In this context, Paul Ricoeur reminds us that "lament

---

[25] Chesnut, *Devoted to Death,* 117.

[26] It should be noted, in this sense, that any devotion, even the most mundane and historically orthodox, can fall into the same patterns as Santa Muerte.

reveals us as victims."[27] Job properly laments because he has done nothing to warrant his situation. As a man declared to be just by God at the beginning of the book, there is no context in which Job could do anything but offer a lament. When we consider many, though clearly not all, Santa Muerte devotees, we might consider that theirs is also properly a position of lament. Particularly as the ethnographic evidence from Chesnut, Kingsbury, Pansters, and others seems to indicate, most devotees still recognize the sovereignty of God, even over Santa Muerte. As such, the turn to Santa Muerte when prayers go unanswered often takes the form of a protest. Especially for those born into poverty or those who are affected by the injustices in their society, the turn to Santa Muerte devotion turns out to be a complaint "that divinity account for itself."[28]

This complaint is offered, perhaps most importantly, when the prevailing religious narratives no longer serve to make meaning of the world in which those who offer the lament live. One of Ricoeur's key insights, here, is that lament is really only possible when a society has moved beyond the level of myth. While Santa Muerte might seem to be an altogether magical way of looking at the world, the language that practitioners offer often belies the presumed magic behind it. Taking Ricoeur's work on the differences between societies of myth and wisdom alongside the ethnographic evidence, we can recognize how devotees to Santa Muerte have moved from a society based primarily in myth to a society grounded in wisdom. In this transition, counterintuitively, operating beyond the bounds of the institutional Church offers the possibility of lament. In this sense, the Church is called to hear the

---

[27] Paul Ricoeur, *Figuring the Sacred: Religion, Narrative, and Imagination* (Minneapolis: Fortress Press, 1995). Kindle location 3715.

[28] Ricoeur, *Figuring the Sacred*, 252.

cries of the poor that are expressed as lament in the devotion to Santa Muerte as well.

Ricoeur describes the stage of myth through the sorts of organizing principles that ordinary people might hear from the pulpit on a Sunday. At the stage of myth, explanations are offered that give structure to the worlds we inhabit, nicely folding the stories of evil as fitting in the context of a much grander design. The mythic stage of society provides a careful ordering of meaning by providing strong narratives of origin. As Ricoeur notes, "By telling how the world began, a myth tells how the human condition came about as something generally wretched and miserable."[29] In the context of the Mexican reality, the mythic stage is a movement toward a unified narrative through careful control of religion by the institutional structures of the Church:

> As Talal Asad argues, ecclesiastical authorities managed the "authorizing discourses," which "defin[ed] and control[led]" religion. The church, in an effort to "subject all practice to a unified authority," could reject some practices and accept others, authenticate certain images and dismiss the rest, "regularize popular social movements into rule-following orders, or denounce them for heresy."[30]

In creating and enforcing a dominant religious narrative, the Church inadvertently created the primordial conditions for the type of lament that we see in Santa Muerte. By creating and controlling dominant narratives in the evangelization of

---

[29] Ricoeur, *Figuring the Sacred*, Kindle location 3706.
[30] Benjamin T. Smith, "Saints and Demons: Putting La Santa Muerte in Historical Perspective," *in La Santa Muerte in Mexico* (Albuquerque: University of New Mexico Press, 2019), 59.

Mexico, as Smith notes, the Church both offered reasonable explanations for why the world functions as it does and an account of why there was evil, sin, and misery in the people's world.

There is a twofold problem with the sort of rudimentary theodicy that we see emerge in Santa Muerte devotion at the mythical level, as Ricoeur envisions it and the way in which the people of Mexico experience it. First, the imposition of a colonial metanarrative on top of an Indigenous metanarrative left little room for the expression of question and lament in terms that made sense to the people to whom the message of the Gospel was brought. As Ambrose Mong notes, evangelization in this context is often most effective when space is left for a new religious perspective to hover over a local cosmology.[31] In the best scenario, Christianity as new religion leaves space for Indigenous, non-Western cosmologies and allows people to experience the in-breaking of the Gospel as a meeting of the two cultures rather than as a conquest. Second, while a theodicy that remains at the mythical level may offer broader responses to the problem of evil in the world, it lacks

---

[31] See Ambrose Mong, *Power of Popular Piety: A Critical Examination* (Eugene, OR: Cascade Books, 2019), 43. Mong rightly notes that evangelization in non-Western cultures is often most effective when it allows the non-European cosmologies which underpin the local cultures to remain intact. In the Philippines in particular, but also in many Eastern cultures, Mong notes that there is often a level on which religion is cosmic, which is to say that there is a level on which it is somewhat animistic in its perspective and carries within it distinctive attitudes toward elemental realities such as earth, water, wind, and fire. At the same time, however, there is also another level on which religion is more meta-cosmic, and concerns itself with questions surrounding soteriology, structure, and ultimate meaning. When religion functions on these two levels Mong notes that cosmic religion serves as a sort of landing pad over which the "helicopter" of the meta-cosmic level of religion can hover. In the case of Santa Muerte, the appeal to the folk saint through ritual common to animistic practice evidences some of the underlying tension between the cosmic and the meta-cosmic levels.

the specificity of a response to why evil happens *to me*. At this level, many Santa Muerte devotees are able to acknowledge the teachings of the Church, the divine sovereignty of God, and the rites of the Church while also maintaining a devotion that has been publicly declared by the Church to be transgressive. The disconnect between belief in the Church and the practice of the devotion to Santa Muerte is, therefore, often not seen by the devotee as a rejection of the Church. Rather, this is a devotion that answers questions, particularly at the personal level, that the institutional narratives do not.

As Ricoeur notes, when we move to the level of wisdom in our theodicy, lament becomes personal. The ethnographic evidence from Santa Muerte devotees reminds us that it's at the personal level that so many find their connection to the folk saint. One devotee in Mexico City, a taxi driver named Ricardo, recounted to Wil Pansters that when he was faced with a family problem and it seemed after prayer that God was either unwilling or unable to resolve it, he went with a friend to the shrine of Santa Muerte that Doña Queta runs in Tepito for the first time. Without being specific about how his prayer was answered, the cabby noted that the answer he did find has caused him to remain devoted to the skeleton saint ever since.[32] Thus, it was in the resolution of a personal matter and not in the context of a broader narrative that Ricardo came to be devoted to the skeleton saint.

While there are devotees like Ricardo, who seem to acknowledge a certain place for Santa Muerte in the communion of saints along with the efficacy of the folk saint when prayers directed to God have failed them, there are others for whom this is an intentionally transgressive devotion of lament. This is a lament that is not just about a relationship to God, but also a

---

[32]Pansters, "La Santa Muerte," 1.

failure of relationship to the Church. As Laura Rausch rightly notes, for many devotees, a turn to Santa Muerte intends to be a statement about organized religion such that: "You're giving a finger to the Church."[33] In that sense, the devotion is not *just* something akin to the lament of Job. It is also a rejection of both the mythic order and the institutions and practices that surround it. In the devotion to Santa Muerte, the rejection often can be of the institutional Church and the order that European missionaries imposed on the Indigenous people.

For Ricoeur, anti-Manichean and anti-gnostic arguments of the Patristic period played a significant role in the development of a formal theological answer to the questions around evil. These arguments echo through the Church's formal response to Santa Muerte. Cardinal Ravasi's arguments above mirror some of Augustine's own arguments about the non-being of evil, thus marking reverence for death, qua evil, futile. The problem that comes with this approach, however, is that, while it points to the futility of the symbol, it neglects the lament that cries out from underneath it. The condemnation of Santa Muerte, when it has come in these terms, has only served to galvanize the cult such that, as David Bromley notes: "There is at least the potential for a coalescing and radicalization of the Santa Muerte devotee base."[34] This base, as both Bromley and Chesnut note, has shown itself to potentially have the roots of a new religious movement in several breakaway groups like the Mexican-US Catholic Apostolic Traditional Church. These groups, while small, have begun to amass some followers in their stalwart devotion to Santa Muerte.[35]

---

[33] Smith, "Saints and Demons," 60.

[34] David Bromley, "Santa Muerte as Emerging Dangerous Religion?" *Religions* (Basel, Switzerland) 7, no. 6 (2016): 10.

[35] Such groups account for only a small percentage of the estimated 1.5 million devotees to the skeleton saint. Pansters, "La Santa Muerte," 11.

The recent crackdown on roadside shrines devoted to Santa Muerte by the Mexican government, with the approbation of the Church, has also given voice to these groups in the local media, only spreading the devotion.[36]

This devotion is, at its core, often a sort of protest directed to a God who is not otherwise speaking or acting in response to dire circumstances and directed to his Church that seems to be deaf to those cries. Beyond acting on the obvious commitments the Church should have to tearing down social structures that perpetuate contexts in which such a devotion as Santa Muerte could flourish, Pope Francis is right to propose a healthier dynamic of lament with the reminder of a patron who promised to listen in Our Lady of Guadalupe. Still, such a lament to Santa Muerte demonstrates clearly that the dark side of devotion is more often a symptom of a deeper problem than a mere act of idolatry.

The real challenge posed by a devotion like Santa Muerte turns out to not be the simple condemnation and control of the associated practices. The real challenge is to consider the realities, theological, ecclesial, and social, that are bound up in it. People, particularly the poor, turn to Santa Muerte when they feel that all other prayer has failed them. In situations of poverty, misogyny, and violence, she becomes as much a place of refuge as lament.

---

[36] R. Andrew Chesnut describes the collaboration between the Mexican government, particularly the Calderón administration, and the Church in this at length in *Devoted to Death*. As a way of combining forces to combat narco-terrorism specifically, the administration had roadside altars to Santa Muerte torn down across Mexico. David Romo, the self-styled bishop of the Iglesia Santa Cattolica Apostólica Tradicional Mex-USA, led public protests against the destruction of the altars, noting the legal right of his Church to practice their devotion to Santa Muerte wherever they see fit. Romo and others have seized such moments as opportunities to further spread their message of devotion to Santa Muerte in the press.

Death as an Idol

There is something perversely consoling about death as an idol. We are weirdly familiar with death, in sometimes unsettling ways. As Joseph Ratzinger notes: "Death is ever present in the inauthenticity, closedness, and emptiness of our everyday life."[37] The commonality of our human experience with death grounds its efficacy as a symbol. That symbol's rich common meaning confers on it a certain power that provides a lens that shapes how we view the world. The *memento mori* of the stoics, for example, is more than a remembrance; it is a motivating worldview. Remembering that we will die binds us to life and to others in a peculiar way. The inexorable draw of death upon us all also bestows a certain internal logic that, as an idol, makes it impossible for death not to ultimately answer our prayers. Finally, as is true of all things that we might put in the place of God, death has acquired a certain fascination by becoming something of a *mysterium tremendum* in the way our society treats it in the current moment. These three considerations provide us with background on why, as an idol, death seems to have a particularly powerful sway such that we can recognize why it might become conceptually confused with Godself in an act of true idolatry.

Death, or the prospect of death, has a certain common power that draws us to each other. Ephraim Radner astutely notes in *A Time to Keep* that there is a certain filiation in life that pulls on us when we walk in the valley of the shadow of death. Building on the work of the historian and poet Jennifer Michael Hecht, Radner notes that those whom we love, and who love

---

[37] Joseph Ratzinger, *Eschatology: Death and Eternal Life*, edited by Aidan Nichols (Washington, DC: Catholic University Press, 1988), 95.

us, call to us on the edges of death. This call reminds us that we are part of a much grander narrative, composed by the generations who have come before us and will be continued by those who come after us. In this sense, a devotion to death stands as a reminder of the ways in which we are situated in and related to the world around us. "Each of us is the child of parents," Radner reminds us, "and the relative of a range of birth lines, all the way down and in the most concrete and also mysterious of ways. To this degree our personhood is essentially generational."[38] In the cultural devotions that surround death in Mexico, in the altars set up to honor the dead on All Souls' Day, that filiation is powerfully felt. As the Catholic funeral liturgy reminds us, the belief is that life has changed, not ended, and that our relationship to the deceased has also not ended, even if only because we come from them and feel them powerfully as a part of us. In that sense, death, because it reminds us of the generations that came before us, pulls on us powerfully to remember that we were loved into being.

Death's symbolic power as a patron also lies in the fact that, with the notable exception of Jesus Christ, it seems to remain undefeated in our world. That is why, in the devotion to Santa Muerte, there is a circular logic that both logically necessarily affirms her efficacy and points to her role in setting justice for the poor. As a fictionalized St. Thomas More says in *A Man for All Seasons*, "Death comes for us all, my lords. Yes, even for kings he comes."[39] For the Santa Muerte devotee, that death comes for us all points to her power. When considering the role of Santa Muerte, particularly in situations of extreme poverty, there is a sense in which she also takes the place of

---

[38] Ephraim Radner, *A Time to Keep: Theology, Mortality, and the Shape of a Human Life* (Waco, TX: Baylor University Press, 2016).

[39] Fred Zinneman, dir., *A Man for All Seasons*. Special ed. (Culver City, Calif: Sony Pictures Home Entertainment, 2007).

divine justice for her adherents. People of every race, class, and gender will die and are, thus, ultimately accountable to Santa Muerte. For those on the margins, that authority over both the rich and the poor, the king and the serf, is the ultimate expression of power. That that power is distributed equally among all is testament to her justice. Supplications offered to Santa Muerte for the death of an enemy or an oppressor are ultimately *always* answered. As a devotion to death, which comes for us all, Santa Muerte never fails. While this logic might seem to lack appropriate nuance, it is a very real reason for devotees to hold to their patroness. Her power reigning equally over all, and to which all must offer an account, adds to the mystery ascribed to her as a patroness in the sorts of incarnate meaning that we discussed in Chapter 2, while offering us a glimpse of why those on the margins would take such a devotion so seriously.

Finally, death bears a numinosity for many of us today because, as Josef Pieper reminds us, we have made it curiously mysterious by bourgeois attempts to ignore it.[40] Ironically enough, the broader absence of the sorts of plague symbols that anthropologists argue might have evolved into Santa Muerte in our society has made death itself a mysterious thing for many of us. When the goal of so many undertakers is to make the deceased look alive in their caskets and when we do our best to mark death as a *mere* inconvenience or a

---

[40]See Joseph Pieper, *Death and Immortality* (South Bend, IN: St. Augustine's Press, 2000), 5. Pieper makes this point throughout his work. Here, however, he poignantly adds: "And, of course, our own thinking as well, before we engage in critical reflection, is in many ways colored by the influence of current attitudes towards death and dying, by the materialistic disparagement of death no less than by the nihilistic defiance of it, *as well as by the crass optimism of simply ignoring it*—as if the dying of human beings were some sort of 'painful episode' that occasionally 'still' happens, something it is best not to talk about, at least not in public."

simple fact of life, the ways in which it has become sheltered and privatized also give it a certain power in its otherness to us. Perhaps most intriguingly, Chesnut notes that this sort of cleaning up of death is not a cultural priority in the Mexican folk culture that surrounds Santa Muerte. Those diverse reactions render a difference in the interpretation of the skeleton saint as a symbol between the more European and upper-class culture of most ecclesial authorities and the expression of devotion to Santa Muerte as it is felt on the streets of Tepito and Cancun. Thus, for those of us who come to the devotion from the outside, devotion to Santa Muerte seems perhaps more foreign and more idolatrous than it would to those who are insiders in a culture where she is venerated.

The Death of God: When the Postmodern Problem Emerges in Our Devotions

The emergence of a devotion like that of Santa Muerte reveals something about the culture in which it takes hold. When the narratives that once ruled our vision of the world dissolve into a lament, people can turn to idolatry. When, at the base of Mount Sinai, the people waited for Moses to descend from the cloud and thought that perhaps the wait was too long and life in the desert was too difficult, they built a golden calf. Idolatry as an outgrowth of misplaced lament reminds us that our structures of meaning can lack the ability to accommodate our reality. When we construct idols, it is often because our concept of God itself has grown idolatrous, and we have cast God in our own image. Thus, God's response to Job functions as a reminder of divine solicitude and of absolute divine sovereignty. We are called beyond the mirror of the idol, through the window of the icon into intimacy with the God who loves us and always escapes our ability to fully know or conceptualize him.

In a line that sounds all too familiar to the way that the ethnographic sources describe the devotion to Santa Muerte, Jean-Luc Marion makes the point that, in the construction of idols, we hope to coax a response from God such that "the idol must fix the distant and diffuse divinity and assure us of its presence, of its power, of its availability."[41] In constructing the idol, we want it to somehow smile back at us and remind us that God is listening. This is the cry of so many Santa Muerte devotees and is the oft-proffered raison d'être of their devotion. There is a sense in which one might argue that most popular religiosity has this practice. A deeper consideration of the matter reveals an important point, though. The real relationship and true patronage is grounded in the radical freedom of God and of the saints and not in our ability to cajole or control them through our devotion.

Remembering that religious patronage is that which draws us into mystery, Marion's work offers three points for consideration. First, Marion reminds us that, for Christian belief, God's distance, rather than God's presence, plays a crucial part in the Paschal mystery. Christ's cries from the cross, echoing a lament of God's absence, reveal the relationship of the Son to the Father and the nature of our relationship to God. It also reminds us that we ought to be careful about how the analogies that we use to talk about God can become idolatrous. Finally, the idol in its proximity also mirrors back to us our own ideas on presence and power and reveals them as fruitless. Considering those three points, something emerges about how understanding Santa Muerte as an idol stands as a

---

[41] Jean-Luc Marion, *The Idol and Distance: Five Studies* (New York: Fordham University Press, 2001), 5.

conviction of both her devotees and of the context in which such a devotion was able to emerge.

The odd familiarity that we feel toward death makes it potent as a symbol and fosters its transition to an idol. The familiarity and the ways that death draws us strangely to each other speak to the ways in which death ironically cannot function as a symbol of the divine. For Marion, the distance between the Son and the Father that is revealed on the Cross, not their closeness, is the sign of their filiation. Radner notes that *we* experience the filiation caused by death as a draw to stay. On the cross, however, it was precisely that filiation that turned our human instinct on its head in the abandonment of the Son to death. "From the bottom of the infernal abyss that opened at the very heart of our history, once and for all," Marion writes, "there issues the insurpassable filiation that eternally confesses the paternity of the Father."[42] Marion goes on to remind us, along with the Church Fathers, that the Father is revealed as Father in the kenotic act of begetting the son. This revelation is not merely a revelation of *what* God is. It is a revelation of *how* God is: "In the Christ, divinity becomes filial."[43] That begetting creates a distance in the pouring out of the Son into the world, and reaches its zenith in the Paschal mystery. Christ is revealed as the Son of the Father not in the closeness that the fear of death inspires but by going forth from the Father to his death. This is the Christian mystery.

The Christian mystery is not marked by proximity and similitude, as devotees of Santa Muerte seem to praise as present in their devotion, but by a distance and otherness that allows for relationship. The sorts of filiation that death itself draws us to on Radner's account requires an otherness. That

---

[42] Marion, *The Idol and Distance*, xxxv.
[43] Marion, *The Idol and Distance*, 109.

otherness implies the window-like nature of the icon, allowing us to look through to an "other," to a person with whom I am in a genuine relationship of patronage. It also points us to what the icon's inverse might be, a mirror in which I see only my own face.

Marion reminds us of the inversion of our expectations for filiation in the face of death. He further reminds us that the "death of God" is, in many ways, a death of the ideas that we have of God. Thus, Nietzsche's (in)famous declaration in *Thus Spoke Zarathustra* that "God is dead" stands for us as the declaration that the ideas that we have about God are, in and of themselves, somewhat idolatrous. Following on the thought of Hans Urs von Balthasar, Marion reminds us that the greatest theological distance "appears when one asks about the 'highest difference that exists between God and the Being of beings.'"[44] He draws our attention to the declarations of Lateran IV. This distance means that "between Creator and creature, no similitude can be expressed without implying a greater dissimilitude."[45] Our concepts of God, when we consider God to somehow be circumscribed by them, are idolatrous in themselves. When we circumscribe God, we create an image of God that is not God. In doing so, we create an idol that merely smiles back at us. We create a figure like Santa Muerte that we appease with an offering that we ourselves desire.

Idols, in their proximity, create something of an existential echo chamber. "Everything," Marion writes, "is set up to allow a Feuerbachian reappropriation of the divine: since, like a mirror, the god reflects back to me my experience of the divine, why not reappropriate for myself what I attribute to

---

[44]Marion, *The Idol and Distance*, 246.
[45]Fourth Lateran Council, DS 806 (1215).

the reflection of my own activity."[46] Such a movement leads to the possibility of an infinite regress of appropriation in which I appropriate the divine unto myself and, having seen myself in the divine, turn once again to gaze upon it. Idols like Santa Muerte do not offer consolation through a relationship. Idolatrous consolation comes through a vague theological narcissism that is lethal. As if gazing down a hall of mirrors, "the image without distance is multiplied and endlessly reproduces man to the point of madness."[47]

Santa Muerte as an idol reminds us of how easy it is to fall into idolatry, either through the veneration of images or the veneration of the images of God that we have built in our minds. As we live our faith, we often forget that we only think of God in terms of analogy, or that, perhaps, our own personal images of God and expectations of how God might act resemble our own image and action a bit too much. Turning from God in a moment of protest or lament, when we feel revealed as victims who might be rightly pleading our cause before a distant or deaf God, we can all too easily find ourselves looking for a patron in the mirrors of idolatry. When we proudly dictate how we think God should act, we turn in upon ourselves and enter the closed cell of the funhouse hall of mirrors at the existential core of idolatry. In that echo chamber, where all narrative and relationship break down, we might even jump to the madness that severs the ears of our enemies or separates our own hearts from the lamentations of the poor.

---

[46] Marion, *The Idol and Distance*, 7.
[47] Marion, *The Idol and Distance*, 98.

4

Trickle-Up Devotion

From Tepeyac to Vatican Hill

The best way to get to the sanctuary is not the main entrance. Of course, you could walk down the sprawling boulevard that leads to the main entrance, which was constructed by the Mexican government. The verdant gardens along the center of the Calz de Guadalupe provide shade and respite for those journeying to the basilica. Sometimes along that path, you will even catch a glimpse of the pageantry of colorfully dressed Indigenous pilgrims dancing while making their way up the boulevard in the last steps of their journey. To encourage an orderly arrival for pilgrims, the gate that the marks the ingress to the grounds of the sanctuary has signs that indicate the entrance and the exit. People mill about in the plaza on either side, all submitting to the organization that the main entrance imposes.

Still, for all its attempts at organized splendor, the main entrance lacks the charm of the back way into the sanctuary. That path winds through the stalls of a marketplace overflowing with paraphernalia offered for sale so that pilgrims can commemorate their visit to the shrine. With even casual glances at the objects on offer, you might find Mary in the form of soap-on-a-rope and her image on hand fans and glow in the dark rosaries. There are large light-up plastic statues portraying the apparition, along with pious cigarette cases and holy water bottles mixed in among the myriad of things that bear the image of the Lady of Guadalupe. Sometimes, the images can be surprising, and the most rudimentary ones that are made by local artisans often also tell stories of how the people who made them and who buy them connect with the narrative of Guadalupe. The tents filled with goods in this little market protect you from the sun. Those tents also give you a sense of how the people have materially and spiritually appropriated the image that resides inside the basilica so that they might rest in the shelter of their devotion while continuing to tell the story of the shrine.

Going through the market is the best way to arrive at the sanctuary of Guadalupe because it reminds us of a crucial part of the narrative that has surrounded the devotion from the beginning. This path reminds us that popular devotions are often a spring of theological richness that bubbles up from the seemingly disorganized and even sometimes garish spaces of a local church to enliven the whole Church.

This chapter argues that popular piety plays a crucial role in the development of doctrine as a locus of the *sensus fidelium* of the Church. By paying attention to the dynamics that were at play at Guadalupe, particularly in the early days of the devotion, we can recognize how the devotion of a small and largely Indigenous community on the outskirts of Mexico City grew from a locally passed pious legend to become the officially recognized patronage of Mexico. The historical exchanges between the laity and the Church hierarchy regarding the devotion clearly demonstrate the value of dialogue and attentive listening within the people of God in ecclesial discernment. This discernment process leaves space for a more robust understanding of what we mean when we say that *the whole Church speaks* on matters of doctrine. Guadalupe and devotions like it demonstrate that popular religiosity is a privileged locus of ecclesial discernment.

The Lady Clothed with the Sun

The image is well known. A woman bears a blue mantle that is spangled with stars. Her pink dress is woven with gold thread and adorned by a sash around her waist. Her features are distinctly non-European, and her hands are folded in prayer. She is lifted up by an angelic figure with multi-colored wings and seems to stand on the moon. Rays of light emanate from her, making her appear to also be clothed in the sun itself.

The original image is said to be on roughhewn cactus fiber, and it currently hangs in a glass frame above the main altar of the modern-day basilica.[1] Devotees are so taken with the image that both government and ecclesial authorities saw fit to install a moving sidewalk underneath it when constructing the basilica in order to keep pilgrims moving and to ensure access for all to the image. The sidewalks could also be there

---

[1] There is some debate over what type of cloth the image is imprinted on. In 1752 the artist Miguel Cabrera was allowed to examine the image in order to be able to paint copies of it. At that time Cabrera testified that the image was imprinted on "a coarse weave of certain threads which we vulgarly call pita," signifying that it was a material similar to that which might have been woven by Indigenous people for garments like the one that tradition says that St. Juan Diego was wearing at the time of the apparitions. Cabrera notes, however, that it was soft to the touch, and so it could not be made of the cactus fiber that tradition had held it to be. Mariano Fernández de Echeverría y Veytia, a historian who was also present, noted that it felt like the material was more likely to be woven "from the thread of palms or of cotton." See D. A. Brading, *Mexican Phoenix: Our Lady of Guadalupe: Image and Tradition across Five Centuries* (Cambridge: Cambridge University Press, 2001), 170.

as a measure of necessary security after Luciano Carpio tried to destroy the image in 1921 by placing a bomb in a bouquet of flowers at the base of the image. The bomb exploded. The windows in the old basilica blew out. The image survived.

The origin of the image is debated.[2] According to pious tradition, it is of miraculous provenance. Many contemporary devotees will point to peculiar features that one finds in the image, or even the very existence of the image itself without much decay after five hundred years, as a sign of God's and the Virgin's presence within it. Of course, many also point to the image's survival of the Carpio bombing as proof of its supernatural origin. Historians, however, will often point to the fact we still have much of the correspondence of the local bishop, who plays an important part in the narrative, and that there is no specific mention of the events of the narrative in those letters. The bishop does, however, laud the faith of Indigenous neophytes in Mexico City and seems to have also asked the Franciscans to establish a hermitage on Tepeyac.[3]

---

[2] While the tradition which comes from the narrative surrounding the image is that it is of divine origin, that seems to have been debated throughout the image's history. Miguel Cabrera, who examined the image and noted the material constitution of the image in 1752, clearly examined the image with an eye to determining the techniques that the artist who painted it used in its manufacture. In other words, Cabrera presumed that the image was of human, and not divine, origin when he examined it and that, as was his charge, he would be able to replicate the image using the same techniques. Cabrera determined that it was a mix of different paints and methods, according to David Brading, professor of Mexican History at Cambridge University: "In effect Cabrera here testified that the elements of paint were as open to analysis as the texture of the cloth and that part of the miracle consisted in their unique combination of European and Indian techniques and materials." Brading, *Mexican Phoenix,* 171.

[3] See Rodrigo Martínez Baracs, "Orígenes del culto en Tepeyac," *Artes de México*, no. 125 (2017): 22–31. Baracs notes that there were no religious references to the site in the government's documents until a reference to a church being built there in 1554. Baracs concludes that it is likely that a small chapel

Other scholars, particularly those of sixteenth-century Spanish and Mesoamerican art, point to the similarities between the image and those produced by schools around Mexico City at the time.

Jeanette Favrot Peterson's work on the subject also suggests that, perhaps, the idea of the Virgin "appearing" in the records of early colonial Mexico could be a result of a poor translation of the Nahuatl word *neci*, which was translated variably as "discovered" or "appeared before our eyes."[4] Peterson clarifies, however, that, in the context of one of the earliest texts that mentions the image of Guadalupe from 1555, "appear" does not imply that an apparition took place: "Reyes Garcia makes abundantly clear, 'to appear' in this and other contexts . . . does not carry a supernatural meaning but rather should be understood as 'to show publicly' or 'to manifest,' sometimes for the first time."[5] For Peterson, the conclusion is that the image could have been made by human hands, contrary to the devotional legend as it was passed down. As we have seen in the first chapter through the example of Our Lady of Copacabana, however, the image being human-made would not *necessarily* have excluded it from being miraculous in the eyes of the early community. It is still possible that, if it was of human, and not divine, origins, the early community could have also ascribed something miraculous to its origins

---

was built there by the Franciscans in the 1520s or '30s as a sort of substitution for the Aztec goddess Tonantzin (a Nahuatl title meaning mother) Cihuacóatl who had been worshipped on the site. The lack of a direct historical record of an apparition on the site in 1531, particularly given that there is a notable record of correspondence between the bishop and both Spanish royal and Roman interlocutors, casts doubt on the veracity of the story of the apparitions for many historians like Baracs.

[4]Jeanette Favrot Peterson, "Creating the Virgin of Guadalupe: The Cloth, the Artist, and Sources in Sixteenth-Century New Spain," *The Americas* 61, no. 4 (April 2005): 581.

[5]Peterson, "Creating the Virgin of Guadalupe," 581.

or to events that surrounded it. The community could have understood that the image was of divine inspiration, even if it was not of divine construction. In this way, it would follow in the long tradition of the role of religious images in the Church. From there, a genuine devotion could have just as easily developed.

So much of the meaning that is ascribed to the image of Guadalupe, as we saw in Pope Francis's juxtaposition of it to Santa Muerte, is grounded in the narrative that surrounds it. Precisely because the narrative proposes the meaning that grounds the image, it has proven to be as important as the image itself. Pope Francis's re-proposal of the devotion to the Virgin of Guadalupe in the context of the growing devotion to Santa Muerte intends to invite devotees back into a relationship with a character in that narrative who invites all the people of Mexico into relationship with her.

The Virgin of Guadalupe, as proposed by Pope Francis in this interplay, is not just "one of us." Rather, she exists more as *an other* with whom I can have a relationship of patronage. As a result, the narrative *combined with the image* proposes the possibility of meaning that can also potentially escape the devotional narcissism of idolatry. The *Nican Mopohua*[6]

---

[6]*Nican Mopohua,* 1649, one of the oldest and most popular narratives of the apparitions of Mary to St. Juan Diego which resulted in the devotion to Our Lady of Guadalupe. First published as a part of a larger devotional, the *Huei Tlamahuiçoltica Omonexiti In Ilhuicactlatóca Çihvapilli Santa Maria Totlaçonantzin Guadalupe In Nican Huei Altepenahhuac Mexico Itocayòcan Tepeyacac* (hereafter *Huei Tlamahuiçoltica*), a manual intended to facilitate pilgrimages at the shrine in the seventeenth century, the story combines European and Mexican Indigenous narrative elements to tell the story of the apparitions. Notably, the copy currently held in the archives at the New York Public Library, which is handwritten and dated ca. 1550–1600—earlier than the 1649 print publication—uses "iron gall ink containing cinnabar, a poisonous mineral that the Aztecs considered sacred, on extremely expensive European paper that priests and royal authorities used for religious and political

and the *Image of Guadalupe*,[7] two of the earliest published sources that contain the narrative as it has been handed down, reveal a Mary who intends to draw the Mexican people into her patronage so that they might be introduced to her Son by her. While historical research casts some reasonable doubt on the events of those narratives being the objective facts of the matter, the narratives themselves reveal the deeper meanings of the devotion.[8] Those meanings may, in the end, be more

---

documents." Thus, even the construction of the document itself implied the connection between Indigenous and European cultures. See *Nican Mopohua*, New York Public Library, https://www.nypl.org/events/exhibitions/galleries/belief/item/5559.

[7]Cf. Miguel Sánchez (México City: Bernardo Calderón, 1648.) This text, in particular, proposed a more explicitly Criollo image of the Virgin; it proposed a link between the Virgin of Guadalupe and the woman of Revelation Chapter 12, and helped fuel the movement that proposed the Virgin of Guadalupe as the patroness of Mexico City and eventually the entirety of the country of Mexico.

[8]See Stafford Poole, "Did Juan Diego Exist? Questions on the Eve of Canonization," *Commonweal* 129, no. 12 (2002): 9. Stafford Poole notes that the veracity of the Guadalupe narrative was challenged as early as 1794 by a Spanish priest named Juan Bautista Muñoz, and that in 1883 Joaquín García Icazbalceta, the foremost historian in Mexico at the time, wrote to the archbishop of Mexico City chronicling problems in the historical accounts. Poole also notes that there are serious reasons to doubt even the existence of the visionary, St. Juan Diego, citing that the 1548 Codex Escalada, which is accepted as a source to demonstrate the existence of Juan Diego, is "full of anachronisms and errors and is most probably a crude nineteenth-century forgery." Poole argues that he is not alone in this thinking and that none of the documents held up as proof of Juan Diego's existence withstand historical criticism. See also Timothy Matovina, *Theologies of Guadalupe: From the Era of Conquest to Pope Francis* (Oxford: Oxford University Press, 2019), 3, where he rather succinctly notes: "No one doubts that a shrine dedicated to Guadalupe at Tepeyac, originally situated north of Mexico City (though today within the domain of the since expanded metropolis), has been active since the mid sixteenth century. The disagreement is whether the shrine or the apparition tradition came first. In other words, did reports of Juan Diego's miraculous encounters with Guadalupe initiate the shrine and its devotion, or is the apparition narrative a later invention that provided a mythical origin for an already existing image and pious tradition?"

important than objective fact, especially given the way the narratives have helped shape a people and amplify their voice.

In his address on Santa Muerte, Pope Francis refers to the *Nican Mopohua*. The *Nican Mopohua* dates to 1649, one hundred and eighteen years after the apparitions that they purport to chronicle occurred in 1531.[9] The Nahuatl title of the account itself points to its place in a larger work, the *Huei tlamahuiçoltica,* which means "By a Great Miracle" in English. "*Nican Mopohua,*" in the original text, is not so much a title in the original Nahuatl as it is the beginning of the text. It simply means "Here is recounted," and it begins the narrative of Juan Diego meeting the Virgin on the hillside. The larger work in which it is contained was written as a sort of devotional manual for pilgrims to the shrine by a diocesan priest named Luis Laso de la Vega, who was also the vicar of the Sanctuary of Guadalupe.[10]

Although this is the most diffuse narrative, it was not the

---

[9] See David Jordan, "Nican Mopohua," in *Readings in Classical Nahuatl*, 2021, https://pages.ucsd.edu/~dkjordan/nahuatl/nican/NicanMopohua.html. Although some sources date the origin of the *Nican Mopohua* to an earlier date than 1648 and support the Indigenous authorship of Antonio Valeriano (d. 1605) as the source of the text, David Brading's assertion that this tradition comes from the undocumented claim of the "enigmatic" historian Carlos de Sigüenza y Gongóra (1645–1700) seems important for establishing the timeline of the narrative. As Brading notes, Sigüenza y Gongóra's desire to find primarily Indigenous sources could have served to motivate claims that someone other than Miguel Sánchez or Luis Laso de la Vega had produced the text. For the purposes of this work, we will cite the first confirmable author, Laso de la Vega, understanding that his sources for the narrative likely came from an extant oral tradition. This work will cite the English translation from the original Nahuatl of Dr. David K. Jordan, professor emeritus of anthropology at the University of California at San Diego.

[10] Luis Laso de la Vega was a seventeenth-century Criollo diocesan priest of Mexico City appointed vicar of the sanctuary of Guadalupe in 1647, a role that he held until he was promoted to the Cathedral Chapter in 1657. In addition to his publication, the *Huei Tlamahuiçoltica,* he was known for having made improvements to the physical plant of the sanctuary.

first to be published. As Timothy Matovina notes, we know that at least one year earlier Miguel Sánchez published *Imagen de la Virgen Maria,* on the subject.[11] As we will see, that text is also crucially important in the development of the devotion. The *Nican Mopohua,* however, offers us insights into how the Indigenous population might have heard, or at least received, the narrative by making "extensive use of poetic devices, diminutive forms, and the Indigenous narrative style of accentuating dialogue."[12] In much the same way that Mary speaking the language of Juan Diego is an important feature of the story of Guadalupe, that the narrative *itself* speaks the Indigenous language seems to be an important part of why it has conveyed meaning to the people who visit the shrine, from the seventeenth century to the present day. Whatever the facts are that surround the origins of the Guadalupe narrative, the way it is told and the movement that grew out of it tell us a rich story about the relationship between God, a people, and the Church.

Here Is Recounted the Story: A Narrative That Binds the Image to a Patroness

Echoing the Christmas declaration in the Roman Martyrology, the text of the *Nican Mopohua* begins by situating the Guadalupe event in a very specific time and context. The Martyrology places the nativity of Jesus in the context of the

---

[11] Miguel Sánchez, 1596–1674, was a Mexican diocesan priest and well-known preacher. His text *Imagen de La Virgen Maria Madre de Dios de Guadalupe, Milagrosamente Aparecida en La Ciudad de México* (México City: Bernardo Calderón, 1648) is the first published text with an account of the apparitions at Guadalupe. Cf. Matovina, *Theologies of Guadalupe,* 3.

[12] Timothy Matovina, "The First Guadalupan Pastoral Manual: Luis Laso de la Vega's Huei Tlamahuiçoltica (1649)," *Horizons* (Villanova) 40, no. 2 (2014): 162.

conquest of the Holy Land by Augustus and the resulting Pax Romana. The *Nican Mopohua* situates the Guadalupe event in the context of the Conquest of the Aztec Empire by the Spanish and makes claims to a certain Pax Hispaniae.[13] Not surprisingly, since Urban VIII would have ordered a revision of the text of the Martyrology just before the time that Laso de la Vega was writing his account of the Guadalupe story, the parallels between the texts point to an important theological point. Theology is contextual. Luis Laso de la Vega first reminds us that the story that he is about to recount takes place at a particular moment within human history. He connects it to a place and a context that is marked both by war and suffering, which is somehow hopeful in the peace that had come to Mexico City.[14] At the same time, by using language that echoes the Roman Martyrology, Laso de la Vega reminds us of the ways that the *kairos* breaks into the *kronos,* and the ways in which God, and those in friendship with God, break into our history.

The narrative continues. In early December of 1531, on a Saturday morning, a devout neophyte, St. Juan Diego, was walking near the base of Tepeyac hill just before dawn. He

---

[13]Cf. *The Roman Martyrology,* 396.

[14]See Miguel León-Portilla, *Broken Spears: The Aztec Account of the Conquest of Mexico* (Boston: Beacon Press, 1990), 152. The Aztec Empire surrendered to the forces of Hernando Cortez and his six hundred soldiers on August 13, 1519, after a short, but bloody, war. The new order under Spanish control seems to have taken hold fairly quickly. There is evidence that at the time of the apparitions, and certainly by the time of the publication of the *Nican Mopohua,* the Indigenous nobility had begun to understand themselves as largely a part of the Spanish Empire with recourse to the king of Spain, especially in matters of religion. In one letter, dated just after the time of the apparitions, some of the Indigenous nobility even petitioned the king to have Bartolomé de Las Casas named their bishop and protector. As León-Portilla notes of this letter, they were writing to a "distant king who though unknown was thought to be good and just to his vassals."

heard something that attracted him to the top of the hill. Reporting that it sounded like the most pleasing songs of birds that he had ever heard, the *Nican Mopohua* recounts that St. Juan Diego wondered if, perhaps, heaven itself awaited him at the top of the hill. Not surprisingly, given the document and its audience, St. Juan Diego's hoped-for heaven is a peculiarly Aztec heaven: "Is it possible that I am in the place our ancient ancestors, our grandparents, told about, in the land of the flowers, in the land of corn, of our flesh, of our sustenance, possibly in the land of heaven?"[15] The sound that first attracted him coalesced into a voice, beckoning him up the hill.

When St. Juan Diego arrived at the top of the hill, he encountered the beckoning voice in the person of the Lady of Guadalupe. The text reports that she resembled the image that is now venerated in Mexico City and that she was ready to engage him as a patroness. Remarkably, in this narrative, there was little doubt in St. Juan Diego's mind as to the person with whom he was speaking. At Lourdes and in many other Marian apparitions, the visionaries either doubt that it is the Virgin or simply attest to the brute facts of the apparitions while they sort out the "who" of it all. In the *Nican Mopohua*, St. Juan Diego seems to indicate to the Virgin of Guadalupe, whom he recognizes immediately as Mary, that he is in a rush to get to religious instruction. "My Lady, my Queen, my Beloved Maiden! I am going as far as your little house in Mexico-Tlatilolco, to follow the things of God."[16]

Perhaps the way in which the apparition is recorded as having occurred is what is supposed to have convinced St. Juan Diego. The whole of existence seemed to vibrate with her presence. She radiated like the sun, and there was a sort

---

[15]*Nican Mopohua*, 21.
[16]*Nican Mopohua*, 24.

of energy pulsating forth from her. St. Juan Diego is said to have perceived the world around her as changed. There is something remarkably eschatological in the account. The text uses images that resonate with the book of Revelation, describing common plants as appearing like precious gems around him, and the earth itself shining with a particular brilliance. Uncommon to more recent Marian apparitions, Mary does not only appear to St. Juan Diego. Rather, the entire world is transformed by her presence.

This might be a theological flourish by Laso de la Vega, or it might be the tradition that those devoted to the sanctuary handed down to him.[17] Either way, St. Juan Diego's acceptance of the apparition and immediate candor with the Virgin seem remarkable. Even as the Lady asked him to tell the priests to build a church on the spot, Juan Diego tells her that he is in a hurry to do what the Church requires of him as a neophyte, and he goes off to do it.

There is something particularly theologically important in Mary's message to St. Juan Diego, even if he seemed unable to understand it. Mary's request that a house be built for her at Tepeyac is immediately deferential toward her Son. Her intent, she tells St. Juan Diego, is to "give him to the people in all my personal love, in my compassionate gaze, in my help, in my salvation, because I am truly your compassionate mother."[18] In her deference to her Son in this narrative, Mary becomes the icon. She desires to be a window through which Jesus Christ will be experienced and, therefore, known. In this way, the narrative makes clear what the image alone cannot: the

---

[17] It is also possible, as we will see, that the images, which bore a resonance to images from the biblical book of Revelation, were already a part of a connection that devotees were making to the woman of Revelation 12.

[18] *Nican Mopohua,* 28–29.

intent of the devotion is iconographic.[19] In making the point that Mary wishes to give her Son to the people of Mexico, the author of the *Nican Mopohua* may have intended to remind us of the internal dynamics of the veneration of Mary and of the saints more generally as it participates in the dynamic of patronage. The intent of the saintly patron is to bring us closer in friendship with Christ.

Following her request, St. Juan Diego immediately went to the newly arrived bishop to put Mary's request before him. The bishop, Juan de Zumárraga, was incredulous in his response to St. Juan Diego. The *Nican Mopohua* recounts that, after two separate conversations, the bishop even sent spies to follow St. Juan Diego to ascertain how genuine he was in making such a claim. At the end of their second conversation, Zumárraga asked St. Juan Diego to produce some sort of sign as proof that he had spoken with the virgin Mary and that a chapel should be built on top of Tepeyac.

St. Juan Diego resolved to ask Mary for a sign but, as he was preparing to go to Tepeyac to ask her, his uncle fell ill. After seeking the help of an Indigenous healer, to no avail, St. Juan Diego decided to go seek the priests to give his uncle last rites. On his way into Mexico City, St. Juan Diego decided that he needed to take another route around Tepeyac Hill in order to avoid the Virgin and more quickly get the help

---

[19] St. John of Damascus (c. 675–749) notes in the *Three Treatises on the Divine Images,* borrowing from a treatise by St. Basil (329–379) on the Holy Spirit, that in the veneration of images, the honor passes from the image to the archetype. He grounds this concept in the idea that Jesus is, himself, the material image of God and that the honor that we give to God in the worship of Christ also passes on to the Father. In the saints, though, John makes the important distinction that we venerate, rather than worship, them by virtue of their friendship with and imitation of Christ. As such, the veneration of the saints is by virtue of their connection to Christ and is intended to direct us to Christ.

of the priests. According to the story, the Virgin met him on his way, asked him where he was going, and told him that his uncle was already healed. She then sent him to the top of the hill to receive the sign for the bishop, Castilian roses blooming in barren soil. Having gathered those flowers, St. Juan Diego presented them to the Lady. She placed them in the fold of the tilma, or cloak, that he was wearing and told him to present the flowers to the bishop as a sign. The *Nican Mopohua* recounts that St. Juan Diego returned to the bishop and presented the flowers. When the tilma that he was wearing was unwrapped to offer the flowers, the image that we know as our Lady of Guadalupe had miraculously appeared on the cloak. As further proof of the apparition, the *Nican Mopohua* reports that Juan Diego's uncle was healed and then brought to the bishop to confirm the sign. The chapel was subsequently built on Tepeyac, and the image was displayed there for the veneration of all the faithful.

Source of Devotion, the *Nican Mopohua's* Purpose

As a source, the *Nican Mopohua* is more than just a story of an Indigenous man meeting Mary on top of a hill. It is a part of a larger devotional manual constructed by the vicar of the sanctuary in an era when devotion was growing among both the Indigenous and Criollo populations of Mexico City. In that context, it does more than provide us with either brute fact or religious edification. Publishing the narrative for the devout in a language and cultural context that they understood was an attempt to both regularize what may have been a preexisting oral tradition and spread the devotion beyond the neighborhoods surrounding Tepeyac.

The *Nican Mopohua* promoted devotion to Our Lady of Guadalupe by providing a narrative that gave its readers reason to believe. The narrative meant that the image on the tilma, which would have been familiar to the contemporary pilgrim, was not the only proof offered for the appearance of Mary at Tepeyac. The narrative recalls the miraculous roses, which would not have grown in that place at that time of year, and the miraculous healing of St. Juan Diego's uncle, Juan Bernadino. Both of these elements of the narrative stand as proofs for the intervention of Mary.

Beyond providing proofs, though, the document itself is intentionally enculturated. The original text was written in the Indigenous language. Furthermore, the images of the ways in which the world is transformed around the apparitions would have intentionally resonated with the Indigenous society.[20] Finally, St. Juan Diego himself becomes something of a sympathetic figure by virtue of his interaction with the skeptical Spanish bishop. The *Nican Mopohua* also regularized the narrative surrounding the devotion for the general population. Through a story that both identifies a member of their com-

---

[20] See Inga Clendinnen, *The Cost of Courage in Aztec Society: Essays on Mesoamerican Society and Culture* (Cambridge: Cambridge University Press, 2010), 15. Clendinnen notes that for the Aztecs, in a manner similar to the role that we saw Tiahuanaco play for the people of the Altiplano in Chapter 1, the city of Tenochtitlán played a particular role in connecting heaven and earth. Citing archaeological evidence and Aztec poetry of the period, Clendinnen concludes: "Its quadripartite divisions and its central temple precinct replicated the shape of the cosmos, while the great temple pyramid which dominated the precinct was a 'cosmogram in stone', asserting that here was the center and creative core of the world, resting indeed upon 'the foundation of heaven', and rising up as the Mountain of Sustenance, the Earth Mother from whose womb the sun leaped, as he does at every dawning, to strike down his murderous sister Moon and to scatter the Uncounted Stars." The woman described in the *Nican Mopohua* and in the image of Guadalupe has this same murderous moon under her feet and the stars in her cloak. In the narrative, Juan Diego asking if Tepeyac is the "place of corn" implies a reference to the Aztec Mountain of Sustenance and the apparitions occurring on successive mornings at sunrise also would have spoken to the Aztec sensibilities surrounding the sunrise.

munity as a protagonist and uses Indigenous symbols, the text sets forth a written narrative that unifies many accounts that may have existed in the oral tradition of the community. As Jeanette Favrot Peterson reminds us, some in the community might have seen the image as simply manmade while others held to some version of the narrative recorded in the *Nican Mopohua*.[21] Peterson's contention that there is space within the Nahuatl language to hold both meanings in the word "appeared" could have easily left space for competing understandings. That a vicar at the sanctuary published the story, in the Indigenous language, in a manual intended for pilgrims at the sanctuary, seems to begin to address that problem.

The project of regularizing the narrative finds its most diffuse expression in the *Nican Mopohua*. Cited by successive generations of devotional material that would follow and by Pope Francis even today, the story directs itself to those on pilgrimage, seeking to stir devotion within their imaginations using common linguistic conventions and a familiar symbolic language. That symbolic language would have been deeply felt in a culture that perdured a century after Spain's Conquest of the Aztec empire. When translated into Criollo understanding in another contemporary text, the Indigenous devotion emanating from the *Nican Mopohua* helps forge a new people out of two former enemies.

The Lady of Tepeyac, the Lady of Revelation, and a New Church

The *Nican Mopohua* might have addressed itself to a largely Indigenous population. Miguel Sánchez's contemporaneous text, *Image of Guadalupe,* spoke to a Criollo audience.[22]

---

[21] See Peterson, "Creating the Virgin of Guadalupe."
[22] Cf. Brading, *Mexican Phoenix,* 55. Brading notes that Sánchez's account

Bringing both the extant Indigenous narrative and his own colonial cultural foundations to his text, Sánchez makes use of European images, methodology, and cultural presuppositions, placing them alongside the Indigenous images in the *Nican Mopohua*. Along with the narrative itself, the text attempts to make an important theological point that seems to be grounded in the religious experience of its author. Sánchez, having read a text that he mistook for a work of St. Augustine, was convinced that the Virgin of Guadalupe and the woman in the desert of Revelation were meant to be seen as one and the same. Included in his narrative surrounding the devotion, this exegetical claim in turn influenced the thought of many of the local clergy. Their preaching, particularly at the sanctuary, made that specific parallel an accepted part of the Guadalupe tradition while elevating the role of the Virgin of Guadalupe in the eyes of the local church. Seeing themselves as a chosen people connected to the visions of Revelation also contextualized the local church's place in salvation history. Some have argued that this contextualization helped to form a concept of a truly "Mexican" people and culture.

Sánchez's connection between the woman in the desert in the twelfth chapter of Revelation came through an insight of personal prayer and study—and some unfortunately confused scholarship. Sánchez claimed that, in reading Augustine's "to Catechumens," he made the initial connection, even though such a connection does not appear in Augustine's writings.[23] D. A. Brading cites Sánchez's own words, using what he thought

---

"enthralled the creole elite of the capital and was calculated to strengthen the already fervent devotion to the Mexican Virgin."

[23] Matovina, *Theologies of Guadalupe*, 36. It should be noted that Sánchez misattributes this connection to Augustine. As Timothy Matovina notes, the proper source was the Augustinian contemporary bishop of Carthage, Quodvultdeus.

to be Augustine's interpretation of the woman in the desert in Revelation as representing *both* the Church and Mary, as a way of making a connection between Sánchez's own devotion and the development of a new national identity. "Since this image of Mary also signified the Church," Brading writes, "it followed that 'this New World has been won and conquered by the hand of the Virgin Mary and the Church established at its head in Mexico.'"[24] The figurative reading of scripture afforded by the commentary allowed Sánchez to appeal to the similarities between the description of the woman in the desert in Revelation and the image of the Virgin of Guadalupe in his own text. In doing so, he emphasized the importance of the apparitions in the context of the new culture that was emerging in Mexico City. Sánchez became convinced that the woman, "clothed with the sun, with the moon under her feet and a crown of twelve stars on her head,"[25] was the woman on the tilma of Juan Diego in Mexico City and, thus, the same woman whom tradition holds that St. John saw in his visions on Patmos.[26]

Although similar images of Mary with the moon under her feet and a crown of stars on her head were already iconographically abundant in the Church, we can understand how someone would make the connection that Sánchez made. The image on the tilma of Guadalupe is of a woman who appears to be

---

[24] Brading, *Mexican Phoenix*, 58.
[25] Revelation 12:1.
[26] Revelation 1:9. Cf. Sor Juana Inés de la Cruz, *Obras completas de Sor Juana Inés de la Cruz*, vol. 1, ed. Alfonso Méndez Plancarte (Mexico City: Fondo de Cultura Económica, 1951), 310. Further illustrating the depths of this connection as it was taking hold in both the devotion and in the culture of the colonial new world, the poet Sor Juana Inés de la Cruz composed a sonnet in the seventeenth century dedicated to the Lady of Guadalupe, which addressed the virgin as "she whose proud foot made the dragon humbly bend his neck at Patmos."

clothed in the sun with the moon under her feet, as described in the text. That the moon is supported by an angel also helped Sánchez to connect the image to St. Michael the Archangel, mentioned a few verses further on in Revelation, and to whom Sánchez had his own particular devotion.[27] The colors used in the image and the Indigenous face of the Virgin make the image on the tilma at Guadalupe specifically Indigenous to Mexico. It appropriates the symbols of Revelation, but it was by no means unique in its use of them. The iconographic tradition that surrounds Mary has long embraced many of the same symbols derived from the twelfth chapter of Revelation, and they are evident in the image of Our Lady of Copacabana as well.[28] Guadalupe is unique, however, because it stands at the nexus of the origin of the particular local church and a culture that embraces a narrative of harmonized Indigenous and colonial influences.

Unlike at Lourdes, where the devotion grew out of a long-established local church, or at Copacabana, where the still emerging locally inculturated church looks to Copacabana as a touch point between cultures, the apparitions at Guadalupe helped to forge a new culture altogether. The emphasis that Sánchez placed on the strong connection between the woman of Revelation and the Lady on the Tilma in the sanctuary was more than a mere personal devotion. It provided a place in salvation history for an emerging local church and gave a mission to its people. As Brading notes, this reading of the devotion endowed the Virgin of Guadalupe, and the colonial Mexican reality within which she emerged, with a purpose and a mission. "In short, Mexico had been conquered by Spain so

---

[27]Brading, *Mexican Phoenix,* 59.

[28]The statue of Our Lady of Copacabana is enthroned on a very large silver moon with a halo that attempts to give the appearance of rays of light behind her head.

that Mary could found the Church through the revelation of her image, a likeness which was simultaneously intensely Mexican and yet a faithful copy of St. John's prophetic vision."[29]

Though Sánchez could have just been offering a justification for the Conquest and subjugation of Indigenous peoples by colonists in Mexico, the care for finding Indigenous sources that emerged as he promoted the devotion seems to reveal the role of the Indigenous members of the community as equal members of a new nation. This new nation, as he experienced it, was already a mix of Indigenous and colonial culture.[30] Matovina directs us to an important point in Sánchez's work, reminding us that, as a priest, he had a clear theological mission in mind. "Sánchez addressed a fundamental issue: the place of the Guadalupe event and, more broadly, the Spanish encounter with the peoples of the American continent in salvation history."[31] Using the apparitions to ground the encounter in the context of salvation history did more than justify the Spanish Conquest. By elevating the role of an Indigenous man in the narrative, it also helped to create a new national identity that was grounded in a narrative of dialogue between the Indigenous people who inhabited the land and the Spanish colonizers. Interpreting the events of 1531 in this way grounded a *mestizo* national identity, speaking to the

---

[29] Brading, *Mexican Phoenix*, 58.
[30] Cf. Brading, *Mexican Phoenix*, 59. Brading offers an important explanation of how Sánchez viewed the Conquest of Mexico in theological terms. Mary's presence in Mexico at Tepeyac in the context of the Conquest was, for Sánchez, a fulfillment of the prophecy of the seventh angel of the Apocalypse, that all of the kingdoms of the earth would become the Kingdoms "of our Lord" (Rev. 11:15). As a product of that reality, one hundred years after the Conquest, Sánchez sought to make sense of the new cultural reality that was emerging in theological terms.
[31] Matovina, *Theologies of Guadalupe,* 11.

foundational values of the culture that emerged.[32] Creating such a narrative, Sánchez himself becomes

> the true founder of the Mexican *patria*, for on the exegetic bases which he constructed in the mid-seventeenth century that *patria* would flower until she won her political independence under the banner of Guadalupe. From the day the Mexicans began to regard themselves as a chosen people, they were potentially liberated from Spanish tutelage.[33]

For Sánchez, the Guadalupe event locates the Conquest beyond the context of the primarily economic arrangements of colonialism by marking it as a moment of providence.[34] Sánchez's work, recording a local tradition that he had likely heard through oral tradition, provides a narrative identity for the people beyond that of the mundane chronology of events since the Conquest. The narrative imbues the events with values. These are a people who are connected to the patronage of Mary, the mother of God. Ways of praying, living, and producing their own art and telling their own stories can be grounded in that fertile soil.

As Terry Eagleton notes, providing the sorts of values inherent in such an identity is the precondition for the birth of a people. "You can see culture as a specific sector of civilization, from brass bands and kindergartens to fashion shows and basilicas; but it also signifies the symbolic dimension of society as a whole, permeating it from one end to another, as

---

[32] A mix of Indigenous and Spanish identities.

[33] Jacques Lafaye, *Quetzalcóatl and Guadalupe: The Formation of Mexican National Consciousness, 1531–1813*, trans. Benjamin Keen (Chicago: University of Chicago Press, 1976), 250.

[34] Cf. Brading, *Mexican Phoenix*, 59.

omnipresent as the Almighty. There can be no distinctively human activity without signs and values."[35] In noting the relationship between culture and civilization Eagleton reminds us of why Lafaye is probably right. The founding of Mexican civilization as we know it is likely bound up in the signs and values that began to emerge from the telling of the story of Guadalupe and the ways in which the story continues to be told by the preachers who take up this message.

Hearing Is Believing:
Preaching a People into Being

It is not enough for a story to be written down to become a foundational narrative. The people must assent to it. While Sánchez and Laso de la Vega recorded their stories as ways of situating the narrative of Guadalupe inside salvation history and spreading and regularizing the devotion, the priests who shared and spread the story through their preaching were essential parts of how a story that was told by a few devotees in a small secondary shrine in Mexico City became the foundational narrative for a local church.[36] The preachers affirmed Our Lady of Guadalupe as the woman of Revelation and, similarly to Sánchez, drew parallels to biblical narratives

---

[35] Terry Eagleton, *Culture* (New Haven, CT: Yale University Press, 2016), 11.

[36] Cf. Victor Turner and Edith Turner, *Image and Pilgrimage in Christian Culture* (New York: Columbia University Press, 2011). Even at the time of the writing of Sánchez's *Image of Guadalupe* the image of Our Lady of the Remedios was vastly more popular than devotion to Guadalupe. Sánchez himself lived close to this other shrine in Mexico City which housed a small saddle statue of the Virgin which was brought by the conquistadors. Victor and Edith Turner note in the second chapter of their work that those who took up the Spanish colonial cause at the time of the Mexican Revolution took Remedios as their patroness, while those embracing a uniquely Mexican identity saw Guadalupe as their patroness.

in order to assert the place of the Mexican people in salvation history.[37] In their assent to the narrative and with the accompanying growth of the devotion, the faithful of the Mexican church affirmed the theological claims of their place in salvation history and solidified Guadalupe as a part of their own national myth.[38] The homilies of one preacher in particular, Bartolomé Felipe de Ita y Parra,[39] provide a clear example of how the priests' preaching helped shape a narrative that went beyond a specific devotion to the identity of the nation itself.

On December 12, 1731, at a celebration of the two hundredth anniversary of the apparitions, Bartolomé Felipe de Ita y Parra rose to preach in the pulpit of the shrine at Guadalupe. His message was straightforward: the woman who had spoken with Juan Diego two hundred years before in the place where

---

[37] Cf. Matovina, *Theologies of Guadalupe,* 44. Matovina notes that there are about 100 extant published Guadalupe sermons from 1660 to 1821. "These preachers borrowed extensively from Sánchez's insights and imagery, such as his association of Moses, Mount Sinai, and the Ark of the Covenant with Juan Diego, Tepeyac, and the Guadalupe image."

[38] It seems helpful to note here that expressions of popular religiosity often carry within them implicit theological claims, including the place of a people within salvation history, commonly held by a people taken as a whole. As the International Theological Commission wrote in 2014: "Both as a principle or instinct and as a rich abundance of Christian practice, especially in the form of cultic activities, e.g., devotions, pilgrimages and processions, popular religiosity springs from and makes manifest the *sensus fidei,* and is to be respected and fostered. It needs to be recognized that popular piety, in particular, is 'the first and most fundamental form of faith's 'inculturation.' Such piety is 'an ecclesial reality prompted and guided by the Holy Spirit,' by whom the people of God are indeed anointed as a 'holy priesthood.' It is natural for the priesthood of the people to find expression in a multitude of ways." International Theological Commission, *Sensus Fidei in the Life of the Church,* no. 110 (2014).

[39] Bartolomé Felipe de Ita y Parra was an eighteenth-century Mexican diocesan priest and native of Puebla. Parra was known as an eloquent speaker and was often called upon to preach in moments of greater importance at the shrine at Guadalupe.

they were standing was none other than the Virgin Mary, the mother of God. Further, her appearance was a clear demonstration of the work of the woman in the desert in Revelation chapter 12. He continued to interpret the image itself and the events that are said to have surrounded its appearance. Ita y Parra concluded by saying that God had made himself known through his mother on the soil of Tepeyac, and the church of Mexico was made of a people chosen to be under her mantle and protection.

Ita y Parra's homily makes the case that there are hidden meanings within elements of the image that reveal the identity of the person portrayed. He says that "forty-six stars . . . adorn her dress," because, as Augustine, Bede, and Cyprian note, Luke counts forty-six generations between Adam and the Incarnation.[40] Ita y Parra points to the one hundred rays of light that surround the woman in the image and the twelve rays of light that surround her head as signs that the Lady of Guadalupe bears the fullness of time within her, since there are one hundred years in a century and twelve months in a year. Finally, in a switch from the way Mary was usually talked about, Ita y Parra points to the symbol of the moon as a throne on which the sun-clad Mary sits as a symbol of the constancy of divine presence in Mexico, illuminating a waxing and waning moon.[41] According to Matovina, Ita y Parra attempted to

---

[40]St. Augustine of Hippo, 354–430, Bishop of Hippo, Doctor of the Church. St. Bede the Venerable, c. 673–735, English monk and church historian. St. Cyprian of Carthage, c. 210–258, Bishop of Carthage. Bartolomé Felipe de Ita y Parra, *La Imagen de Guadalupe, Señora de los Tiempos* (Mexico City: Imprensa Real del Superior Govierno de los Herederos de la viuda de Miguel de Rivera, 1732), 6.

[41]Ita y Parra cites Innocent III's image of Mary as the moon, and intentionally builds on that image. Rather than being an archetype of the Church, which is commonly associated with the moon reflecting the light of God into the world, Mary stands as a source of light herself.

demonstrate for his congregation that "Guadalupe illumines all of humanity and all times past, present, and future. In Ita y Parra's words, the conjoining of the heavenly lights—stars, sun, and moon—make Guadalupe a 'beautiful image [that] gathers in itself all times, unites all years, encompasses all centuries.'"[42]

Ita y Parra's point, if perhaps overwrought, was not *just* to show the importance of the image and lay claim to divine origins for it. Ita y Parra was concerned to make the gathered congregants aware of their place in salvation history. He wanted his congregants to know that the Lady present on the tilma, who had visited one of their own, was none other than the mother of Jesus. That visit, in which she promised to hear their "weeping, their sadness, to remedy, to cleanse and nurse all their different troubles, their miseries, their suffering," placed them under her direct patronage and care and gave them their own identity in salvation history by virtue of a special relationship to her.[43] Ita y Parra emphasizes this idea when he calls St. Juan Diego "the Jacob of our Indians," underscoring his role as a patriarch of a new chosen people.[44] Ita y Parra also situated the image of the Virgin in the basilica among the other great images of Mary throughout Europe, comparing her to the statues cast in porphyry in Greece, in marble in Italy, and in bronze in Germany. He elevates Mexican culture to the level of Classical and European cultures. He added that the fact that a fragile cactus fiber tilma has survived for two hundred years stood as proof that the image is of divine origin, further cementing his claim that devotees are a new chosen people.[45]

Ita y Parra's homilies were not simple declarations of his

---

[42]Matovina, *Theologies of Guadalupe*, 97–98.
[43]*Nican Mopohua,* 32.
[44]Ita y Parra, "La Imagen de Guadalupe, Señora de los Tiempos," 11.
[45]Ita y Parra, "La Imagen de Guadalupe, Señora de los Tiempos," 13.

devotion to the virgin of Guadalupe. Eventually, the people directly assented to his message. His homily in 1731 contributed to a movement that grew in Mexico City and the colony of New Spain to name the Virgin of Guadalupe as their universal patroness. A 1737 sermon of Ita y Parra's led to the city council declaring Our Lady of Guadalupe, and not the Lady of Los Remedios, who had been brought by the Spanish, as the patroness of the city. The city council first petitioned the archbishop, who consulted his cathedral chapter, which agreed that Guadalupe should be named patroness of the city. Once the archbishop agreed, the city council and the canons of the cathedral, which included Ita y Parra, swore an oath on April 27, 1737, accepting her as the patroness.[46] A month later, the people of the city celebrated.

> It was on 24 May 1737 that the city publicly celebrated the election of its new patron by staging a great procession through the streets in which the confraternities, both Spanish and Indians, the religious communities, members of all civil institutions, both royal and municipal, and the secular clergy all accompanied a life-size silver statue of the Mexican Virgin.[47]

One observer even stated that the scene reminded him of an ancient acclamation of an emperor or king.[48]

The preaching of Ita y Parra and others, built on the narratives recorded by Sánchez and Laso de la Vega, did more than just tell a story to edify the faithful or demonstrate the virtues

---

[46] In accepting the devotion, the archbishop also made clear that, at that moment, the scope of the patronage of Our Lady of Guadalupe would be limited to just the city. The devotion grew over the course of the next two hundred years such that Pope Pius XII would name her patroness of the Americas in 1946.

[47] Brading, *Mexican Phoenix*, 125.

[48] Brading, *Mexican Phoenix*, 125.

of religious conversion. Through their preaching they built on the cultural values that were first proposed by the written narratives. The homiletic theology used the narrative of a divine in-breaking, through the person of the Mother of God, among the Mexican people. By situating the narrative very carefully within salvation history, Ita y Parra reminded the people both that they were bound by the maternal affection of the mother of God and that that affection gave them a mission as a particularly chosen people. Having had this almost covenantal relationship preached to them, the people responded by taking up the Virgin of Guadalupe as their patroness in their religious observance and in their political movements.

Preaching and assent constitute a dynamic of the Word handed down and the ways that the people are consulted and how they appropriate the Word. This dynamic is not unique to Mexico, and the adoption of the Virgin of Guadalupe is a useful way to understand this dynamic in other contexts. Similar circumstances have often played out throughout the Church when a particular community accepts a patroness, as the archbishop of Mexico City himself reminded the devotees of Guadalupe when they chose her as their intercessor before God. These dynamics, which rely both on the local culture's cosmology *and* the dynamics of religious patronage, also position the local Church as a sort of guarantor of the devotion when it is attentive to the dynamics of faith in the context.

In the case of Guadalupe, we can recognize a devotion that is attentive to the local culture, bound in the dynamics of patronage, and affirmed by the Church. In this case, the Church is attentive to the *sensus fidelium* as it is expressed in the people's desire for Guadalupe as a patroness that yields a healthy expression of that same people's life within salvation history. Examining how the Church can be attentive to the people of God through the voice of the *sensus fidelium*, as it was in naming Guadalupe as the patroness of Mexico City, reminds us of how a hierarchy that is attentive to the devotions of the people can help create the conditions for a Church of dialogue.

Sensus Fidelium: The Dynamic Assent of the People of God

As the ascendancy of the devotion to Our Lady of Guadalupe demonstrates, popular religiosity is one of the clearest ways that the people of God express and reinforce theological belief. In the life-giving tension between popularly held belief and magisterial approbation, popular religiosity often provides both the theoretical framework for and the ritual expression of the *sensus fidelium*. At Guadalupe, the rich interplay of the preaching of the devotion, the assent of the people, and the meaning made of the narrative situated the event uniquely in salvation history and demonstrates how a devotional culture is born; it shows one way that those responsible for the teaching office of the Church consult and integrate the beliefs of the faithful into authoritative magisterial teaching. In such a consultation, popular devotion can stand as an assent that helps define the beliefs of the whole people of God and can function, as it did in Mexico, as that which individuates a local church, defining its interaction with the broader *ecclesia*.

The way that the early Church chose to refer to itself—ecclesia—reminds us that the development of doctrine is never, nor really ever has been, merely that which comes down from the hierarchical leadership of the Church. Joseph Ratzinger asserts that ἐκκλησία is a title that the early Church gave itself, with roots that go deeper than the Greco-Roman political understanding of a gathering or an assembly. Tracing this title through the Greek and to the Old Testament equivalent, Ratzinger points out that the Hebrew word that best accommodates this reality is קהל, *qahal*. On Ratzinger's reading of the word, this was more than *just* a gathering. Recalling the assembly of the whole people of Israel at the base of Mt. Sinai[49] and again before Ezra at the end of the exile,[50] Ratzinger understands the *qahal* as a dialogical gathering, listening to and agreeing to abide by God's word. Citing Linton, Ratzinger continues: "A closely connected fact is that in Greece it is the males who determine by their decisions what is to be done, while the assembly of Israel gathers 'to listen to what God proclaims and to assent to it.'"[51] The assent of the whole of the people to the revelation of the Law was foundational to the self-understanding of the Early Church. The reception of a teaching is an essential movement of the people of God. In that assent, doctrine finds its fullest expression as the belief of the whole Church. That assent marks an exchange between God and God's people. Those moments finally also stand as a corporate act of faith in which the Word is heard, the people assent, and, in that very act of assent, they become a people through and in whom God speaks.

St. John Henry Newman, when considering this same dynamic, relied heavily on the thought of his professor at the Gregorian University, Giovanni Perrone.[52] Peronne's work

---

[49] Exodus 35.

[50] Nehemiah 8.

[51] Joseph Ratzinger, *Called to Communion: Understanding the Church Today* (San Francisco: Ignatius Press, 1991), 31, 97–98.

[52] Rev. Giovanni Perrone, SJ (1794–1876), was an Italian Jesuit priest and theologian at the Pontifical Gregorian University in Rome. A regular correspondent with Newman on the matter of the development of doctrine, Perrone was also instrumental in the 1854 dogmatic declaration of the Immaculate Conception by Pope Pius IX, the importance of which was discussed at some length in Chapter 2. While it is still widely whispered around the august halls of the old venerable Roman institution that the now saint, and then already

became particularly important for Newman when considering the process around Pius IX's promulgation of *Ineffabilis Deus*.[53] Newman, noting how the laity had been consulted in the process, wanted to clarify how it had occurred, what weight it held doctrinally, and how it might further illustrate the ways in which the people of God give their assent. Newman's work reminds us that the sorts of dynamics that we see at play in the consultations of the people of God around the Catholic Church's teaching on the Immaculate Conception were by no means novel. The interplay between the hierarchy and the laity after Guadalupe stand in the line of a much longer tradition.

Newman specifically goes to great lengths to help us understand what is, and is not, meant by being consulted. Going back to the work of Perrone helps clarify Newman's understanding. Perrone was clear that "the constitution of the Church is in no way democratic," noting further that the hierarchy itself, along with the role it serves in leading the Church, receives its mission from God.[54] Perrone does, however, take up the Pauline image of the body, an image that Newman himself will later use in describing the dynamic of the interchange between the laity and the hierarchy.[55] The body and soul always

---

highly regarded scholar and theologian, rarely attended class in those days, it is clear that at least Perrone made an impression on him. Newman once commented in a letter to his friend Dalgairns of Perrone, Mazio, and Passaglia that: "There is no doubt that the Jesuits are the only persons here."

[53] See *Ineffabilis Deus*, December 8, 1854. The 1854 Papal Bull in which Pope Pius IX solemnly defined the virgin Mary as having been Immaculately Conceived: Mary, "by the singular grace and privilege of almighty God and in view of the merits of Jesus Christ, the Savior of the human race, was preserved immune from all stain of original sin."

[54] Giovanni Perrone, *Praelectiones Theologicae Joannis Perrone e Societate Jesu ab Eodem in Compendium Redactae* (Torino: Hyacinthi Marietti, 1840), 92. Translation mine from: "nullo modo democraticum esse ecclesiae constiutionem."

[55] 1 Cor 12:12–31.

act and react with one another. Perrone draws an analogical parallel between the laity and the hierarchy and the body and soul in the Church.[56] They always act and react to each other and, just as body and soul in their entirety make a person, so the laity and the hierarchy in their entirety make the Church. Perrone's image echoes Aristotle's work in *De Anima*. The soul stands as the main principle of motion for the body, yet it also relies on the body for its progress. From the movements of the body, we can infer the movements of the soul.[57] Thus, if the pastors of the Church stand as the analogical soul of the Church, we may discern also that which moves the Church's pastors through the movements of the whole of the people of God, namely "sanctifying grace, faith, hope, charity and the other virtues attached to or flowing from it."[58]

Developing Perrone's image of the body of the Church, Newman writes that "a physician consults the pulse of his patient; but not in the same sense in which his patient consults *him*. It is but an index of the state of his health."[59] In the same way that a doctor searches for objective fact to make sense of reported symptoms, Newman argues that the magisterium looks for objective signs of belief among the people of God when consulting the *sensus fidelium*. It is not so much that

---

[56]Cf. Perrone, *Praelectiones Theologicae,* 94. Translation mine from: *"Ut igitur envicamus inter utramque ecclesiae partem intercedere commercium, restat ut ostendamus et corpus in animam et animam in corpus agere."*

[57]Aristotle, *On the Soul*, edited by Richard McKeon (New York: Random House, 1941), 406a:30. "Further, since the soul is observed to originate movement in the body, it is reasonable to suppose that it transmits to the body the movements by which it itself is moved, and so, reversing the order, we may infer from the movements of the body back to similar movements of the soul."

[58]Perrone, *Praelectiones Theologicae,* 94. Translation mine from: *"gratia santificante, fide, spe, caritate caeterisque virtutibus adnexis aut profluentibus constare."*

[59]John Henry Newman, "On Consulting the Faithful in Matters of Doctrine," *The Rambler,* July 1859, 199.

the faithful are asked for their opinion by the hierarchy as much as "the fact of the matter, viz. their belief *is* sought as a testimony to that apostolical tradition, on which any doctrine whatsoever can be defined."[60] At Guadalupe, for example, the attendance of the people on the anniversary of the apparitions and the celebrations subsequent to the declaration would have stood as clear signs of belief in the consultation of the *sensus fidelium*.

While members of the hierarchy often have their own devotions based in popular religiosity, a distinction between those holding a particular belief and the magisterial office held by some in the Church is still helpful for understanding how this dynamic works. Newman makes an important distinction that is still helpful for understanding this peculiarly dialogical reality.[61] Newman distinguishes between *ecclesia docens,* the teaching church, taken to mean the hierarchy in the ordinary exercise of the magisterium, and the *ecclesia dicens* or *docta*, the learning church, taken to mean the laity, to help us understand the parties involved in the consultation. Newman agrees with Perrone that the Church does not function as a democracy, but he fruitfully uses the distinction to illustrate that the laity often prove to be more faithful than the hierarchy in matters of doctrine.[62]

---

[60] Newman, "On Consulting the Faithful in Matters of Doctrine," *The Rambler,* July 1859, 199.

[61] Since Vatican II the Catholic Church has eschewed as clear a distinction as the one that Newman makes, preferring to emphasize a more egalitarian vision of the people of God grounded in our common baptism. For our purposes, the distinction that Newman makes still has some utility in naming distinct dialogue partners.

[62] Cf. Newman, "On Consulting the Faithful in Matters of Doctrine," 199. Newman is clear that the manner of consulting is not about asking of the laity "their advice, their opinion, their judgment on the question," but rather about asking about the fact of a belief. That point demonstrates the utility of popular devotion, particularly in matters like synods and councils, which

A Communion of Love: **Sensus Fidelium** *in the Narrative Heart of the Church*

Newman's main, and somewhat painstaking, example of the utility of the *sensus fidelium* is the way in which the *ecclesia docens* and the *ecclesia dicens* interacted during the Arian controversies. Newman first identifies instances when the hierarchy fell into heresy and instances when the laity affirmed orthodoxy. Then, Newman writes:

> I mean still, that in that time of immense confusion the divine dogma of Our Lord's divinity was proclaimed, enforced, maintained, and (humanly speaking) preserved, far more by the *"Ecclesia docta"* than by the *"Ecclesia Docens";* that the body of the episcopate was unfaithful to its commission, while the body of the laity was faithful to its baptism; that at one time the Pope, at other times the patriarchal, metropolitan, and other great sees, at other times general councils, said what they should not have said, or did what obscured and compromised revealed truth; while, on the other hand, it was the Christian people who, under Providence, were the ecclesiastical strength of Athanasius, Hilary, Eusebius of Vercellae, and other great solitary confessors, who would have failed without them.[63]

Newman is doing two things here. First, he grounds the *sensus fidelium* firmly in the tradition and history of the Church. Second, he provides a theological foundation for the ecclesial

---

Newman himself notes often use the devotional life of the Church to demonstrate the fact of the belief that is observed through the devotional practice of the people of God.

[63]Newman, "On Consulting the Faithful in Matters of Doctrine," 199, 213.

practice of the consultation of the *sensus fidelium*. By situating the *sensus fidelium* in the history of the Church, Newman reminds us that this concept is not some novel innovation that arrived with the consultation of Pius IX around the question of the Immaculate Conception.[64] Rather, the practice of consulting the laity in the nineteenth century connects back to one of the very earliest and most critical theological controversies of the Patristic era. In our analysis, the ascent of Guadalupe from a hyperlocal devotion to the patronage of Mexico City and on to the patronage of the Americas is consistent with the pattern of consultation in the Church down through the ages.

The International Theological Commission, in their 2014 reflection "*Sensus Fidei in the Life of the Church*," also explores Church history when tracing the first signs of a genuine *sensus fidelium* in the Church. Thinking through its scriptural foundations, the commission cites the commissioning of members of the Church, "with the consent of the whole Church," to accompany Paul and Barnabas to Antioch in Acts 15:22. The commission further points to examples where something similar to the understanding of the *sensus fidelium* clearly existed both in the time of Augustine and into the Middle Ages.[65] They identify that the more formal definitions of the concept arose with the need for clarification during the Reformation. By clarifying the formal distinctions between laity and hierarchy that Newman would later use, the Catholic Counter-Reformation at the Council of Trent solidified the distinction in the twenty-third session of the council.

---

[64]Newman, "On Consulting the Faithful in Matters of Doctrine," 228.

[65]St. Augustine of Hippo, 354–430, bishop of Hippo, student of St. Ambrose of Milan, most famously is known as the author of the *Confessions, De Trinitate,* and as an interlocutor of the Pelagians. International Theological Commission, *Sensus Fidei in the Life of the Church*, nos. 27–28.

And if any one affirm, that all Christians indiscriminately are priests of the New Testament, or that they are all mutually endowed with an equal spiritual power, he clearly does nothing but confound the ecclesiastical hierarchy, which is as an army set in array; as if, contrary to the doctrine of blessed Paul, all were apostles, all prophets, all evangelists, all pastors, all doctors.[66]

While that might seem dogmatic, the Catholic Counter-Reformation strikes a balance that emphasizes the unity of *ecclesia docens* and *ecclesia dicens* in order to further assert the infallibility of doctrine when it is held *de fide* by the whole Church.[67] These definitions, offered by the likes of Melchior Cano and St. Robert Bellarmine, provided a foundation for the theologians of the Catholic Counter-Reformation to argue for the perdurance of the ancient Church in the Catholic Church of the sixteenth and seventeenth centuries.[68] The theological

---

[66] The Council of Trent occurred from 1545 to 1563. Considered the nineteenth ecumenical council by the Catholic Church, the council met in Trent, Italy, in an attempt to answer the controversies of the Protestant Reformation. It also sought to renew the Catholic Church from within by addressing the abuses that had led to the Reformation.

[67] International Theological Commission, *Sensus Fidei in the Life of the Church*, no. 32.

[68] Melchior Cano, OP, 1509–1560, was a Spanish Dominican bishop and theologian. His most famous work, *De Locis Theologicis,* sought to elaborate a theological method that was connected to scientific method. St. Robert Cardinal Bellarmine, SJ, 1542–1621, was an Italian Jesuit cardinal and theologian. He was known for his work as a Counter-Reformation controversialist, an interlocutor with Galileo, and, at one time, a potential pope. It seems important to note that these conversations were occurring contemporaneously with the origin narratives and development of the devotion to Our Lady of Guadalupe. While the Reformation and Counter-Reformation were occurring in Europe, the colonization by the Spanish, and their establishment of a church in the Americas was clearly directed in part by the clear delineations of laity and clergy emphasized by the Counter-Reformation and by Trent. We likely see some of that clear delineation at play in the interactions between St. Juan Diego

commission's historical survey of the use of the concept, in part, illustrates that the *sensus fidelium* is not *only* a concept with deep roots within the Church. It also had an important theological utility in the Counter-Reformation as it supported a theoretical foundation for a unified history within the Catholic Church for the counter-reformers.

Newman did more than simply assert the historicity and utility of the tradition of consulting the *sensus fidelium*. He further argued that the value of that consultation is the discernment process by which the *Ecclesia Docens* listens to the Spirit who is speaking in the Church. Perrone's corporeal analogy already admits of the role of the Spirit in animating the body of the Church, and Newman builds on the concept and clarifies the foundation for the Spirit's movement through the *sensus fidelium*. "The more devout the faithful grew, the more they showed themselves devoted to this mystery. And," he wrote, "it is the devout who have the surest instinct in discerning the mysteries of which the Holy Spirit breathes the grace through the Church, and who, with as sure a tact, rejects what is alien from teaching."[69] The International Theological Commission clarifies this growth in terms of a development of a relationship of faith that properly prepares and hones the *sensus fidelium* in the life of the individual believer as a sort of connaturality. "Generally speaking, connaturality refers to a situation in which an entity A has a relationship with another entity B so intimate that A shares in the natural dispositions of B as if they were its own."[70] Growth in devotion in the life of

---

and the bishop in the *Nican Mopohua*. We can likely also trace some of the theological understanding of history in the manner in which Sanchéz and Ita y Parra choose to situate the events of the narrative both in their preaching and writing.

[69]Newman, "On Consulting the Faithful in Matters of Doctrine," 172.

[70]International Theological Commission, *Sensus Fidei in the Life of the Church,* no. 50.

the individual believer, then, is a matter of love such that one knows the mind of Christ through the Spirit in a particularly intimate and immediate manner. As Newman notes, when devotion grows connaturally, the *sensus fidelium* can emerge as worthy of consultation because of its foundation in the relationship presupposed by the act of faith.

Connaturality offers us a way to think about how the *sensus fidelium* functions in the context of ecclesial discernment. Newman's reminder that the Holy Spirit sustained the communities that fought against the Arian heresy also outlines the boundaries of what qualifies as true discernment in an ecclesial context. Connaturality cannot be a matter of knowledge that we acquire by our own efforts through careful study. Rather, the sort of connaturality that supports the *sensus fidelium* derives from an act of faith. Any act of faith implies a relationship that reminds us of the importance of the role of the Holy Spirit in revealing the heart of Christ to us. The *sensus fidelium*, as an instinct born of the act of faith that directs us toward connaturality, requires an intimate knowledge of Christ that might not be otherwise available to us except through the Spirit of love. As Romano Guardini[71] points out, the actual distance between our current context and the event of the life of Christ in chronological history poses some problems for the act of faith. As generations pass, Guardini points out, the events of the life of Christ become more veiled to us.

> The more this indirect revelation spread, the thicker, simultaneously, grew its veil, woven of the human weaknesses of its messengers and the distortions and abuses

---

[71] Rev. Romano Guardini, 1885–1958, was a German Catholic priest and theologian. He is famous for works such as *The Saviour*, which challenged Nazi ideology and asserted the Jewishness of Jesus, and *The End of the Modern World,* which is cited repeatedly in the encyclical *Laudato Si'* of Pope Francis.

of human history. The problem of the later-comers, that of excavating the living Son of God from sermon, book and example, from the sacred measures of divine worship, from work of art, pious practice, custom and symbol, is difficult, certainly, but probably not more difficult than that of recognizing him in the son of a carpenter.[72]

We may not experience the revelation of God's presence in the immediacy of relationship to Christ as did those who knew him before the ascension. Guardini points out that the Spirit, as the Spirit of love, breaks down the barriers such that we are able to experience the intimacy implied by connaturality. Guardini likens the experience of the Spirit to a falling in love such that "the I-not-you, mine-not-thine barrier begins to dissolve. Now no particular virtue or effort is necessary to join the beloved; he is already 'there.' What is his suddenly belongs to the other, and what affects the other suddenly touches him, for a new unit has been created."[73]

The *sensus fidelium* is grounded in relationship with Christ, through the Spirit of love. Through the *sensus fidelium*, we recognize that communion is the mission of faith. As it aids the faithful in discerning that which is, and is not, helpful to the practice of faith, the *sensus fidelium* ideally serves as a means to connect the people of God in the present and across time to the love that underpins faith itself. Consulting of the *sensus fidelium* in the ordinary exercise of the magisterium, at its best, stands as a guarantor of communion among those who might fruitfully receive the teaching of the Church.

In Guadalupe, the devotion grew over time and found itself recognized officially after two hundred years. That connection

---

[72]Romano Guardini, *The Lord* (Washington, DC: Regnery, 1982), 298.
[73]Guardini, *The Lord*, 170.

to the Church throughout the two hundred years of the devotion's development was essential. That the devotion produced communion among the people was, itself, also a manifestation of the Spirit of Love speaking through the *sensus fidelium*. While these local devotions manifest the deliberations of the *sensus fidelium* of a local church, these instincts can be, and have been, consulted by the universal Church to help shape Christian doctrine.

Consultations of the Sensus Fidelium: *How Popular Devotion Affirms Doctrine*

The distinction between popular devotion and doctrine can often be subtle. When a devotion is an expression of commonly held belief, after consultation among the people of God, the distinction seems to disappear. The deeply held beliefs expressed through devotion, when submitted to the wisdom of the universal magisterium and found to be worthy of universal assent, often function as the means to measure the *sensus fidelium* so as to provide evidence for the solemn definition of new dogmas. Newman began his investigation into this process in the context of the formal definition of the Immaculate Conception by Pius IX in 1854.[74] Following on the model of the consultations conducted by Pope Pius IX, Pope Pius XII also conducted his own investigation in 1946 into the devotion of the people of God when considering the Church's teaching on the Assumption in the days leading up to the 1950 Apostolic Constitution *Munificentissimus Deus*. That both popes engaged in this process of consultation reminds us of the importance of the *sensus fidelium* as an instrument

---

[74] This is the same process, and definition, that was discussed at length in Chapter 2 and which, in many ways, set the stage for the understanding of what occurred at Lourdes in 1858.

of communion that can unite the devotions of distinct local churches with the faith of the universal Church.

On May 1, 1946, Pope Pius XII penned a letter to all the Catholic bishops of the world. He recounted the tradition within and devotion of the Church to the idea that Mary, the mother of Jesus, had been assumed body and soul into heaven upon the completion of her earthly life. He further recounted the movement to solemnly declare this as the teaching of the Catholic Church at Vatican I. Pius XII, then, stated to all of the bishops of the world:

> We want to know as much as possible, Venerable Brothers, of your extraordinary wisdom and prudence, if your view that the corporeal Assumption of the Blessed Virgin can be proposed and defined as a dogma of the faith, and whether you would desire it (along) with your clergy and people.[75]

Pius XII was asking the bishops of the world not simply whether he might be able to propose such a teaching without opposition. He was asking specifically whether the belief already existed among the people of God and whether or not, as such, he would be correct to define it as a dogma of the faith.

Of course, this was by no means a novel moment in the history of the Catholic Church. We might even note a resonance with how the bishop of Mexico City came to name the Virgin of Guadalupe as the patroness of the city after consultation among the people and the pastors. These practices of consulta-

---

[75] Pope Pius XII, *Deiparae Virginis Mariae*, no. 5, May 1, 1946. Translation mine from: "Praesertim autem nosse quam maxime cupimus, a vos, Venerabiles Fratres, pro eximia vestra sapientia et prudentia censeatis Assumptionem corpoream Beatissimae Virginis tamquam dogma fidei proponi ac definiri posse, et an id cum clero et populo vestro exoptetis."

tion were common, not just to the papacy, but generally in the Church by the time of the solemn affirmation of the dogma of the Assumption. When Pius XII finally wrote *Munificentissimus Deus* after this consultation was complete in 1950, he noted that his dogmatic declaration that Mary, "having completed the course of her earthly life, was assumed body and soul into heavenly glory," was for "the joy and exultation of the entire Church."[76] Pius XII could assert that his proclamation would cause such joy and exultation with confidence, at least in part, because he had consulted the people of God.

The consultation among the people of God before the two infallible dogmatic declarations by Pius IX and Pius XII, which remain the only dogmatic declarations of this nature, demonstrate an understanding that the authority involved in papal infallibility requires the consultation of the *sensus fidelium*. In these two instances in particular, however, the consultation clearly met evidence from popular devotion. As the bishop of Quebec wrote to his diocese shortly after the solemn declaration of the Immaculate Conception in presenting the reasons for *Ineffabilis Deus*:

> It is indeed Mary, inasmuch as she was conceived without sin, whom you have ever honored and invoked, when celebrating the solemn festival of the Conception. What a triumph, what a holy consolation for you to hear, on this occasion, this magnificent title confirmed by the oracles of Heaven.[77]

---

[76] *Munificentissimus Deus,* no. 44, the Apostolic Constitution promulgated by Pope Pius XII on November 1, 1950, dogmatically declared that Mary had been assumed, body and soul, into heaven. This declaration affirmed a long-held devotion in both the Christian east and west. Pius XII, like his predecessor Pius IX, consulted all the bishops of the Catholic Church seeking the *sensus fidelium* before making this declaration. *Munificentissimus Deus*, no. 41.

[77] Cf. DH 2800. *Ineffabilis Deus*, discussed in Chapter 2, is the 1854 Papal

In the context of the Virgin of Guadalupe, similar sentiments would have been felt. The image itself evokes the Spanish devotion to the Immaculate Conception such that, as Patricia Barea Azcón notes, she is sometimes referred to as an "Immaculate Indian."[78] The gathering of these devotions, and the evidence that bishops like the bishop of Quebec would have produced to Pius IX, show how crucial popular devotion is when consulting the *sensus fidelium*. These devotions offer the objective fact of the matter when it comes to the faith of the People of God.

The participants of the First Vatican Council understood this dynamic of papal infallibility itself as including a path for the *sensus fidelium* to be expressed in infallible teaching, however subtly, by noting that the need for papal infallibility itself is based in consultation and aimed at communion. Notably, *Pastor aeternus* emphasizes the right of the pope to communicate with the rest of the Church and that everyone in the Church should "have recourse to his judgment in all cases pertaining to ecclesiastical jurisdiction."[79] The council continues: moments of difficulty in the Church required consultation among the people, the bishops, and the pope both in ecumenical councils and in "sounding out the mind of the Church throughout the world."[80] As Newman notes, Ephesus

---

Bull promulgated by Pope Pius IX that dogmatically declared that Mary had been immaculately conceived, "always and absolutely free from every stain of sin." *Pastoral Letter of His Grace the Archbishop of Quebec, for the Promulgation of the Dogmatic Decree of the Immaculate Conception of the Blessed Virgin : Peter-Flavianus Turgeon, by the Mercy of God and the Grace of the Holy Apostolic See, Archbishop of Qu.* S.l. : s.n., 1855. 4.

[78]Patricia Barea Azcón, "La iconografía de la Virgen de Guadalupe de México en España," *Archivo español de Arte* 80, no. 318 (2007): 187.

[79]*Pastor aeternus,* no.8, July 18, 1870.

[80]*Pastor aeternus,* no. 9.

was a seminal example of the need for such a council. Quoting his friend John Dalgairns, Newman reminds us that the affirmation of Mary as the mother of God against Nestorius at the council began among the people of God: "While devotion in the shape of a dogma issues from the high places of the Church, in the shape of a devotion, it starts from below."[81]

Both Pius IX's 1854 dogmatic declaration of the Immaculate Conception in *Ineffabilis Deus* and Pius XII's dogmatic declaration in *Munificentissimus Deus* remind us of the power of the *sensus fidelium* and of its importance in the development of doctrine. When considered that way, the growth of the devotion to Our Lady of Guadalupe was not just a nice moment in the history of the Latin American Church. The different phases of the development of the devotion, including the formal approbation of the patronage of the Lady of Guadalupe, demonstrate how, on a local level, the consultation between the hierarchy, in the exercise of its magisterial office, and the people of God can affirm beliefs that are present within the people of God in order to clarify doctrine. On the macroscopic level, especially when there is a consistent belief held among many devotions, popular devotions can speak to the presence of a belief among the whole people of God. When, as in an instance that we have covered in this chapter, there are many images of Mary that indicate a connection to the woman in the book of Revelation, the presence of those

---

[81] Rev. John Dalgairns, 1818–1876, was a convert to Catholicism, a good friend of St. John Henry Newman, and a priest at the London Oratory. Dalgairns was primarily known for his work as a Thomas Aquinas scholar. Nestorius of Constantinople, c. 386–c. 450, was a bishop of Constantinople and the first to espouse the eponymous Nestorian heresy, which claimed that Mary, because she was human, could not be the mother of God. This heresy was refuted by the council of Ephesus, which solemnly declared Mary to be the "Θεοτόκος," or God bearer. Newman, "On Consulting the Faithful in Matters of Doctrine," 229.

symbols of Revelation that are present in an image tell us something about the connection that the People of God already make between the otherwise unnamed woman in Revelation and the mother of Jesus.

Bubbling up from Below: From Tepeyac to the Universal Church

Whatever happened on Tepeyac in 1531, it seems clear that Miguel Sánchez and Luis Laso de la Vega did not create the stories of the origins of a popular religious image out of thin air. The people told stories of the image "appearing"; they likely recounted favors done at the shrine; and narratives evolved with each pilgrimage up Tepeyac. The local stories that they heard from the people in the streets surrounding the small Franciscan hermitage atop the hill came into contact with the theological formation of the two priests such that, in recording the oral traditions that surrounded it, they were able to help form the local devotion for future generations. When preachers such as Bartolomé Felipe de Ita y Parra submitted the theological interpretation for those events to the people for their assent through homilies at the sanctuary, the devotion grew such that the local bishop chose to assert the special care of Mary as the Virgin of Guadalupe through the declaration of her patronage. The back and forth between the people and the clergy in this particular case allowed a story told on the margins of Mexico City to grow into a devotion for the universal Church. That devotion, in turn, stood alongside others such as Our Lady of Copacabana and Our Lady of Lourdes in the development of doctrine when popes consulted the people of God.

The case of the Virgin of Guadalupe, as a devotion, reminds us of the role of the *sensus fidelium* throughout the history of the Church and how a doctrine's development often owes a great deal to consultation of the people of God in the magisterium's deliberations. It is also a reminder that the development of doctrine, rather than simply being a matter of the assertions of learned scholars, is an essentially dialogical reality between the hierarchy and the laity. Ultimately, as Newman reminds us and as Guardini reinforces, the act of faith grounds the development of doctrine out of the *sensus fidelium*. Here, faith is understood as a love that grows into a connaturality that looks to take as its own the mind of Christ, which is grounded in the belief that the Spirit moves in and with the people of God.

The *sensus fidelium*, in that sense, is not simply a matter of consultation. It is an attempt to understand the movements of the Spirit in the body of the Church, animating it and bringing it a newness of life. The *sensus fidelium* opens the path for a genuine synodality that arises "whenever we listen with the heart: people feel that they are being heard, not judged; they feel free to recount their own experiences and their spiritual journey."[82] Popular religiosity is an essential source for synodal listening in the Church because, through their devotions, people express their experience of God.

The synodal exercise of listening will be the subject of the next chapter, demonstrating how the Church can listen to an intercultural dialogue that is already occurring in its devotions. This practice, in turn, reminds us of our common acceptance of the faith from different cultural origins, our need for a sense

---

[82] Pope Francis, "Opening of the Synodal Path: Homily of His Holiness Pope Francis," October 10, 2021.

of patronage to make meaning of the world, the pain when God seems deaf to our prayers, and the movements of belief that make us unique peoples in order to help make us a truly synodal Church, seeking communion across our differences.

5

E Pluribus Unum

When Many Faces Become One

One of the largest Catholic churches in the Americas rises over the Washington, DC, neighborhood of Brookland. Miles away from the grandeur of the national monuments that evoke ancient Rome, Greece, and Egypt, this dome evokes a Byzantine grandeur and the triumph of Christian faith over pagan ideals.[1] Like so many large churches in Catholicism, many side chapels line the aisles. Unlike those other churches, though, the chapels are all dedicated to one person under many titles. The basilica has altars dedicated to Our Lady of the Miraculous Medal, Our Lady of Częstochowa, Our Lady of Guadalupe, Our Lady of Knock, and Our Lady of Lourdes, to name a few. There, out of many images, one common concept emerges in the name of the building itself, the Basilica of the Immaculate Conception. A principle of the inclusion of all under one roof emerges out of the many titles, cultures, and faces of Mary. Out of many, one.

---

[1] See Gregory W. Tucker, *America's Church: The Basilica of the National Shrine of the Immaculate Conception* (Huntington, IN: Our Sunday Visitor Press, 2001), 31–32.

This concluding chapter examines how culturally located devotion, meaning-making through patronage, attention to lament, and attention to the ways in which local stories can change a global Church can lead us to greater dialogue across the entirety of the *ecclesia*. The symbolic dialogue that occurs between cultures in the practices of popular religiosity, which has been at the heart of this work, can be a pathway to greater dialogue within the Church. The fruit of this dialogue could be a genuine *synodality* between local churches such that "our own cultural identity is strengthened and enriched as a result of dialogue with those unlike ourselves."[2] Such a diversity is able to express itself as synodality when it is grounded in our commonality. With Avery Dulles, we recognize our life together through a Church that "is not in the first instance an institution or a visibly organized society. Rather it is a communion of men, primarily interior but also expressed by external bonds of creed, worship, and ecclesiastical fellowship."[3] Popular religiosity, because it allows for the expression of diverse cultural identities in symbols that are recognizable to those who share a common creed, worship, and ecclesiastical fellowship, is therefore itself a rich model for synodality and one of the surest indications of synodality already at work in the Church. Thus, popular religiosity can point to how synodality, despite perhaps being a "linguistic

---

[2] Francis, *Querida Amazonia*, no. 37, February 2, 2020. International Theological Commission, *Synodality in the Life and Mission of the Church*, no. 6, March 2, 2018: A neologism from the Greek συν and ὁδός, in this case together and walking, "synodality" refers to an "ecclesiological context, synodality is the specific *modus vivendi et operandi* of the Church, the People of God, which reveals and gives substance to her being as communion when all her members journey together, gather in assembly and take an active part in her evangelising mission."

[3] Avery Dulles, *Models of the Church* (New York: Doubleday, 1991), 47–48.

novelty," is not a new reality for the Church.[4] Synodality has been present among the people of God from the very beginnings of the Church in the existence of shrines, images, and devotions, which are grounded in a particular place or culture but are common across the Church.

Understanding popular religiosity as a sort of incipient synodality requires us to consider how the vast array of shrines, images, pilgrimages, and devotions can lead to dialogues across differences. As Pope Benedict XVI reminds us, any meaningful dialogue must first be grounded in a notion of truth:

> *Truth*, in fact, is *lógos* which creates *diá-logos*, and hence communication and communion. Truth, by enabling men and women to let go of their subjective opinions and impressions, allows them to move beyond cultural and historical limitations and to come together in the assessment of the value and substance of things.[5]

If popular religiosity is the product of so many locally and culturally bound popular devotions, it seems crucial to consider how the dynamics of truth might ground the dialogue it inspires. When we recognize that dialogue is inherent in popular religiosity, we are prompted to ask how and in what ways we are enabled to walk together as a Church. As Benedict reminds us, however, there are two distinct aspects that show us that such a dialogue is present: communication and communion. Considering two images, that of an elephant and that of gravity, as a heuristic lens for understanding the problem might allow us to better understand the ways in which popular

---

[4] International Theological Commission, *Synodality in the Life and Mission of the Church*, no. 5.

[5] Pope Benedict XVI, *Caritas in Veritate,* no. 4, June 29, 2009.

piety fosters communion and communication so that we all, through synodal dialogue, might together move closer to the *logos* underpinning all truth.

The Parable of the Elephant: Communication from Different Perspectives

In the Tittha Sutta of the Udāna, the Buddha famously offers the parable of the blindfolded men and the elephant.[6] The well-known parable describes a scenario in which, to make a point about truth, a king brings an elephant into the midst of a group of blindfolded men who have had no experience of an elephant and simply tells them that this thing before them is an elephant.[7] Not being able to see the whole of the creature, the blindfolded men feel what is before them and each makes a different judgment about what an elephant is. One of the blindfolded men, in grasping the elephant's ear declared that the elephant is like a winnowing fan. Another, in grasping the elephant's leg declared it to be like a post. Still another, in grasping the elephant's tusks declared it to be like a ploughshare. Finally, another, coming up against the elephant's torso, declared it to be like a wall. Having heard each other's judgments about what an elephant is "like," an argument broke out among the men that, in the parable, even went so far as to involve fisticuffs.[8]

---

[6]A text of Buddhist scripture that is a collection of inspired sayings of the Buddha dating back to the first century, CE. The parable of the elephant, however, is found in the Tittha Sutta which dates to 500 BCE. See "Udāna," in *The Princeton Dictionary of Buddhism* (Princeton, NJ: Princeton University Press, 2013), 932.

[7]There are versions of this parable where the men are blind rather than blindfolded.

[8]"Tittha Sutta: Sectarians (1)" (Ud 6.4), translated from the Pali by John

In the past, proponents of Spanish colonialism took up the patronage of Our Lady of Los Remedios as a counter to the Mexican nationalists' devotion to Our Lady of Guadalupe. One also still might hear a playful rivalry between devotees to Our Lady of Lourdes and devotees to Our Lady of Fatima in their respective shrines. Even in these cases, our understandings of our devotions rarely lead us to blows, like the quarrel among the men describing the elephant. Like the blindfolded men in front of the elephant, though, our devotions tell the story of our Catholic faith from our own perspectives.

In Mary, the mother of Jesus, devotion to whom we have traced throughout this work, we see different perspectives on the same person. For some, like at Copacabana, she is a connection to their history and a way of expressing a continuity with a history that is marked by cataclysmic change. For others, like devotees of Lourdes, she is a hope of intercession and healing when they are submerged into the baths by the grotto. Still, for others, like those who venerate her image at Tepeyac, her patronage is a unifying force for their cultural and national identity. The person of Mary simultaneously stands as a symbol of divine solicitude in each of those diverse ways, and in many other ways, across cultures.

Beyond being able to provide descriptions from cultural perspectives, popular religiosity valuably grounds local perspectives in a global *ecclesia*. The global perspective allows the blindfolds to ultimately be removed so that, rather than arguing for a narrow conception of Mary based on a particular culturally specific devotion, one looks beyond to the whole. As John J. Thatamanil notes in his work on the parable of the elephant in the context of broader religious diversity, "The diversity of perspectives is a positive good. Each is right about

---

D. Ireland. Access to Insight (BCBS Edition), September 3, 2012.

what he affirms but wrong about what he denies. Error results from overreaching."[9] The tension between the local and the universal within the Church allows us to richly understand how the faith is variously experienced in local churches through the popular devotions of those Churches. It also limits the types of overreaching that result in error in the context of the global reality of the Church. The first question—how does one unifying symbol mean so many things across so many cultures?—still sits at the heart of this dynamic.[10]

An Abundance of Meaning: Mary as a Made Symbol

As a referent for the universal Catholic Church, Mary is a unifying symbol beyond her role as a character in scripture. For the global Catholic Church, Mary is essential as the starting point for Christian faith, in the context of the Church's current reality, and in the hope for the Church's fulfillment. In the early era of the Church, the Fathers of the Council of

---

[9]John J. Thatamanil, "Introduction: Revisiting an Old Tale," in *Circling the Elephant* (New York: Fordham University Press, 2020), 7.

[10]Leslie Newbigin, *The Gospel in a Pluralist Society* (Grand Rapids, MI: William B. Eerdmans, 1989), 10. It seems helpful to note here that, because we are talking about many different perspectives on a unified narrative, this particular use of the parable of the blind men and the elephant escapes the concern posed by Leslie Newbigin that because the parable speaks from the perspective of a sighted individual observing the actions of a group of individuals without sight that "it embodies the claim to know the full reality which relativizes all the claims of the religions and philosophies." In other words, while Newbigin's point is well taken when we are discussing the elephant as the sum of all religious belief and considering each religion as a different part of the elephant being perceived, because, for our purposes, we are using the parable to *only* explain a reality which presupposes communion in the way that Dulles describes it above, we understand that each of the blindfolded individuals has at least some knowledge that the part of the elephant that they are perceiving is a part of a unified whole, or *at least* that it is not the totality of the whole. How this is the case will be discussed further below.

Ephesus understood Mary's role in salvation history as one of the key unifying principles for Christians. Making meaning of Mary as the Θεοτόκος—Theotokos—the Fathers argued that, by virtue of the fact that she was the "bearer of God," they could affirm the divinity of Christ.[11] To understand the nature of the Church, Vatican II talks about her as "the image and beginning of the Church as it is to be perfected in the world to come."[12] John Paul II later affirmed this by clarifying that she is "the eschatological fulfillment of the Church," adding that she also serves as the "star of the sea," guiding all of us on a journey of faith.[13]

Multifaceted doctrinal meaning has clearly been ascribed to Mary on the global level. In the preceding chapters, we have examined just a few of the myriad other meanings that individuals and communities have placed on the person of Mary as they situate their relationships with God and with the Church. The elephant has many sides and parts that, only when fruitfully combined, are understood as and mean "elephant." Such a reality is true of the deeper symbolic underpinnings of devotions. When they are symbols for the local church, together they help us understand the Church, at its best, in its

---

[11] The definition comes in a letter from Cyril of Alexandria to Nestorius, which was later included in the acts of the council: "Οὕτως τεῦαρσήκασι, θεοτόκου εἰπεῖν τήν ἁγία παρθένον, οὐχ ὡς τῆς τοῦ Λόγου φύσεως ἤτοι τῆς θεοτητος αὐτοῦ τήν ἀρχήν τόῦ εἶναι λαβούσης ἐκ τῆς ἁγίας παρθένου, ἀλλ' ὡς γεννηθέντον ἐξ αὐτῆς τοῦ ἁγίου σώματος ψυχωθέντος λογικῶς ὦ καὶ καθ' ὑπόστασιυ ἐνωθεὶς ὁ Λόγος υευεννήσθαι λέγεται κατά σάρκα." ("Accordingly, they boldly called the holy Virgin "God's mother" not because the nature of the Logos or the deity took the start of its existence in the holy Virgin but because the holy body which was born of her, possessed as it was of a rational soul, and to which the Logos was hypostatically united, is said to have had a fleshly birth.")

[12] Paul VI, *Lumen Gentium*, no. 68, November 21, 1964.

[13] John Paul II, *Redemptoris Mater*, no. 6, March 25, 1987.

totality, as multifaceted, as polyhedral. Such an understanding of the Church

> reflects the convergence of all its parts, each of which preserves its distinctiveness. Pastoral and political activity alike seek to gather in this polyhedron the best of each. There is a place for the poor and their culture, their aspirations and their potential. Even people who can be considered dubious on account of their errors have something to offer which must not be overlooked. It is the convergence of peoples who, within the universal order, maintain their own individuality; it is the sum total of persons within a society which pursues the common good, which truly has a place for everyone.[14]

This polyhedral vision of the Church is fed by popular religiosity because it allows distinct communities to define their individuality in ways that allow their own unique identities to be situated within the context of the whole. Each side is recognizable to the others as a part of the whole because, in the context of the symbols and images used in popular devotion, the nature of the symbols that are used allows us to derive meaning beyond the brute fact of what we see before us. Bernard Lonergan can help us wrestle with how we grasp a common concept of meaning behind the diverse symbols that are present in popular devotion.

The value of a symbol is that it can stand for a concept. A symbol is vacuous, and, therefore, not a symbol at all if it has no conceptual content. Those images of Mary that we have discussed, and even the image of Santa Muerte, are all useful for a conversation about meaning-making processes within

---

[14]Pope Francis, *Evangelii Gaudium*, no. 236, November 24, 2013.

the Catholic Church because they are conceptually bound. Something about each of those images qua symbol potentially relays to us something more than the brute aesthetic fact. We can describe all of the various features of an image, but, to arrive at the concept of "Mary" in that image, we need to grasp that the combination of all of the various parts of the symbol before us gives us a representation of the mother of Jesus.

In considering these sorts of connections, Lonergan invites us to think about how we come to understand that the wheel of a cart is a circle. It is not sufficient, in this case, to simply name the brute fact of the sensory impressions pertaining to a cartwheel. That a cartwheel has a hub and spokes connected to a rim does not, of course, *necessarily* entail that the thing we perceive when we perceive a cartwheel is also circle. Something could have a hub, a rim, and spokes and also be a circle or a triangle.

On Lonergan's account, when we come to the insight that the thing before us is a circle, we will have first surmised several key things, including that we are seeing an infinite number of perfectly equal radii that have a common center that produce a perfectly round curve.[15] The insight, for Lonergan, "is the act of catching on to a connection between imagined equal radii and, on the other hand, a curve that is bound to look perfectly round."[16] In other words, drawing a connection between the concept of a circle—defined by the infinite number of radii of the same length with a fixed and common center—and the cartwheel that I see before me that seems to look perfectly round gives meaning to the assertion that the cartwheel is a circle.

However, not all images, and indeed in the case of the

---

[15] Bernard Lonergan, *Insight: A Study of Human Understanding* (Toronto: University of Toronto Press, 1992), 33.

[16] Lonergan, *Insight*, 33.

circle probably no images, are perfect representations of the concept. We must allow for the approximation between the two. In the case of a cartwheel, most of us would assert that the cartwheel is still circular even when the wheels might be damaged and not be perfectly circular. Think back to the elephant at the beginning of this section. We can still gain the insight that the elephant is still an elephant even if the tusks of the elephant had been cut by poachers. This elephant would not perfectly match the blindfolded man's definition of an elephant as being like a ploughshare because of the trauma of poaching, but we would not lose the ability to recognize that it is, in fact, an elephant.

This sort of approximation between image and concept is hugely important, especially when we delve into a conversation about religious images. We can admit both that an image of Mary at Guadalupe, in which she appears to be Indigenous and Aztec, and an image of Mary at Lourdes, in which she appears to be French and Occitanes, are one and the same person because of this ability to understand through approximation. Insight connects the concept of Mary that is present in both images, even if the one-to-one equivalence is not obviously evident.

This, of course, leads us still further to consider what happens when we are talking about symbolic meaning. The representations offered by a symbol invite a different type of insight from the insights that are drawn from an instantiation of an object. For Lonergan, religious images can have value as either a sign or as a symbol. Signs are the sorts of things that have a more definite correspondence to a concept, object, or action. Signs on the streets direct us by indicating how we are to walk, drive, or behave in relation to other people on the street. In religious contexts, signs have a similar function. Their meaning is, in some way, exhaustible. A pilgrimage, for example, has its signs about what one must do to complete the tasks that make up the pilgrimage. Shrines, like the one at Lourdes or in DC, have signs that indicate the name of a space or a chapel.

Symbols, however, function in an altogether different sphere of insight on Lonergan's account. Grounded in the reality that each of us is bound by the "detached and disinterested desire to know" as we arrive at insights about our world, Lonergan reminds us that symbols are bound by the reality that "in fact, our questions outnumber our answers, so that we know of an unknown through our unanswered questions."[17] The *known unknown* in the use of symbols admits of the sort of humility with which we have to approach the symbols. The ability to offer a more definite description of a symbol's meaning escapes us. Surely, we can and must say something about them, but symbols, and religious symbols in particular, will always escape our ability to fully define them, no matter how long we search to make meaning of them. Religious symbols, by their very nature, are inexhaustible and cannot admit of anything resembling analytic, incontrovertible certainty.

This inexhaustibility is perhaps why the symbol of Mary that is lifted up at Guadalupe means something different to a generation of immigrants who are desperately seeking a new life and safety in the United States than it did in the two-hundred-year development following St. Juan Diego. Robert Orsi reports that immigrants give accounts of seeing visions of her on the US/Mexico border.[18] In filling out the narra-

---

[17]Lonergan, *Insight*, 555.

[18]Robert Orsi, *Between Heaven and Earth* (Princeton, NJ: Princeton University Press, 2005), 70: "Stories are told today that Our Lady of Guadalupe comes in the middle of the night to distract guards along the border between the United States and Mexico, allowing migrants to slip past them undetected. How does she capture the attention of these rough men so late at night?"

tive of a caring mother of the Mexican people it, of course, makes sense that Our Lady of Guadalupe would be with them in their struggles in the treacherous terrain of Arizona, California, Texas, and New Mexico. That inexhaustibility of the symbol is also perhaps why so many Hindu immigrants to Europe make pilgrimage to Lourdes each year and lay flower garlands at the feet of the statue of Our Lady of Lourdes as they take ritual baths there. The symbol might have slipped the bounds of traditional Catholic practice in that moment, but something about the water, the cleansing, and the healing that people receive at the site speaks beyond the theologies that we might ascribe to the shrine.[19]

Lonergan reminds us that our insights, the connections that we arrive at between concepts and images, can be imprecise things. Yet those insights are still reliable indicators of actual meaning behind the images that we perceive, the signs that give us direction, and the symbols that fill our world. As a result of this dynamic, our polyhedral pachyderm reminds us that the symbols and signs of our own devotions are a part of the whole religious practice and devotion of the Church. Each of these symbols is perceived from our own perspective. Our ability to perceive them well and derive meaning from them is marked by our own cultural perspective. Still, the unity of the polyhedron reminds us that no single culturally grounded

---

[19] I have personally witnessed Hindu pilgrims engaged in their own distinctive practices at Lourdes while doing research at the sanctuary over four successive summers from 2016 through 2019. The statue of Our Lady of Lourdes that resides outside of the baths, in particular, often has a marigold garland placed around it. My own conversations with members of the Hospitalité de Notre Dame de Lourdes, the confraternity which runs the baths and many of the day-to-day functions at the shrine, note that many of the members of the confraternity have continued to see this recent trend on a consistent increase. Thanks to Ginafranco Brescia, Marco Coppero, and Giordano Torresi, three of the confraternity members responsible for running the ceremonies and the baths, for sharing this insight with me.

devotion or symbol can exhaust the entirety of meanings that pertain to any given conceptual reality, doctrine, or person to which it refers.

Specifically religious symbols always participate in that known-unknown to which Lonergan invites our attention. As Lonergan says, we are invited to the numinosity that Rudolf Otto reminds us is at play in so many of our religious experiences.[20] When we understand the limits of our ability to express what is behind our practices of popular piety, we can articulate how our desire to know draws us to better understand the meanings of our practices. As a result, we are able to ask how we express meaning *as truth*. Our careful attention to truth makes space for the fruitful dialogue that Pope Benedict discusses. Symbols, then, invite conversations about what they represent in the broader ecclesial reality because of how these symbols function.

Gravity: A Thought Experiment

Consider again that basilica in Washington, DC. It draws your attention in a thousand different directions. The Byzantine mosaicked dome sits atop a church that is held up by heavy Romanesque arches. Its altars and chapels, icons, statues, and mosaics are a feast for the eyes. The burning candles and flow-

---

[20] Bernard Lonergan, *Insight*, 556: "Thirdly, on the intellectual level the operator is concretely the detached and disinterested desire to know. It is this desire, not in contemplation of the already known, but headed towards further knowledge, orientated into the known unknown. The principle of dynamic correspondence calls for a harmonious orientation on the psychic level, and from the nature of the case such an orientation would have to consist in some cosmic dimension, in some intimation of unplumbed depths, that accrued to man's feelings, emotions, sentiments. Nor is this merely a theoretical conclusion, as Rudolf Otto's study of the nonrational element in *The Idea of the Holy* rather abundantly indicates."

ers before some of the images fill your nose. Heat floats off the votive candles to warm you on a chilly day. The sounds of the carillon high in the bell tower, playing a song known as the Lourdes hymn, "Immaculate Mary," fill your ears on the hour. As the mosaics and music draw you up, the flowers and votive candles draw you down. You are stuck between many centers of sensory gravity and symbolic meaning, each pulling on your religious sensibilities.

As you enter, you could feel pulled up into the golden mosaics adorning its ceiling, beckoning you into communion with the saints depicted. At the same time, you might feel bound to the earth under the weight of the grand structure. The effect can be both awe-inspiring and unsettling. The different aesthetic gravities, including the many faces of Mary that emerge from the vast array of the cultures in which she is venerated and which adorn the space that surrounds you, spark your curiosity.

The imposing mosaic above the main altar—Christ as an eschatological judge—seems to be the main pull forward for most visitors. Even still, once inside the basilica, the side chapels and icons draw pilgrims side to side as they progress forward. The many centers inexorably lure the attention of the faithful. The basilica draws its power from those many centers of meaning, intended ultimately to point toward Christ. Out of the many ways of making meaning of the world and cultures that surround the people and our popular religiosity, one concept emerges. As happens in many iconodule worship spaces, that attractive, unseen force within and throughout the basilica feels like a gravity of meaning-making.

Gravity is a helpful heuristic lens for considering how popular devotion functions as a privileged locus of synodality because, as a model, it invites us to consider both principles of attraction and organization. It is a model that can account for the connections between devotions that we make in a moment of insight, and it can help organize those connections such that we can speak across cultural difference. Just as all matter in the universe is bound by the gravity and as gravity compels the movement and organization of the universe, so the symbolic language of the Church can compel and organize Catholic thought.[21] In so doing, it can help us better understand how we enter into a dialogue across difference with confidence in the commonality that we share.

We know that the force of gravity was, of course, famously described by Sir Isaac Newton in 1687 in the *Philosophiæ Naturalis Principia Mathematica* as a principle of attraction between two points of mass.[22] The famous insight is linked to the legend that, at some point in 1665 or 1666, Newton observed an apple falling from a tree while he was at home because of an outbreak of plague at Oxford. Having either observed the apple or been struck by it, Newton asked why it was that the apple fell straight to the earth rather than falling up or to the side.

Galileo had already proposed a law about the nature of objects falling to Earth, and Johannes Kepler had already suggested that the observable planets were governed by the same laws of motion. Newton argued that the same principle was at play in both instances. The novelty in Newton's approach was that it provided a *universal* law of gravitation. As Fritz

---

[21] Note: While Einstein's theory of relativity has superseded Newton's as the principal model for understanding gravity, for the purposes of the heuristic exercise here, the Newtonian understanding of gravity is sufficient. That said, there is nothing in Einstein's special theory of relativity which contradicts the very basic way in which gravity will be used here and playing out the analogy in terms of relativity might only further clarify the point.

[22] Isaac Newton, *Philosophiæ Naturalis Principia Mathematica* (London: Jussu Societatis Regiae ac Typis Josephi Streater, 1687), 197.

Rohrlich notes: "One cannot underestimate the tremendous revelation it must have been for people to learn that the same law of gravitation underlies *both* the heavenly motions of planets and the earthly motions of falling apples."[23] Gravity, as a force of attraction and organization, forms a sort of connection between all things that exist. It allows for each to act on the other in a manner proportional to both the mass of a thing and the proximity of a thing.

Consider Jupiter. The largest planet in our solar system is eleven times the mass of Earth and is orbited by sixteen moons. At least one of those moons, Io, has its own moons.[24] Jupiter's mass means that its gravity functions such that, in a particular way, it practically constitutes its own small planetary system. Yet Jupiter is still vastly dwarfed by the Sun, the massive size of which exerts pull over seven other planets,[25] including our own, and exerts a gravitational pull that extends far further into the universe. Still, observation of other stars and galaxies indicates with scientific certainty that our sun is also moving through the void of space, likely around a black hole at the center of our galaxy. Each celestial body moves through space and time, and, the greater the mass, the more influence a given celestial body exerts, with farther-reaching influence.

Consider also our moon. Compared to the Sun, it is a mere speck, yet the moon is full of craters. Each pock mark that we view on its surface from our own planet demonstrates that the moon has its own proper gravity and that that gravity attracts other smaller objects that sometimes crash into its surface. Even if the motion of those crashing objects were due purely to

---

[23]Fritz Rohrlich, *From Paradox to Reality: Our Basic Concepts of the Physical World* (Cambridge: Cambridge University Press, 1987), 28.

[24]Frederick W. Price, *The Planet Observer's Handbook* (Cambridge: Cambridge University Press, 2012), 211.

[25]And the satellite formerly known as the planet Pluto.

the motion that they were set in by the Sun's massive gravity, we still observe the effects of lunar gravity, particularly for those of us who live in coastal areas, as the tides progress and regress under the pull of the moon. Even some of the smallest objects exhibit their ability to change the course of events for other celestial bodies through their relative gravity.

For our purposes, if we consider the different cultures within the Church to function analogously to the planets and stellar systems, we might fruitfully observe how certain cultures might seem to exert more influence. We may also bear witness to the real pull of even the seemingly least significant event. Finally, we might consider the possibility that a universal constant urge for communion is the principle that binds and sets the Church in motion.

The Draw of Devotions

Huge devotions—like the devotion to Padre Pio or to Our Lady of Guadalupe—seem, from some perspectives, to eclipse even the worship of the Holy Trinity. The devotion to St. Padre Pio of Pietrelcina, for example, is massive. Many Italians address their prayers to him requesting his intercession.[26] Particularly in the south of Italy, this devotion means that Padre Pio's own specific piety and worldview, found in the words of his preaching and the legends that surround him, hold sway over how his devotees make meaning of the world. Yet his devotion exercises little influence among many Catholics in other places.

---

[26] A 2006 poll conducted by the Italian newspaper *Corriere della Sera* found that 31 percent of Italians had asked in prayer for Padre Pio's intercession, while only 2 percent reported having addressed Jesus directly. See John Allen, "Padre Pio Tops Jesus, Mary in All Saints' Day Poll in Italy," *National Catholic Reporter*, November 1, 2006.

Padre Pio is to Catholic devotion what Jupiter is to our solar system. The sheer mass of the devotion exerts such a force of attraction for its devotees that those who are near it cannot help but to be attracted to it or, at the very least, interact with it. Yet for those of us who might be at a distance, much like Jupiter, the devotion to Padre Pio can be remote even as it is still one of the large lights illuminating our night sky. Such remoteness can make the stories of his bi-locating, of his suffering the stigmata, or of his appearing in the clouds during World War II to stop Allied air force bombing runs over the hospital he was building, seem bizarre to our different cultural sensibilities, much as the planetary properties of Jupiter seem peculiar.[27]

Smaller devotions, like the one to Our Lady of Copacabana, might not seem to exert as much pull beyond their very local communities, but we still see the effects of them in the ways that their host cultures interact with other cultures. As we noted in the first chapter, Our Lady of Copacabana is remote, and the pilgrimage to get there can be trying. Juxtaposed with the hustle and bustle of the market near the shrine of Guadalupe, Copacabana can seem like a sleepy village. On a visit to the shrine in 2017, I was the only person in the church building. Still, Peruvians and Bolivians who immigrated to Brazil in search of work brought their devotion with them. Today,

---

[27]See Ella Stelluto, "The Story of a Flying Monk: Myth, Legend, or Reality?" *Italian Tribune.* April 6, 2021. The legend attached to Padre Pio is that during World War II Allied bombing runs would never meet with success when trying to drop bombs over his town of San Giovanni Rotondo. According to one telling of the legend, near the conclusion of the war, the commanding general of the United States Air Force in the area, General Nathan F. Twining, witnessed one of these events. After the end of the war Twining is said to have gone to the village to see Padre Pio. The saint is reported to have quipped: "So you are the one that wanted to destroy everything."

one of the most famous beaches in the world, Copacabana, is named for its neighborhood, which is named for the local church community in that neighborhood, which is, finally, named for the devotion on the other side of the continent high in the mountains. Even small and remote devotions exert influence on other cultures and places, often in somewhat surprising ways.

Each planet in our solar system stands as a center of gravity, and similarly each of our devotions stands as a center of a culture for a local church. Devotions like the one to our Lady of Guadalupe can function as a symbol that unites a community. Other devotions, like the one at Lourdes, can help a community in turmoil come to a sense of peace. Even still, a devotion like the one to Our Lady of Copacabana can ground a new community as it emerges through the interactions of two cultures. Finally, even devotions like that to Santa Muerte have their draw because they express human realities, however difficult or challenging those realities are. Each of these devotions exerts a gravitational pull within its own cultural sphere of influence, helping organize individuals into a local community.

Analogous to how heavenly bodies gravitationally influence each other, devotions exert their own pull on other devotions. As Edith and Victor Turner note, there was a certain sense in which, for the people of France, the rather reclusive life of St. Bernadette after the time of the apparitions lent credibility to her claim because of the contrast it struck with the lives of the visionaries of La Salette. Those visionaries, Mélanie and Maximin, lived ultimately scandalous lives after their purported apparition in 1846.[28] We have also seen how

---

[28]See Victor Turner and Edith Turner, *Image and Pilgrimage in Christian Culture* (New York: Columbia University Press, 2011), 223. Maximin Giraud

devotional practices pull on each other in Mexico; where the versions of Santa Muerte that appear in the dress of Our Lady of Guadalupe are almost immediately intended to strike a resonance for the devout, with each shaping the other in current devotional practice. It is little wonder why, when denouncing Santa Muerte, Pope Francis chose to re-propose the devotion to Our Lady of Guadalupe.

Finally, certain common themes seem to hold for all devotions. Consider the three Marian devotions we have examined. Each understands Mary as having been immaculately conceived, as evidenced either iconographically—Copacabana and Guadalupe—or verbally—Lourdes. Each relies on stories of healing to lend credibility to the overall narratives surrounding the devotion, and each shapes the ways that a local church interacts with the broader ecclesia. While devotions can form a center of the community, they generally bear the signs of participating in a dynamic larger than themselves. Each of these examples emerge through interpreting the symbols of the individual popular devotions. As Paul Ricoeur might argue, this common dynamic is central to the function of symbolic communication.

---

and Mélanie Calvat, the two children who are purported to have seen Mary in the Alps on the French and Italian Border in 1846, unfortunately experienced great hardship later in life. Maximin was known to exhibit problems with alcohol and suffered from periods of homelessness at one juncture. The Turners report that "being fond of more than a glass or two of wine, he became involved with a wine merchant and 'hustler,' who persuaded him to join in selling, at high prices, an herb-flavored liqueur called Salettina, with his name on the label." Mélanie became a nun, eventually settling in Italy. The Turners report that she would often put forth her experience as a visionary to enable an unexemplary, and sometimes controversial, living of religious life. By contrast, Bernadette's desire to retire to a life of prayer after the apparitions to a cloistered convent is sometimes cited as a supporting reason for the legitimacy of the apparitions at Lourdes by its devotees.

Naming the Gravity: The Dynamics of Symbolic Dialogue

Drawing out our analogy, we have tried to map correspondences between celestial objects and devotions, considering how devotions, like heavenly bodies, both influence each other and stand as unique centers of gravity for their own cultures. We have yet to name the force that binds the whole together. What, like gravity, can function as a principle of both attraction and organization among diverse cultures?

Paul Ricoeur offers an account of that connection between metaphorical language and symbolic mediation that allows us to grasp something of the gravity for which we search. For Ricoeur, it is not simply that symbols speak to us. We can use symbols to speak to others. Symbols have a necessarily communicative nature because "symbolism only works when its structure is interpreted."[29] This type of communication, unlike the blindfolded men describing the elephant by touch who thought they had understood the whole, understands that the meaning conveyed by symbolic communication is inexhaustible. In the context of popular devotion, we can identify three movements for our analysis. First, we must consider the nature of the interpretation that is possible for symbolic mediation. Second, we must embrace the concept of mystery-as-inexhaustibility that is required for symbolic mediation's connection to interpretation. Third, we must reflect on the particular nature of religious symbols. As we grasp these three movements, we can recognize how the gravity of popular piety reveals itself as the sort of symbolic dialogue that is richly present in the history of the Church and already at the heart of synodality.

---

[29]Paul Ricoeur, *Interpretation Theory: Discourse and the Surplus of Meaning* (Fort Worth: Texas Christian University Press, 1976), 62.

Ricoeur reminds us that, for it to be meaningful, our use of symbols must be bound up with linguistic expression through metaphorical language: "The symbol, in effect, only gives rise to thought if it first gives rise to speech."[30] Interpretation thus requires an ability to express both the literal meaning behind a symbol and its figurative meaning. Symbols, and religious symbols especially, need to be interpreted beyond the brute fact of their appearance. In each chapter of this text, we have considered a literal meaning of the symbols at hand. Descriptions have been given of Our Lady as she is venerated at Lourdes, Copacabana, and Tepeyac, and we have also heard descriptions of Santa Muerte. Still, if we considered *only* those descriptions, there would be no real meaning behind the symbols to discuss, and this would have been a considerably shorter work. The structures of metaphor that are inherent in our symbols allow us to make meaning by grasping a connection to something else and by understanding the insufficiency of a *mere* literal sense of interpretation.

The connection between things that arises out of metaphoric utterances is a matter of both naming and of comparison. For Aristotle, "metaphor consists in giving the thing a name that belongs to something else; the transference being either from genus to species, or from species to genus, or from species to species, on grounds of analogy."[31] When, for example, we say "time stood still," we are not saying literally that time has an ability to stand still. We are, rather, making a connection between time, which has no corporeal substance such that it could stand still, and organisms, which have that potential. Naming time as a thing that could stand still connects where there previously was no connection, explaining the thought

---

[30]Ricoeur, *Interpretation Theory*, 62.

[31]Aristotle, *Poetics,* edited by Richard McKeon (New York: Random House, 1941), 1475b:7.

that time seemed not to move. Still, the way that we think of metaphor is not simply a matter of denomination, but predication. Following Ricoeur, we take account of the entirety of an utterance to understand a literal sense, which is often an absurdity like time being able to stand still, and a figurative sense, which relies on a concept of resemblance to "tell us something new about reality."[32]

The symbols of individual popular devotions participate in this dynamic of resemblance by re-presenting a person or reality. One of the values of religious symbols is that they warn us "from the very beginning that here we are crossing the threshold of an experience that does not allow itself to be completely inscribed within the categories of *logos* or proclamation and its transmission of interpretation."[33] As such, our stance toward religious meaning is not that we name the experience itself, but rather that we speak *out* of an experience of the revelation of the sacred. In a certain sense, we do not *make* meaning. We *speak out of* the meaning that we have experienced.

For Ricoeur, "the capacity to speak is founded in the capacity of the cosmos to signify."[34] This is why, for example, in each of the devotions that we have studied, there is some elemental component present either in the foundation of the devotion itself or in the current devotional practice. In the *Nican Mopohua*, the story tells us that the world was transformed and seemed to vibrate with the presence of the Lady of Guadalupe. At Lourdes, pilgrims bathe in healing waters which remind them of their baptism, which in turn has resonances with the waters of birth. At Copacabana, the straits of Tiquina in Lake Titicaca are said to have parted in order

---

[32] Ricoeur, *Interpretation Theory*, 53.
[33] Ricoeur, *Interpretation Theory*, 60.
[34] Ricoeur, *Interpretation Theory*, 62.

to allow the image to pass. In each case, "the sacredness of nature reveals itself in saying itself symbolically."[35] As such, we are able to engage in discourse around meaning. Rather than being a means of communicating, the symbols of popular devotion enable us to begin communicating such that "interpretation of a symbolism cannot even get underway if its work of mediation were not legitimated by an immediate liaison between the appearance and the meaning of the hierophany under consideration."[36] The symbol starts the dialogue, but the ability of the created universe to symbolically signify the sacred requires the interpretation of the symbol.

Popular religiosity allows us to make connections between the sacredness of the universe as it is revealed to us. It does this for each of us in our own place, time, and culture, requiring that we begin to express the sacred in metaphorical terms. In some sense, the kind of symbolic mediation that occurs allows popular religiosity to function as a gravity that can hold particular churches in the orbit of the larger Church. As Joseph Ratzinger noted when considering the nature of *communio* as a descriptor for that which binds the Church together, "The Church came into being when the Lord had given his body and his blood under the forms of bread and wine, whereupon he said, 'Do this in remembrance of me.' . . . The Church is Eucharist."[37] The symbolic mediation of the sacrament lives at the core of the Church, echoed in the sacramentals of popular devotion, which both connect us to the hierophany that is the revelation of the Father and the Spirit through the Son, demanding that we speak of it. We must genuinely walk together through dialogue that recognizes the realities present within

---

[35]Ricoeur, *Interpretation Theory*, 63.

[36]Ricoeur, *Interpretation Theory*, 63.

[37]Joseph Ratzinger, *Called to Communion: Understanding the Church Today* (San Francisco: Ignatius Press, 1991), 75.

the symbols as we have experienced, interpreted, and communicated them. Though no interpretation will circumscribe the meaning that we are trying to convey, our dialogue makes space for our journey together.

Walking Together: Popular Piety toward a Synodal Church

The car license plates "SCV1" are, or at least used to be, a particularly well-known set of plates in Rome. Standing for *"Status Civitatis Vaticanus 1,"* they are the plates that, until the pontificate of Francis, had been normally affixed to the papal car. Sometimes they might also be attached to the popemobile as it winds its way through St. Peter's Square as the pontiff greets the faithful. Usually, when you see those license plates, it means that the pope is in the vehicle. On one particular night early in his pontificate, the plates were affixed to a pickup truck that wound its way up the Esquiline Hill of Rome, from the Basilica of St. John Lateran to the Basilica of St. Mary Major, with a monstrance holding a consecrated host in the truck bed. Pope Francis walked behind the truck. Up the hill the car went, followed by the striking image of the pope, the priests, the religious, and the laity all walking together in the Corpus Christi procession as a sign of their eucharistic devotion. Many people, from many different parts of the life of the Church, were *walking together* as a sign of their popular devotion, as one.[38]

Popular religiosity, as an expression of the life of the people of God, can speak across cultures, inviting us to walk together and be properly *synodal*. It requires both recognition

---

[38] This event took place on May 30, 2013. I was, myself, present to witness this event.

and interpretation, the dynamics at play in both Lonergan's conception of an insight and Ricoeur's understanding of symbolic mediation. Popular religiosity has always been a type of synodal dialogue in and across the Church that models for us ways of speaking that respect difference such that we can better understand the nature of internal unity. It is a matter of walking together, but it is also a matter of allowing ourselves to speak to each other in and through the symbols that make us who we are. In this sense, as we have seen throughout this work, the symbols of popular piety allow us to see the world and our church as relational and to consider ways to speak across difference. As was the case during the procession that night in Rome, popular devotions also allow us to speak beyond necessary hierarchical distinctions within the Catholic Church and to be understood in a common language. Our many paths with Mary, journeying through Bolivia, France, and Mexico, can still speak to the broad diversity of the Church in both its culture and position.

Synodality, as understood by those preparing for the synod of 2021–2024, requires that a dialogical posture grounded in "love, respect, trust, and prudence" be embodied such that the Church views itself as essentially relational.[39] As a matter of seeing the world through the eyes of love, the preparatory document for the synod notes that such a relational worldview then "becomes a form of shared knowledge, vision through the eyes of another and a shared vision of all that exists."[40] As we have noted, popular devotion is, in its essence, relational. Popular devotion's most basic form is found in the context of the patronage of the communion of saints. Understanding that the Church is extended globally and through salvation history

---

[39] International Theological Commission, *Synodality in the Life and Mission of the Church*, no. 111, March 2, 2018.

[40] *Synodality in the Life and Mission of the Church*, no. 111.

demands that we walk with each other with all the saints who have gone before us. We do this because we understand that we are still in relationship to and with them. As we have seen, though, beyond its vertical and eschatological extension of relationship to the Church triumphant and the Church suffering, popular religiosity also creates ecclesial communities with their own distinctive understanding of the ways that the divine has acted in their lives. Narratives and symbols of localized devotions often give the faithful the ability to express their own hierophanies to the Church as it exists in other cultures, for the benefit of the broader *ecclesia*.

Still, we recognize that, within the Church, there is diversity within the unity. This tension must be respected through a common dialogue so that the Spirit can be heard. As the International Theological Commission reminds us:

> Synodal dialogue depends on courage both in speaking and in listening. It is not about engaging in a debate where one speaker tries to get the better of the others or counters their positions with brusque arguments, but about expressing whatever seems to have been suggested by the Holy Spirit as useful for communal discernment, at the same time being open to accepting whatever has been suggested by the same Spirit in other people's positions, "for the general good" (1 Corinthians 12, 7).[41]

The hope of being understood such that "tensions and opposites can reach a pluriform unity which generates new life, making it possible to 'build communion amid disagreement'" gives us that courage.[42] Consider how, in our three Marian devotions, and in many of the devotions present in the basilica

---

[41] *Synodality in the Life and Mission of the Church*, no. 111.
[42] *Synodality in the Life and Mission of the Church*, no. 111.

in Washington, there are many different cultural instantiations of Mary that point to the basilica's namesake doctrine. In each instance, we are able to experience the insight that the diverse images are Mary. Visually, she is presented in a diversity of ways. Linguistically, she speaks in diverse tongues. Relationally, her message of patronage is carried to diverse peoples. Yet the many Marian symbols that suffuse Catholic devotional life have caused the global Catholic Church to speak such that, when consulted by Pius IX, they affirmed the title under which she is venerated within that basilica, the Immaculate Conception. While there are many different ways of understanding Marian devotion, popular religiosity affords the possibility of a pluriform unity, so that, out of many peoples, the Church might speak with one voice, affirming the belief that, because of who she was and still is for them, Mary must be without the stain of original sin.

"Synodality" may be a neologism of a postconciliar Catholic Church, but its underpinning dynamics have long been a crucial function of the Church's life together. From the *sensus fidelium* made manifest through the people's devotions during the Christological controversies of the first millennium of the Church, to the consultations of the faithful on the matters of Mary's Immaculate Conception and Assumption into heaven, popular religiosity has long accomplished what the synod now seeks to capture. Popular religiosity creates the conditions to faithfully and better proclaim the Gospel in a truly global Church that respects diversity through sharing a unifying narrative. This Church finds its home in diverse places such that it can be a sign of unity for a world in conflict. As the International Theological Commission's preparatory document for the synod understands it, this concretely means that:

> In fact, today, when growing awareness of the interdependence between peoples forces us to think of the world as

our common home, the Church is called to demonstrate that her Catholicity and the synodal way in which she lives and works are a catalyst of unity in diversity and of communion in freedom. This is a significant contribution that the life and synodal conversion of the People of God can make to the promotion of a culture of encounter and solidarity, respect and dialogue, inclusion and integration, gratitude and gift.[43]

While *synodality* is a "new" word, popular religiosity demonstrates that its aims and hopes are not novel. Synodality is not a new way of proceeding for the Church. Rather, it has a precursor in popular religiosity that goes back to the very foundations of the particular churches that would come to make up the broader Church. Unity in diversity has been a part of the Church's own self-understanding from the beginning, and popular religiosity has often been one of those unifying factors. We should not be too sanguine about popular religiosity as a panacea for all of the Church's woes, as both the divisions within the Church that sometimes surround it and the problems that it can sometimes propound demonstrate. However, at its best, it has always been a way to listen to the voices of the faithful and to the Spirit potentially speaking within them.

The principle and practice of listening maps the way forward from this study. By highlighting the role of the Spirit speaking through the devotions of popular religiosity, I argue that we need to continue to develop the use of alternative sources, like those afforded to us through anthropology, sociology, and history, as properly theological sources. Refining methods to use those sources as a way of listening might allow the Church to

---

[43]*Synodality in the Life and Mission of the Church,* no. 118.

better listen to, and consult, the voice of the Spirit speaking through the *sensus fidelium*. Specifically when we seriously engage ethnography and critical historical research to better understand the dynamics at play in popular devotions, listening to the people of God within the Church might offer a sounder methodology for the sorts of consultations in which the current practice of synodality hopes to engage. Those methods might prove especially useful when the lessons to be learned might be difficult ones that seem to skirt the bounds of the Church or even outright reject it. Finally, more careful attention to the ways in which these properly sacramental practices shape and change the views of the people of God surrounding the seven sacraments of the Church might help identify the theologian's task in the present age in order to continue to encourage "fully active and conscious" participation in the life of the Catholic Church and its sacraments.[44]

Many Paths with Mary

This work ends where it began. "Here," or "in this place," the Word became flesh. As a matter of religious symbolism, popular devotion understands that our experiences of God breaking-in through places and events in our lives demand an expression for the world. This understanding throws us into a *dialogos* that issues forth from the divine *Logos*. In the holy house at Loreto, the struggle is to express the belief that God became man within the confines of the walls that have been transported to that hill off the coast of the Adriatic Sea. It is a common struggle for the believer because we cannot help but express the reality that God has moved among us. In

---

[44] Paul VI, *Sacrosanctum Concilium*, no. 14, December 4, 1963.

listening to each other's stories, in understanding the value in those narratives, and in allowing those symbols to form and shape us, we become a people who express ourselves as known and beloved by God.

As we journey with Mary through, from, and with all of the cultures that have been wrapped around the mystery of God's indwelling in the world, we express truths from our own perspectives that enlighten and enliven the whole of the Church. Popular religiosity directs us to the unity of the Church as it is adorned in its rich diversity, attentive to how the many voices of the people of God echo forth the Spirit into the world.

Bibliography

Primary Sources

Albó, Xavier. "Suma qamaña = convivir bien. ¿Cómo medirlo?" *Revista de Estudios Bolivianos* 25 (2019): 99–113.

Allen, John. "Padre Pio tops Jesus, Mary in All Saints' Day poll in Italy." *National Catholic Reporter*, November 1, 2006.

Aubert, Marius. *Manuel de Enfant de Marie—ou moyens de conduite de royaume des cieux: A l'usage des pensionnants.* Paris: Perisse Frères, 1856.

Bertrin, Georges. *Histoire critique des événements de Lourdes, apparitions et guérisons.* Lourdes: Bureaux et Magasin de la Grotte, 1922.

Colque, Abraham. "Sobre papas que lloran y otras cosas: Diaologo sobre la espiritualidad ecológica andina." *Fe y Pueblo* (Instituto Superior Ecuménico Andino de Teología) 19 (October 2011): 5–13.

Estrade, Jean-Baptiste. *The Apparitions of Lourdes.* Lourdes: Imprimerie De La Grotte, 1958.

Francis. "Iter Apostolicum in Mexicum: Ad Episcopos Mexici apud ecclesiam Cathedralem Mexicopolis." *Acta Apostolica Sedia* 108, no. 3 (2016): 255–266.

Irenaeus of Lyon. *Against Heresies.* Translated by John Keble. London: James Parker, 1872.

Ita y Parra, Bartolomé Felipe de. *La Imagen de Guadalupe, Señora de los Tiempos.* Mexico City: Imprensa Real del Superior Govierno de los Herederos de la viuda de Miguel de Rivera, 1732.

John Paul I. Audience, September 3, 1978.

John Paul II. Homily at the Basilica of Zapopán. January 30, 1979.

Jordan, David. "Nican Mopohua." In *Readings in Classical Nahuatl.* 2021. https://pages.ucsd.edu/~dkjordan/nahuatl/nican/NicanMopohua.html.

Juana Inés de la Cruz. *Obras completas de Sor Juana Inés de la Cruz.* Editado por Alfonso Méndez Plancarte. Vol. 1. Mexico City: Fondo de Cultura Economica, 1951.

León-Portilla, Miguel. *Broken Spears: The Aztec Account of the Conquest of Mexico.* Boston: Beacon Press, 1990.

Sánchez, Miguel. *Imagen de La Virgen Maria Madre de Dios de Guadalupe, Milagrosamente Aparecida en La Ciudad de Mexico.* Mexico City: Bernardo Calderón, 1648.

Thomas Aquinas, *Summa Theologica.*

Thomson, Sinclair, Rossana Barragán, Xavier Albó, Seemin Qayum, and Mark Goodale. *The Bolivia Reader: History, Culture, Politics.* Durham, NC: Duke University Press, 2018.

Toor, Frances. *A Treasury of Mexican Folkways.* New York: Crown, 1947.

Tucker, Gregory W. *America's Church: The Basilica of the National Shrine of the Immaculate Conception.* Huntington, IN: Our Sunday Visitor Press, 2001.

Turgeon, Peter-Flavianus. *Pastoral Letter of His Grace the Archbishop of Quebec, for the Promulgation of the Dogmatic Decree of the Immaculate Conception of the Blessed Virgin : Peter-Flavianus Turgeon, by the Mercy of God and the Grace of the Holy Apostolic See, Archbishop of Qu.* S.l.: s.n., 1855.

Van Biervliet, Mélanie. *Les Délices des Enfants de Marie*. Tournai: H. & L. Casterman, 1837.

Secondary Sources

Aristotle. *On the Soul.* Edited by Richard McKeon. New York: Random House, 1941.
Aristotle. *Poetics.* Edited by Richard McKeon. New York: Random House, 1941.
Balthasar, Hans Urs von. *Explorations in Theology I: The Word Made Flesh.* San Francisco: Ignatius Press, 1989.
Balthasar, Hans Urs von. *Heart of the World.* Edited by Erasmo Leiva. San Francisco: Ignatius Press, 1979.
Balthasar, Hans Urs von. *In the Fullness of Faith.* San Francisco: Ignatius Press, 1988.
Balthasar, Hans Urs von. *Theo-Drama: Theological Dramatic Theory,* vol. 3: *The Dramatis Personae: Persons in Christ.* San Francisco: Ignatius Press, 1992.
Balthasar, Hans Urs von. *Truth Is Symphonic.* San Francisco: Ignatius Press, 1979.
Baracs, Rodrigo Martínez. "Orígenes del culto en Tepeyac." *Artes de México*, no. 125 (2017): 22–31.
Barea Azcón, Patricia. "La iconografía de la Virgen de Guadalupe de México en España." *Archivo español de Arte* 80, no. 318 (2007): 186–199.
Bede, and Lewis Gidley. *Bede's Ecclesiastical History of the English Nation.* Oxford: James Parker, 1870.
Benedict XVI. *Caritas in Veritate. Acta Apostolicae Sedis* 101, no. 8 (2009): 641–709.
Brading, David A. *Mexican Phoenix: Our Lady of Guadalupe: Image and Tradition across Five Centuries.* Cambridge: Cambridge University Press, 2001.
Bromley, David. "Santa Muerte as Emerging Dangerous Religion." *Religions* 7, no. 6 (2016).

Chesnut, R. Andrew. *Devoted to Death: Santa Muerte, the Skeleton Saint.* Cambridge: Cambridge University Press, 2018.

Clendinnen, Inga. *The Cost of Courage in Aztec Society: Essays on Mesoamerican Society and Culture.* Cambridge: Cambridge University Press, 2010.

Covey, R. Alan. *Inca Apocalypse: The Spanish Conquest and the Transformation of the Andean World.* Oxford: Oxford University Press, 2020.

Damascus, John of. *On the Divine Images: Three Apologies against Those Who Attack the Divine Images.* Translated by David Anderson. Crestwood, NY: Saint Vladimir's Seminary Press, 1980.

Damascus, John of. *Three Treatises on the Divine Images.* Translated by Andrew Louth. Crestwood, NY: St. Vladimir's Seminary Press, 2003.

Dulles, Avery. *Models of the Church*. New York: Doubleday, 1991.

Eagleton, Terry. *Culture.* New Haven, CT: Yale University Press, 2016.

Eliade, Mircea. *The Sacred and the Profane: The Nature of Religion.* Translated by Willard R. Trask. New York: Harcourt, 1987.

Francis. *Evangelii Gaudium.* November 24, 2013.

Francis. *Laudato Si'.* May 24, 2015.

Francis. *Querida Amazonia.* February 2, 2020.

Guardini, Romano. *The End of the Modern World.* Translated by Elinor C. Briefs. Wilmington, DE: ISI Books, 1998.

Guardini, Romano. *The Lord.* Washington, DC: Regnery, 1982.

Harris, Ruth. *Lourdes: Body and Spirit in the Secular Age.* London: Penguin, 1999.

Huanca, Tomás. *El yatiri en la comunidad aymara.* La Paz, Bolivia: Ediciones CADA, 1990.

International Theological Commission. *Sensus Fidei in the Life of the Church*. 2014.

International Theological Commission. *Synodality in the Life and Mission of the Church*. March 2, 2018.

James, William. *The Varieties of Religious Experience: A Study in Human Nature: Being the Gifford Lectures on Natural Religion Delivered at Edinburgh in 1901–1902*. New York: Modern Library, 1902.

John Paul I. Audience. September 3, 1978.

John Paul II. *Redemptoris Mater*. March 25, 1987.

Justin. *The First Apology of Justin Martyr: Addressed to the Emperor Antoninus Pius*. Translated by John Kaye. Edinburgh: J. Grant, 192.

Kingsbury, Kate. "At Death's Door in Cancun: Sun, Sea, and Santa Muerte." *Anthropology and Humanism* 46, no. 2 (2021): 244–265.

Lafaye, Jacques. *Quetzalcóatl and Guadalupe: The Formation of Mexican National Consciousness, 1531–1813*. Edited by Benjamin Keen. Chicago: University of Chicago Press, 1976.

Laurentin, René. *Lourdes: Histoire Authentiques*. Paris: P. Letielleux, 2002.

Laurentin, René. *Pilgrimages, Sanctuaries, and Icons*. Edited by William Fackovec. Milford, OH: Riehle Foundation, 1994.

Lonergan, Bernard. *Insight: A Study of Human Understanding*. Toronto: University of Toronto Press, 1992.

Lonergan, Bernard. *Method in Theology*. Toronto: University of Toronto Press, 1971.

MacCormack, Sabine. *Religion in the Andes: Vision and Imagination in Early Colonial Peru*. Princeton, NJ: Princeton University Press, 1991.

Marion, Jean-Luc. *Givenness and Revelation*. Translated by Stephen E. Lewis. Oxford: Oxford University Press, 2016.

Marion, Jean-Luc. *The Idol and Distance: Five Studies.* New York: Fordham University Press, 2001.

Matovina, Timothy. "The First Guadalupan Pastoral Manual: Luis Laso de la Vega's Huei Tlamahuiçoltica (1649)." *Horizons* (Villanova University) 40, no. 2 (2014): 157–170.

Matovina, Timothy. *Theologies of Guadalupe: From the Era of Conquest to Pope Francis.* Oxford: Oxford University Press, 2019.

Mong, Ambrose. *Power of Popular Piety: A Critical Examination.* Eugene, OR: Cascade Books, 2019.

Newbigin, Leslie. *The Gospel in a Pluralist Society.* Grand Rapids, MI: William B. Eerdmans, 1989.

Newman, John Henry. *On Consulting the Faithful in Matters of Doctrine.* London: Geoffrey Chapman, 1961.

Newman, John Henry. "On Consulting the Faithful in Matters of Doctrine." *The Rambler*, July 1859.

Newman, John Henry. "Sermon 22: Witnesses of the Resurrection." In *Parochial and Plain Sermons*. London: Longmans, Green, 1907.

Newton, Isaac. *Philosophiae Naturalis Principia Mathematica.* London: Jussu Societatis Regiae ac Typis Joseph Streater, 1687.

Nican Mopohua ("Here It Is Told"). New York Public Library. 2022. https://www.nypl.org/events/exhibitions/galleries/belief/item/5559.

Oliveira, Maria Izabel Barboza de Morais. "Entre a Espada e a Cruz: Bartolomeu De Las Casas em Defesa do modo Pacífico de Evangelização dos Indígenas na América Espanhola." *Revista Brasileira do Caribe* 19, no. 37 (2018): 7–28.

Origen. *Letter to Gregory.* In volume 4 of *Ante-Nicene Fathers*, edited by Alexander Roberts, James Donaldson, and A. Cleveland Coxe. Buffalo, NY: Christian Literature, 1885.

Orsi, Robert. *Between Heaven and Earth.* Princeton, NJ: Princeton University Press, 2005.

Otto, Rudolph. *The Idea of the Holy: An Inquiry into the Non-Rational Factor in the Idea of the Divine and Its Relation to the Rational.* Translated by John W. Harvey. Oxford: Oxford University Press, 1936.

Pamphili, Eusebius. *Evangelicae Praeparationis.* Edited by E. H. Gifford. Oxford: Oxford University Press, 1903.

Pansters, Wil. "La Santa Muerte: History, Devotion, and Societal Context." In *La Santa Muerte in Mexico: History, Devotion, and Society*, ed. Wil Pansters. Albuquerque: University of New Mexico Press, 2019.

Paul VI. *Evangelii Nuntiandi.* December 8, 1975.

Paul VI. *Lumen Gentium.* November 21, 1964.

Perrone, Giovanni, SJ. *Praelectiones Theologicae Joannis Perrone e Societate Jesu ab Eodem in Compendium Redactae.* Tornio: Hyacinthi Marietti, 1840.

Peterson, Jeanette Favrot. "Creating the Virgin of Guadalupe: The Cloth, the Artist, and Sources in Sixteenth Century New Spain." *The Americas* 61, no. 4 (April 2005): 571–610.

Pieper, Joseph. *Death and Immortality.* South Bend, IN: St. Augustine's Press, 2000.

Pius XII. *Deiparae Virginis Mariae.* May 1, 1946.

Pius XII. *Munificentissimus Deus.* November 1, 1950.

Poole, Stafford. "Did Juan Diego Exist? Questions on the Eve of the Canonization." *Commonweal*, December 2002.

Price, Frederick W. *The Planet Observer's Handbook.* Cambridge: Cambridge University Press, 2012.

Proulx, Travis, and Michael Inzlicht. "The Five 'A's of Meaning Maintenance: Finding Meaning in the Theories of Sense-Making." *Psychological Inquiry* 23, no. 4 (2012).

Radner, Ephraim. *A Time to Keep: Theology, Mortality, and the Shape of a Human Life.* Waco, TX: Baylor University Press, 2016.

Rahner, Hugo. *Greek Myths and Christian Mystery.* London: Burns and Oates, 1963.

Rahner, Karl. *Foundations of Christian Faith.* Translated by William V. Dych. New York: Crossroad, 2019.

Ramos Gavilán, Alonso. *Historia de Copacabana y de la Milagrosa Imagen de su Virgen.* Lima: J. Enrique del Campo, 1867.

Ratzinger, Joseph. *Called to Communion: Understanding the Church Today.* San Francisco: Ignatius Press, 1991.

Ratzinger, Joseph. *Eschatology: Death and Eternal Life.* Edited by Aidan Nichols. Washington, DC: Catholic University Press, 1988.

Ratzinger, Joseph. *Introduction to Christianity.* San Francisco: Ignatius Press, 2004.

Ricoeur, Paul. *Figuring the Sacred: Religion, Narrative, and Imagination.* Edited by Mark Wallace. Minneapolis: Fortress Press, 1995.

Ricoeur, Paul. *Interpretation Theory: Discourse and the Surplus of Meaning.* Fort Worth: Texas Christian University Press, 1976.

Rohrlich, Fritz. *From Paradox to Reality: Our Basic Concepts of the Physical World.* Cambridge: Cambridge University Press, 1987.

Roush, Laura. "Santa Muerte, Protection, and *Desamparo*: A View from a Mexico City Altar." *Latin American Research Review* 49 (2014): 129–148.

Rudolph, Kurt. *Gnosis: The Nature and History of Gnosticism.* Edited by Robert McLachlan Wilson. Edinburgh: T&T Clark, 1987.

Salles-Reese, Verónica. *From Viracocha to the Virgin of Copacabana: Representations of the Sacred at Lake Titicaca.* Austin: University of Texas Press, 1997.

Smith, Benjamin T. "Saints and Demons: Putting La Santa Muerte in Historical Perspective." In *La Santa Muerte in*

Mexico, ed. Wil Pansters. Albuquerque: University of New Mexico Press, 2019.

Stelluto, Ella. "The Story of a Flying Monk: Myth, Legend, or Reality?" *Italian Tribune*, April 6, 2021.

Tenace, Michelina. *Cristiani si Diventa: Dogma e Vita Nei Primi Tre Concili*. Rome: Lipa, 2013.

Tertullian. "*De praescriptione haereticorum*." In *Ante-Nicene Fathers*, vol. 3, edited by Alexander Roberts, James Donaldson, and A. Cleveland Coxe. Buffalo, NY: Christian Literature, 1885.

Thatamanil, John J. "Introduction: Revisiting an Old Tale." In *Circling the Elephant*, 1–20. New York: Fordham University Press, 2020.

Turner, Victor, and Edith Turner. *Image and Pilgrimage in Christian Culture*. New York: Columbia University Press, 2011.

Vatican II. *Dei Verbum. Acta Apostolicae Sedis* 57 (1965).

Vatican II. *Lumen Gentium. Acta Apostolicae Sedis* 57 (1965).

Vatican II. *Sacrosantcum Concilium. Acta Apostolicae Sedis* 57 (1965): 5–89.

Velazquez, Oriana. *El Libro de la Santa Muerte*. Mexico City: Editores Mexicanos Unidos, 2009.

Whitehouse, Harvey. *Modes of Religiosity: A Cognitive Theory of Religious Transmission*. Walnut Creek, CA: AltaMira Press, 2004.

Zinneman, Fred, dir. *A Man for All Seasons*. Produced by Sony Pictures. 2007.

Index

Acquavivo, Claudio, 71
Acts of the Apostles, 7*n*7, 152
Adversus Haereses, 15
Albó, Xavier, xix, 27–28
Alexander VI, 17*n*22
Ambrose of Milan, 33, 152*n*65
apokalypsis, 83–84. *See also* revelation
Apologia (Justin Martyr), 15
aporia, 14, 49–50, 81, 83
Apostolic Constitution (1950), 157, 159*n*76. *See also Munificentissimus Deus*
apparitions
  as communal experiences, 58–59, 62
  and meaning-making, 63, 75
  and resurrection, 46–48
  as revelation, 45–46, 82
  in scriptural tradition, 46–47
  seeing vs. perceiving, 82, 134
Aquinas, Thomas, 20, 25, 44, 55*n*17, 161
Arian controversies, 151, 155
Aristotle, 149, 186
Arizmendi López, Daniel, 87–88
Arriaga, José de, 18
Asad, Talal, 106
Association of the Immaculate Conception of the Blessed Virgin Mary. *See* Children of Mary
Assumption, 47–48, 157–59, 161
Augustine of Hippo, 33, 83, 109, 135–36, 142, 152
Aymara, xxiii, xxiv, 27–29
Aztec civilization, 128, 133*n*20, 134

Balthasar, Hans Urs von
  on communion of saints, 79
  on filiation, 117
  hope as Christocentric, 77
  on magic, 99
  on Mary, 31–32
  on significance of Cross, 10
Baracs, Rodrigo Martínez, 122*n*3
Barea Azcón, Patricia, 160
Basilica of the Immaculate Conception, 165, 177–78, 191–92
Basil the Great, 131*n*19
Bede the Venerable, 142
Bellarmine, Robert, 153
Benedict XVI. *See also* Ratzinger, Joseph
  on evangelization, xxviii
  On Heroic Virtue, 55*n*17
  on truth in dialogue, 167, 177
Bernadino, Juan, 131–33
Bertrin, Georges, 54–55
Betanzos, Juan de, 8*n*8
Brading, David, 122*n*2, 134*n*22, 135, 138*n*30
Bromley, David, 109

Cabrera, Miguel, 121*n*1
Calvat, Mélanie, 183–84
Cancun, 91–93

Candelaria, Our Lady of the, 12, 22, 35–36, 38
Cano, Melchior, 153
Canticle of the Sun, 28
Carpio, Luciano, 122
Catholic Counter-Reformation. *See* Counter-Reformation
Chesnut, R. Andrew, 88*n*3, 94–95, 97, 104–105, 110*n*36, 114
Children of Mary, 54, 71–74, 84
Clendinnen, Inga, 133*n*20
Cobo, Bernabé, 35
Codex Escalada, 125*n*8
cognitive psychology, 49–50, 59
Colque, Abraham, 28
communion of saints, 68, 77–78, 84–85, 156–58, 167
Company of Jesus. *See* Jesuits
connaturality, 154–56, 162
consultation
  and doctrine, 157–59
  and laity, 149–50
  and popular devotions, 146, 157, 159
  and sensus fidelium, 150, 152, 154, 156, 159, 162, 192
Contiti Viracocha. *See* Viracocha
Copacabana (Brazil), 21–22, 182–83
Copacabana, Our Lady of
  and Indigenous communities, 23, 26–27
  and intercession, 38
  and missionaries, 26
  name, 21
  and Pachamama, xxiv, 27, 38
  pilgrimage to shrine, 22–23
  statue, 23–24, 38
  as symbol of cultural negotiation, 34
  and Viracocha, 3
Cortez, Hernando, 128*n*14
Cortile dei Gentili, 101
Council of Ephesus, 43–44, 160–61, 170–71

Council of Trent, 71
Counter-Reformation, 152–54
Covey, R. Alan, 5*n*5, 37
COVID-19 pandemic, and Santa Muerte, 91–92
Cyprian of Carthage, 142
Cyril of Alexandria, 171*n*11
Cyril of Jerusalem, 10

Dalgairns, John, 161
De Anima, 149
Dei Verbum, xiv
De la Cruz, Juana Inés, 136*n*26
De las Casas, Bartolomé, 17, 128*n*14
Délices des Enfants de Marie, 71–72
De Locis Theologicis, 153*n*68
De praescriptione haereticorum, xxii
Dialogues (Gregory the Great), 73*n*44
Didache, 10
Diego, Juan
  accepts apparition, 129–30
  existence questioned, 125*n*8
  healing of Juan Bernadino, 131–33
  importance of Indigenous identity, 102, 121*n*1, 127, 138, 143
  meets Mary, 126, 128–29
  as neophyte, 128, 130
  requests construction of shrine, 131
  tilma, 132–33, 136
disanxiousuncertlibrium, 63–64, 77
doctrine
  and consultation, 157–59
  development of, 120, 146, 150, 161–62
  infallibility, 153, 159–60
  and popular devotions, 146, 157
  and preaching, 145

and sensus fidelium, 160–62
doctrine of discovery, 16*n*22
Doña Queta. *See* Romero, Enriqueta
Dulles, Avery, 166, 170*n*10
Duns Scotus, John, 44

Eagleton, Terry, 139–40
ecclesia
   dicens vs. docens, 150–51, 153–54
   docta, 150
   and popular religiosity, 146, 169
Echeverría y Veytia, Mariano Fernández de, 121*n*1
Eliade, Mircea, 9–14, 19, 21, 34
encomienda system, 16–17, 19–20
enculturation, 30
End of the Modern World, The, 155*n*71
Enlightenment, xxv, 41, 60
Ephesus. *See* Council of Ephesus
Estrade, John-Baptiste
   meaning violations in narrative, 59, 64–65
   motivation for narrative, 52
   narrative as apologia, 51
   religious experience, 51, 57–58, 62–63, 82
   role in Lourdes, 50, 61
   travels to verify apparitions, 55–57
Eusebius of Caesarea, 25–26
Evangelii Gaudium, xviii
Evangelii Nuntiandi, xvii

Fatima, Our Lady of, 169
filiation, 115–16
Flammingue, Jean-Léon, 71
Francis
   and Canadian residential schools, 17*n*22
   condemnation of Santa Muerte, 90, 101–103, 110, 124, 126, 184
   on evangelization, xxviii
   Laudato Si,' 28–29, 155*n*71
   on natural world, 28–29
   on *Nican Mopohua*, 126, 134
   on popular piety, xvii, xviii
   on popular religiosity, 78–79
Francis of Assisi, 28

Galilei, Galileo, 153*n*68, 179
García Icazbalceta, Joaquín, 125*n*8
Giraud, Maximin, 183–84
Giselbert of Westminster, 33
gravitational theory, as heuristic tool, 178–80
Gregory the Great, 7, 54*n*16, 73*n*44
Gregory XIII, 71
Guadalupe, Our Lady of
   and Aztec deities, 123*n*3
   Criollo image of, 125*n*7, 134
   debate over provenance, 122–23, 125*n*8, 134
   deference to Christ, 130–31
   first meeting with Juan Diego, 128–30
   and healing, 131–33
   iconographic nature of devotion, 130–31, 137, 142–43
   importance for Mexican culture, 136–37
   and Indigenous communities, 120, 122–23, 127, 133–34
   vs. Lady of Tepeyac, 35
   and Mexican Revolution, 140*n*36
   and migrants to US, 175–76
   miracle of roses, 132–33
   and Nahuatl language, 24, 123, 127, 134
   and *Nican Mopohua. see Nican Mopohua*
   officially recognized patronage, 120, 144, 158, 162
   original image, 121–23
   pilgrimage, 119–22, 124*n*6, 162
   vs. Remedios, 140*n*36, 144, 169

and Revelation 12, 125*n*7, 130, 135–37, 140, 142, 161
and salvation, 140–41, 145
vs. Santa Muerte, 87, 96, 101–102, 110, 124, 184
shrine bombed, 122
shrine established, 122–23, 125*n*8, 130, 132
tilma, 136–37
Guardini, Romano, 13–14, 19–21, 155–56, 162

Harris, Ruth, xxv, 42–43, 53
Hecht, Jennifer Michael, 111–12
hierophanies, 9, 12, 188, 191
Holy Spirit, 155–57, 162
huacas, 2, 4, 18–19
Huei Tlamahuiçoltica, 124*n*6, 126

Idea of the Holy, The, 177*n*20
idolatry, xxv, xxvi, 38
  and concept of God, 114, 117
  and death, 116
  and lament, 114–15, 118
  as mirror, 117–18
  and oppression, xxvi
  and patronage, 118
  in popular devotions, 87, 124
  as protest, 115
  and relationality, 117
  Roman, 15
  Santa Muerte, 99–100, 102, 110, 114–15
  in scriptural tradition, 114
  and theodicy, 87
Ignatius of Loyola, 90–91
Imagen de la Virgen María. See Image of Guadalupe
Image of Guadalupe
  colonial influence on, 135, 138
  Criollo audience, 134
  Indigenous sources, 138
  and mestizo identity, 138–39
  vs. *Nican Mopohua*, 135
  theological purpose, 125, 138
Immaculate Conception
  and Children of Mary, 72–74
  as dogma, 43–44, 72, 147*n*52, 152, 157, 159–61, 192
  and Lourdes, 43
Inca civilization
  colonization of earlier cultures, 12–13
  cosmologies, 6–9
  culture clashes, 18–19
  and missionaries, 6–7
  rites and pilgrimages, 37
  and Spanish Conquest, 5–6
Inca Roca, 37
inculturation, 20, 24–25, 141*n*38
Indigenous communities
  cosmologies, 6, 8, 29
  culture clashes, 19–20
  under encomienda system, 16–19
  evangelization, xxiii, 2, 16, 26
  Marian devotion, 26–27
Ineffabilis Deus, 44, 72, 148, 159, 161
Innocent III, 142*n*41
Inter Caetera, 17*n*22
intercession, 79, 90–91, 103–104
International Theological Commission, 141*n*38, 152, 154, 191–92
Inzlicht, Michael, 52, 60–64, 66, 68–69, 81, 84
Irenaeus of Lyon, 14–15
Island of the Sun, 3, 5, 37–38
Ita y Parra, Bartolomé Felipe de, 141–45, 154*n*68, 162

Jacomet, Dominique, 74*n*45, 80
James (Apostle), 1, 42
James, William, 57
Job, 103–105, 114
John (Apostle), 136, 138
John of Damascus, 30*n*36, 84, 131*n*19
John Paul I, xvii–xviii
John Paul II, xviii, xxiii, xxviii, 171

Index

Jordan, David K., 126*n*9
Justin Martyr, 7, 14–15

Kingsbury, Kate, 91–93, 105
Knock, Our Lady of, 42, 75–76
known unknowns, 80, 175

La Catrina, 89
Lafaye, Jacques, 140
Lake Titicaca, xv, 2, 4, 7–8, 22, 28, 34, 38, 187
lament
  and God's perceived indifference, 86–87
  and idolatry, 114–15, 118
  and myth, 109
  and popular devotions, 87, 114
  as protest, 115, 118
  Santa Muerte, 103–104, 106, 108–110
  and theodicy, 105, 108
Landy, Thomas, xix
La Salette, 183–84
Laso de la Vega, Luis, 126, 128, 130, 140, 144, 162
Latapie, Elsa, 73
Lateran IV, 81, 117
Laudato Si,' 28–29, 155*n*71
Laurentin, René, 48, 73*n*45
León-Portilla, Miguel, 128*n*14
liminality, 22, 25
Lonergan, Bernard
  on incarnate meaning, xvi, 81–82, 84
  on insight, 176, 190
  on meaning through symbols, 172–75, 177
  on mystery, 79–80
Lourdes, Our Lady of
  apparitions as communal experience, 58–59, 62
  as Aqueró, 43, 57
  description of appearance, 73–74
  vs. Fatima, 169
  flambeau processions, 68–69
  and healing, 43, 62*n*28, 66, 69, 176, 187
  Hindu pilgrims, 42, 176
  as Immaculate Conception, 43, 58, 74
  and meaning-making, 60, 68–69
  and resolution of societal tensions in Lourdes, 59
Lourdes
  and communitas, 67, 69
  and Enlightenment, 50, 60
  established culture of supernatural belief, 42–43, 54
  interpretations of apparitions, 54, 63, 74
  meaning-making through ritual, 68–70
  place in French society, 52–53
  skepticism toward Bernadette, 54, 80
  societal tensions in, 41, 49–50, 59–60, 63

Man for All Seasons, A, 112
Manual for the Daughters of the Virgin. See Manuel des Enfants de Marie
Manuel des Enfants de Marie, 72–73
Marion, Jean-Luc, xxvi, 79–80, 83–84, 100, 114–17
Martínez Baracs, Rodrigo, 122*n*3
Mary
  and eschatology, 49, 171
  and inculturation, 24–25
  and intercession, 90–91
  and lunar symbols, 31, 33, 133*n*20, 136, 142–43
  Magna Mater, 32
  and missionary work, 24–25
  and Pachamama, 29–33, 38
  resurrected, 47, 49
  role in salvation history, 29–30, 33, 171
  as Theotokos, 171
  tradition of processions, 68–69

as universal referent, xv–xvi, 170–71
Matovina, Timothy, xix, xxiv, 125n8, 127, 135n23, 141n37, 142–43
McCormack, Sabine, 8
meaning-making
  and aporia, 49
  and cognitive dissonance, 59
  and colonization, 13
  corporate response to, 59, 66
  and epistemology, 61
  as evolutionary instinct, 67–68
  inexhaustability of, 78
  and meaning violations, 59, 61–62
  palliative function of, 60, 64–65, 81
  and patronage, 76, 84
  and revelation, 83
  and ritual, 66
  and salvation, 85
  teleological foundation of, 61
  and transcendence, 25, 75–76
  as translation, 21
  "what" vs. "why," 60–62
meaning violations
  and communal experience, 59
  and conversion, 52
  as disanxioususncertlibrium, 63–64
  and equilibrium, 63–64
  lack of neutrality in, 63
  and patronage, 84
  physiological responses to, 63–64
  and ritual, 68–69
  Travis and Inzlicht on, 52
  "what" vs. "why," 61–64
Mendez, Yuri, 93–94, 96
Mexican Revolution, 140n36
Mexico
  as chosen people, 135–37, 139, 141–43, 145
  devotions around death, 112
  and mestizo identity, 138–39
Milhet, Jeanne-Marie, 73–74
Mochaorejas. *See* Arizmendi López, Daniel
Mong, Ambrose, xix, 107
More, Thomas, 112
Mother Earth, 27–28, 30, 33. *See also* Pachamama
Mountain of Sustenance, 133n20
Munificentissimus Deus, 47, 157, 161. *See also* Apostolic Constitution (1950)
mystery
  and death, 114
  inexhaustability of, 185
  Paschal, 115–16
  and patronage, 79–82, 115
myth
  and lament, 109
  Ricoeur on, 105–106
  and theodicy, 107–108

narco-religiosity, xxv, 94
Nestorius of Constantinople, 161, 171n11
Newbigin, Leslie, 170n10
Newman, John Henry
  on connaturality, 155
  on consultation, 147–50, 152, 157
  on ecclesia, 150–51
  on Ephesus, 160–61
  on resurrection appearances, 46–47
  on sensus fidelium, xx–xxi, 152, 154–55, 162
Nican Mopohua
  as devotional manual, 126–27, 132–34
  on Guadalupe apparition, 129, 187
  vs. *Image of Guadalupe*, 135
  on Juan Diego's tilma, 132–33
  parallels with Roman Martyrology, 127–28

situation of Guadalupe event, 128
on skepticism toward Juan Diego, 131
Nicene Creed, 29, 32, 77–78
Nicholas V, 16*n*22
Nietzsche, Friedrich, 117

On Consulting the Faithful in Matters of Doctrine, xx–xxi
On Heroic Virtue, 55*n*17
Origen of Alexandria, 33
Orsi, Robert, xix, 75–76, 175–76
Otto, Rudolph, 9, 34, 177

Pachamama, xxiv, 27–34, 38
Padre Pio, 181–82
Pansters, Wil G., 89*n*5, 105, 108
Paschal mystery, 115–16
patronage
  and communion of saints, 77–78
  dynamics of, 41, 45, 70, 76, 78, 84, 131, 145
  and eschatology, 78–79
  and idolatry, 87, 118
  as intercession, 79, 90–91, 103–104
  and meaning-making, 64, 70, 75–76, 84
  and mystery, 79–80, 82, 115
  and otherness, 116–17
  and popular religiosity, 78–79
  predisposition toward, 59–60
  processions, 68–69
  relationality in, 77, 99–100
  as theodicy, 87, 96, 99
Paul VI, xvii
Perrone, Giovanni, 147–50, 154
Peterson, Jeanette Favrot, 123, 134
Philippines, 107*n*31
Philosophiae Naturalis Principia Mathematica, 179
Pieper, Josef, 113
Pio of Pietrelcina. *See* Padre Pio
Pius IX

  defines Immaculate Conception, 44, 72, 147*n*52, 148, 152, 157, 159–61, 192
  Ineffabilis Deus, 44, 72, 148, 159, 161
  Munificentissimus Deus, 157
Pius XI, 44
Pius XII
  defines Assumption, 47, 157–59, 161
  on Mary resurrected, 47–48
  Munificentissimus Deus, 47, 161
  names Guadalupe patroness of Americas, 144*n*46
Pizarro, Francisco, 5
Ponce Monolith, 12–13, 20
Poole, Stafford, 125*n*8
popular devotion
  as corporate meaning-making, 59, 65–66
  and cultural interaction, 120
  and death, 111–12
  and doctrinal consultation, 146, 157, 159
  gravity metaphor, 178–79, 181–83, 185, 188
  and heterodoxy, 104*n*26
  and idolatry, 87, 99, 110, 124
  and Indigenous communities, 2–3
  as lament, 87, 114
  as protest, 109–110
  and synodality, 178, 185, 189
  as theodicy, 87, 99
  and use of symbols, 187–88
popular piety
  as act of faith, xx
  as Christianization of folk religion, xxiv
  and communion, 167–68
  and development of doctrine, 120–21
  excesses in, 46*n*3
  and inculturation, 141*n*38
  as *locus theologicus*, xvii

vs. popular devotion, xv, xix, xxii, xxv
vs. popular religiosity, xix
as response to gender disparity, 93–96
and sensus fidelium, 120–21
popular religiosity
and dialogue, 167
documentary sources, xx
and dynamics of patronage, 70
and ecclesia, xv, 169
and ethnographic research, xix–xx
and idolatry, 87
incarnate nature of, 78–79
and local perspective, 170, 172
and meaning violations, 52
and salvation, 141n38
and sensus fidelium, 146
and synodality, 162, 166–67, 193
and theodicy, 87
Proulx, Travis, 52, 60–64, 66, 68–69, 81, 84
Purification, Our Lady of, 36

Querida Amazonia, xxiv
Quispe, Calixto, xxiii, 4, 21, 27–28

Radner, Ephraim, 111–12, 116
Rahner, Hugo, 26, 29, 31, 33
Rahner, Karl, 83
Ramos Gavilán, Alonso, 35, 37–38
Ratzinger, Joseph. *See also* Benedict XVI
on Assumption, 48
on Christianity as synthesis of cultures, 7n7
on death, 111
on ecclesia, 146–47
on Nicene Creed, 77–78
Rausch, Laura, 109
Ravasi, Gianfranco, 101, 109
Redemptoris Missio, xxiv
Reformation, 91, 152, 153n68
Remedios, Our Lady of, 140n36, 144, 169

resurrection, 46–49
revelation, 45, 83–84
Revelation 12, 125n7, 130, 135–37, 140, 142, 161
Ricoeur, Paul, 104–108, 184–87
Rohrlich, Fritz, 180
Roman Martyrology, 127–28
Romanus Pontifex, 16n22
Romero, Enriqueta, 88, 92–98, 101, 108
Rudolph, Kurt, 45

Saint Bernadette. *See* Soubirous, Bernadette
Salles-Reese, Verónica, 6n6, 16–18, 37
salvation history, 29–30, 140–46, 171
Sánchez, Miguel, 126n9, 127, 134–40, 144, 154n68, 162
Santa Muerte
as agent of justice, 96–99, 113
and animism, 107n31
in Cancun, 91–92
condemnation of, 90, 100–101, 108–110, 124, 126, 184
connection to plague imagery, 89, 113
as contractual relationship, 96–97
devotees' self-perception, 89–90, 104–105, 108
efficacy of devotion, 90, 104, 108, 112
and empowerment, 98–99, 113
vs. Guadalupe, 87, 96, 101–102, 110, 124, 184
and healing, 96–97
as heterodoxy, 90, 104
iconography, 88–89
and idolatry, 99–100, 102, 110, 114–15, 118
Indigenous roots, 89, 107
and lament, 103–106, 108–110, 118
love spells, 94–95

and narco-culture, 94
origins, 87–89, 94
in prisons, 88*n*3
as protest, 109–110, 115, 118
relationality of, 97, 100, 116
socio-economic context of devotion, 89, 91–96, 101–103, 110, 112–13
symbol of death, 88, 100–101, 111–12, 114
in Tepito, 92–93
as theodicy, 90, 96, 99, 103–105, 107–108
and women, 92–96
Santiago de Compostela, 1, 12
Saviour, The, 155*n*71
Sensus Fidei in the Life of the Church, 152
sensus fidelium
in Church history, 152, 154
as communion, 157–58
and connaturality, 155
and consultation, 145–46, 149–51, 154, 156, 159, 162, 192
defining, 152
and doctrine, 160–62
and Holy Spirit, 155–57, 162
and popular devotion, xxi, xxii, xxiii, xxvi, 120–21, 141*n*38, 157
and synodality, 162
"Sermon to the Catechumens," 135
signs, 174–75
slavery, 16–17, 19
Smith, Benjamin T., 106–107
Soubirous, Bernadette
canonized, 44
description of Mary, 73–74
enters convent, 44, 71, 183
Estrade witnesses ecstasy, 56–57
first vision, 41–43, 82
interrogated, 74*n*45, 80
visions doubted, 54–55
Spanish Conquest

appropriation of local cultures, 12
Aztec empire, 128, 134
and evangelization, 18, 138
Inca empire, 5–6, 26, 37
as providence, 139
Spedding, Alison, xix
Spiritual Exercises (Ignatius of Loyola), 90
suma qamaña, 27–28
symbols
as communication, 185
inexhaustability of, 175–77
and insight, 174
interpreting, 186
as known unknowns, 175
nature of, 21, 172–74
and popular devotion, 187–88
vs. signs, 174–75
synodality, xix, 162, 166, 178, 189–94
Synod of 2021-2024, 190, 192–93

Tenace, Michelina, 15
Tepeyac, xxvi, 35, 122–23, 128, 133*n*20
Tepito, 88, 91–93
Thatamanil, John J., 169–70
theodicy
defining, 103
lament as, 87, 105, 108
myth and wisdom levels, 107–108
and Santa Muerte, 99, 103–105, 107
Theologies of Guadalupe, 125*n*8
Theotokos, 171
Three Treatises on the Divine Image, 131*n*19
Thus Spoke Zarathustra, 117
Tihuanaco, 5–6, 8–9, 12–14, 20, 33–34
tilma, 132, 136–37
Time to Keep, A, 111–12
Toor, Frances, 94*n*12
transcendence, 25–26, 75–76, 85

Turgeon, Peter-Flavianus, 159–60
Turner, Edith and Victor
  on communitas, 66–67
  on Guadalupe, 140n36
  on Lourdes, xxv, 183
  on pilgrimage, 11–12, 66–67
Twining, Nathan F., 182n27

Urban VIII, 128

Valeriano, Antonio, 126n9
Vatican I, 158

Vatican II, xiv, xvii, 18, 150n61, 171
Viracocha, 3, 13, 35

Whitehouse, Harvey, 20, 53, 66–68

yatiris, 3n2, 4, 27
Yupanqui, Francisco Tito, 38

Zapopán, Our Lady of, xviii
Zumárraga, Juan de, 122, 131–33